Praise For 'Why Don't You

'I just felt such a degree of empathy for the situations he faced, ... and pleasures. A lot of other writers seem to me to be more superficial. They never seem to let you in on how they are feeling and the observations seem stilted because of it. It is a long time indeed since I have read and enjoyed a book so much.'

Peter Green

'Fascinating and inspiring stuff. Ralf's philosophy is interesting, to say the least! Great story and great writing.'

Jonathan Litton

'I have been on an incredible journey! It only took two days, I was on a bike to China. Sometimes I laughed out loud, others I lapped up the history and atmosphere of unexplored lands. I then realised that actually I was still on my sofa reading an amazing book within the comfort of my own home. It's books like these that make me want to sell my car, flat and life (not body), and motor round the world in a Winnebago. Sometimes it takes a book like this to realise what is sadly lacking in one's own life, and the parameters in which we live. Thanks so much, Chris, it's hard to find inspiring people these days, celebrities bore me!'

Denise Acton

'Thoroughly enjoyable!! He's got a really nice, warm style and made me laugh out loud.'

Kieron Callow

'A few days ago I finished reading *"Why Don't You Fly?"* and felt compelled to write to you. What a book! What a fantastic journey / achievement! You have my full admiration. I obviously enjoyed the book immensely and it will remain in the recesses of my memory as one of my "best ever" travel reads. I have been immersing myself in travel literature for most of my adult life, not to mention undertaking quite a few journeys of my own, and every once in a while a "real gem" of a book comes along: for me, *"Why Don't You Fly?"* was one of them. Normally, in these "exceptional cases", I write to the author to convey my thanks and appreciation for the enjoyment and pleasure received – hence this letter to you.'

Martin Davies

'I enjoyed your book immensely, loved the small snippets of history you added about each country you visited.'

Scott Dodgson

"Why Don't You Fly?" is a very refreshing approach to producing a record of this mind blowing journey. I loved the way that Chris shares his excitement with the reader – comparing the anticipation of entering a new country to the feelings remembered from childhood when about to open a window on an Advent Calendar. He truly shares his joy and extreme vitality. I look forward to reading the book for a second time in 2006. What an adventure! What a man! What a book!'

Cynthia Pearson

'Just to say that I really enjoyed your book. It's one of the very few cycle touring books that I have read that really brought the memories flooding back of what it's like to be on a long tour.'

Stuart Lundy

'This is a truly sensational book, and what makes it stand out is that it keeps on getting better weeks after finishing the book. This is a tale of a man whose life circumstances transpire to let him choose to make one of those life quest journeys. The narrative is fast paced and insightful and the pages effortlessly fly by. Where Lance Armstrong's book *It's Not About The Bike* is inspirational as one mans triumph over adversity, Chris Smith's *"Why Don't You Fly?"* lets us grapple with the question we all struggle with from time to time of "why?" or "what's it all about?"'

Anonymous, Amazon

'First I'd like to say how impressed I am with the quality of your writing. I've naturally read (or skimmed) a number of cycle travel books and they are usually poorly written, so only interesting for technical detail. Excellent book. I am recommending it to everyone currently. Even those uninterested in cycling.'

Mark Swain

'I have just finished your amazing book. I could hardly put it down! You certainly do write well and have tremendously interesting things to say. It is a great mixture of a vivid description of your journey, the people you met, just the right amount of background info and your thoughts and feelings.'

Sarah Harrison

'I really enjoyed reading your book. A really good mixture of adventurous cycling, humour and perceptive intelligence.'

Debbie Brady

'Your book is being re-read straight off. That's a first for me even though most of my reading is individual travel accounts. Yours is exceptionally well written. I think your evocation of wind v cycling is brilliant.'

C.A. Murray

'This has to be one of the most interesting travel books I have read. Congratulations, such stamina and resolution.'

Graham Smith

'Consistently entertaining, interesting, informative and well written. I do like your very spare economical style, now increasingly rare, and you have an attractive descriptive vocabulary also.'

Robert Dudley

'Smith is a gifted writer in that he not only knows how to craft a very nicely turned phrase but is also outwardly and inwardly perceptive. There is a strong ontological element to the book; separated from the possessions and jobs that define most of us in the West, he questions the very nature of being, as well as his own motivations.'

Sue Page

I read your book at the weekend. I thought that it was the best cycling book I've ever read and I buy every one I see. Wind is on a par with call centres for my grumpy old woman fury. I hope you've found the love of your life since coming home.

Heather Russell

'Why Don't You Fly?'

BACK DOOR TO BEIJING – BY BICYCLE

CHRISTOPHER J. A. SMITH

Pen Press Publishers Ltd

First published in Great Britain by
Pen Press Publishers Ltd
25 Eastern Place
Brighton
BN2 1GJ

Second Edition

ISBN 1-905203-25-X

Printed and bound in the UK by Cpod, Trowbridge, Wiltshire

A catalogue record of this book is available from
the British Library

Maps by David Court, Severnside Studios, Bewdley

Front cover photograph: Klompjes tackles a section of the Karakoram
Highway near Passu, Northern Pakistan

For my father, who has always encouraged me to do it My Way.

CONTENTS

ACKNOWLEDGEMENTS

I would like firstly to thank all those wonderful people – far too numerous to list individually – who offered me companionship and hospitality during the long ride. Thanks are also due to those who kept me in their thoughts while I was travelling and sent me their reactions and their news; even the briefest emails were a joy to read.

I owe a special debt to my father for dealing with my correspondence while I was abroad; to Malcolm and Luisa Cashmore for caring for some of my more valuable possessions and providing temporary accommodation immediately after the return home; and to Henk Buzink of Fransen Transport – both by taking me on and letting me go you made dreams come true.

I am deeply grateful to Jo Sturges, Lindsay Ridley, Shaun Rana, Chris Whall, Robert Dudley, Carole Ann Rice, Malcolm Cashmore, Helen Jones, Vanessa Little, Peter Green, Stephen Webb, Shirley Clarke, and Alan and Jan Ferguson for allowing themselves to be badgered into reading draft chapters. Their encouragement, criticism and advice have been invaluable during the writing of this book.

I am indebted to David Court for providing the maps; to David Dean for designing the Website; and to the team at Pen Press for transforming manuscript into book.

I would like also to express my gratitude to the couple from London I met at the restaurant in Surmaq who were kind enough to send on their photographs; if I hadn't stupidly lost your address I would certainly have been in touch long before now.

Finally I would like to thank you, the reader, for your decision to travel with me. You will find a photographic accompaniment to the journey at **www.cycleuktochina.com**

Enjoy the ride!

ABOUT THE AUTHOR

By the age of seven Chris Smith was coming top in any Geography test that involved countries and oceans and rivers and capital cities. While at university he hitchhiked the length and breadth of Europe and ventured into Africa and Asia during the long summer vacations. After graduating he spent a hideous three months squirting jelly into pork pies in order to fund a visit the USA, where he drove from New York to San Francisco and back.

He went on to drive six-axle lorries all over Western Europe, the Communist Bloc, Scandinavia, the Soviet Union and – after the USSR's dissolution in 1991 – to Russia, Lithuania, Latvia and Kazakhstan. The roads would be under sheet-ice a foot thick during the Russian winters, and from Moscow to Kazakhstan an armed Russian policeman would guard vehicle and driver against attacks by bandits.

He eventually swapped this nomadic existence for work in a number of management positions but never really took to the office environment of computer and telephone. Following a split with a long-term girlfriend and redundancy he announced – to general disbelief – that he was going to attempt to cross the Eurasian landmass by bicycle.

He lives in the picturesque town of Bewdley and cycles twenty-five miles a day to and from work.

'Why Don't You Fly?'

BACKDOOR TO BEIJING – BY BICYCLE

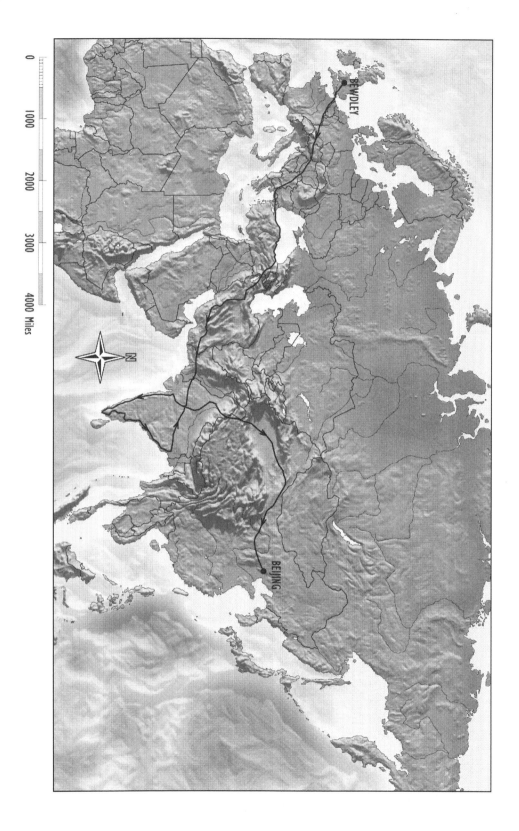

Prologue: Riding Home in the Rain (I)

As soon as the alarm clock goes off at 5.20 a.m. he heaves himself to his feet and switches on Radio Five and the kettle, making the unwelcome discovery that he's aching all over, for the August Bank Holiday Monday was spent in frenzied activity. They had got up early, saddled the horses, and ridden them at a terrific pace around the neighbouring Wyre Forest. Ellen's horses are a little like the classic Jaguar parked in the garage: fast, flashy, unreliable, and hideously expensive to run. The riding accounts for the tenderness around his inner thighs and a thirty-five-minute run in the forest has left him with stiff calves and ankles. An afternoon spent chopping wood and digging foundations for the strengthening of the horses' shelter has contributed sore shoulders and blistered hands to the inventory of discomfort.

After listening to the news and sport he pours himself a coffee and puts on the headphones, aches and pains forgotten as he immerses himself in the first movement of Bach's triple concerto for flute, violin and harpsichord. Twenty minutes later, galvanised by his addictions to music and caffeine, he kisses the sleepy Ellen good-bye, re-sets the alarm to a more congenial seven and scrunches across the gravel to the garage.

There is a magical clarity and freshness to the dawn that makes it a privilege to be up and awake so early. A doe turns and sprints elegantly away as he walks his bicycle (a more practical form of transport than the Jaguar) up the muddy track to the road. Some people might consider cycling twenty-four miles a day to be obsessive, but he feels that if you can't find any passion for whatever you choose to do with your life there is little point in existing.

During the fifty-minute ride through countryside of rolling farmland and forest he uses a number of different routes to vary the routine, preferring wherever possible to use country lanes instead of main roads. There is little traffic about and cats, rabbits and squirrels scurry for the safety of the concealing verges at his approach, some avoiding his front wheel only in the nick of time. A young rabbit races along the road in front of him before bolting into a gateway on the right. 'Use your indicators!' he calls after it. Occasionally he might be lucky enough to see deer or a badger or a fox.

His mind possesses a lucidity at this early hour that matches the dawn sky. This is usually when he gets ideas for the book he is attempting to write, an account of pioneering journeys made by lorry to Central Asia during which he was accompanied by an armed guard from Moscow onwards to fend off attacks by bandits. An idea might arrive in the form of a word that he likes the sound of and mentally files for future use, such as *ersatz* or *ergonomically* or *euphemism*. Or a whole phrase might suddenly come to him unbidden, or he might decide to alter the way he describes an event as he dredges his memory for half-forgotten incidents. Sometimes he thinks that writing a book is a little like starting out with a great, shapeless lump of clay and attempting to fashion something useful or decorative from it.

Energised by the exercise, radiating heat and tingling with well-being, he parks the bicycle in the tyre store a few minutes before seven and unlocks the office. After taking a shower he changes into his office clothes and makes himself another coffee. Then he switches on the computers, records some of his morning reflections on the word processor and, at 07.30 precisely, switches the phones over from the mobile.

His colleagues drive in between eight and half past, entering the office with bleary eyes and slept-in faces, and the phone begins to ring more insistently. His job is merely the means by which he subsidises his passions and the earlier contentment fades.

At 3.45 p.m. the sky turns dark and there are rumbles of thunder. Five minutes later the rain is hammering down outside.

'Do you want a lift home, Chris?' shouts the managing director from his office. He occasionally cycles in himself.

'No thanks, Henk! We're not *all* fair-weather cyclists!' he points out.

At four o'clock he gets changed and heads out into the monsoon. The first five minutes are mildly unpleasant, but once he's as wet as he can possibly get the rain doesn't bother him any more. Slowing down is a more immediate problem, for after a rare dry spell in this awful summer he has momentarily forgotten the effect that wet weather can have on brakes and twice he very nearly collides with cars. They are everywhere, filling the air with the smell of their exhaust, forming long queues at traffic lights and roundabouts, and pulling out in front of him from side roads (either because their drivers underestimate his speed or – more worryingly – because they fail to see him altogether).

The daily grind of the office seems as usual to have sucked all the creativity out of him and the mental sharpness of the morning has disappeared. Somewhere beyond Stourport the rain stops and he pauses before the first steep hill to take off his waterproofs. The ride home is completed under a warm sun on waterlogged lanes.

Part One: The Road to India

The way of cowardice is to embed ourselves in a cocoon, in which we perpetuate our habitual patterns. When we are constantly recreating our basic patterns of behaviour and thought, we never have to leap into fresh air or onto fresh ground.

Chogyam Trungpa 'Shambhala: The Sacred Path of the Warrior'.

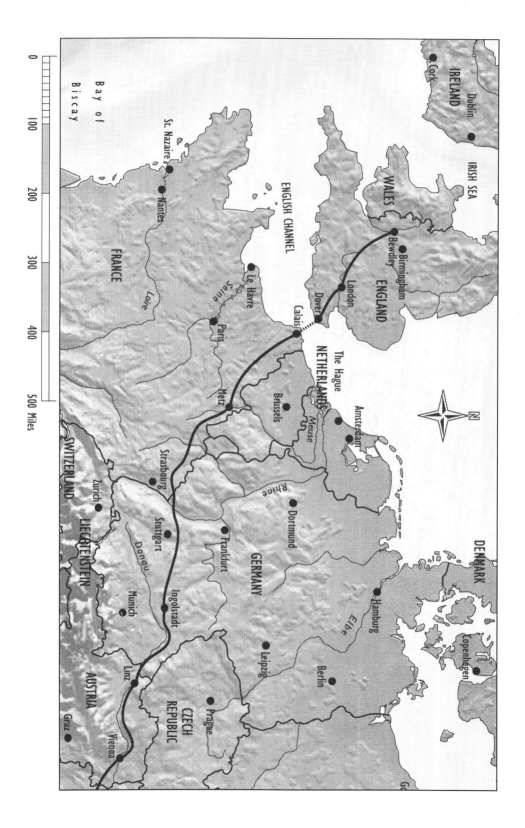

Chapter One
<u>'Never Right'</u>

The only thing I remember about the barman is his voice.

I have stopped cycling because the pain has become intolerable. Sitting at a table, not in Calcutta, Quetta or Kashgar but in the Café du Centre in a village in Northern France between Calais and St Omer, I am trying to escape the inadmissible truth that I can't go on; the adventure of a lifetime has foundered only two days after I left London to a chorus of emotional good-byes. The distinction between tragedy and comedy is often a narrow one and I can visualise the Intrepid Traveller's humiliating return all too clearly: not only will there be more sympathy from some quarters than I can handle, but I imagine that my unexpected reappearance might also provoke some malicious amusement amongst one or two so-called friends.

The discomfort began yesterday on the A20 somewhere near Maidstone as a dull ache on the inside of my right knee, impairing the ability to accelerate and to tackle hills. It became so severe, stabbing like a skewer each time I pressed down on the pedal, that I was obliged to dismount and push the heavily laden bicycle up the steep hill outside Folkestone. A meal of fish and chips on the 14.30 sailing from Dover to Calais filled the void in my stomach and I fell into conversation with two Australian cyclists spending six months touring Europe. In Calais, where it was raining steadily and the surfaces were greasy, the bicycle's front wheel lodged in a tramline crossing one of the roads in the docks. I fell with a jarring crash onto the unyielding wet tarmac at 10 mph, wrenching my shoulder and cutting my knee, my clothes absorbing dirt and water like blotting paper. Shaken, battered and filthy, I untwisted the forks and right-hand brake lever and wondered what on earth had possessed me to bring a *white* polo shirt. Then, unable to find any signs for St Omer or the RN43, I got thoroughly lost and even wetter in the town. Hardly the start I'd envisaged.

*

The unusual response to redundancy had neatly polarised reactions amongst family and friends. My sister and youngest brother had loved the concept of a bicycle ride across Asia and their enthusiastic support helped me through those times when, assailed by doubts, I wondered if I ought to go through with it.

My other brother, though, was less sure. 'It seems a very *Chris Smith* type of thing to do,' he remarked dubiously when he phoned from his apartment in Manhattan.

My father pronounced himself undecided as to whether it was a good or a daft idea, or a combination of both.

'I don't think you should go,' declared a former girlfriend. 'It's too dangerous.'

'Eighteen months by *bicycle*?' exclaimed a friend who clearly thought that I'd finally lost my sanity. 'Why don't you fly, Christopher?' he continued with the exaggerated patience normally reserved for the very young or the mentally retarded. 'Instead of taking eighteen months to get to Sydney you'd be there in eighteen hours!'

Undaunted by the jibes, I pinned roadmaps to walls. Europe was in the bedroom, Turkey and Iran in the bathroom, Pakistan, India and Southeast Asia in the study, China in the living room, and a general map of Asia in the kitchen. Frequently I would break off whatever I was doing to study them, trying to imagine what it would be like to cycle across the Taklamakan Desert and wondering if I'd ever make it across Europe to Istanbul, let alone reach Esfahan, Delhi, Beijing or Singapore. Guidebooks warned of extremes of terrain and climate, officialdom at its most obstructive, sandstorms, stone-throwing children, poisonous snakes, lunatic drivers and mad dogs, and that I could expect voracious bugs, all sorts of nasty diseases and torrents of diarrhoea. I studied glossy mail-order catalogues advertising outdoor clothing and camping equipment, and I parted with my prize possession – a classic Jaguar – to raise extra money.

To pay the bills while I made the necessary preparations I drove lorries to supermarkets throughout the Midlands. I never really came to terms with working at night and sleeping during the day but – vitally important – I was able to continue my physical training by cycling the twenty-five-mile round trip between home and work five or six times a week. Word spread amongst my colleagues and I became known as *that crazy f***er who cycles in from Bewdley every night*.

Occasionally though, I fancied that I detected a touch of grudging admiration. On one particularly filthy night I was approached by one of my fellow drivers as, dripping with sweat and rainwater, I was locking my bicycle in the shed. Floodlights cast a sepulchral glow on a hellish scene, illuminating the raindrops cascading from the blackness above and glinting off the reflective safety jackets worn by spectral figures milling around in the gloom. Headlights flared, hazard-warning lights flashed, and the demented symphony of revving engines, hissing airbrakes and bleeping reversing alarms was interspersed with the regular percussive crash of tractor units being coupled to thrumming refrigerated trailers. 'Christ, mate!' he bellowed above the din. 'You're reelly...' (there was a pause while he ransacked his vocabulary for an adjective which would adequately express his opinion of me) '...*hard!*'

'Hard' I'd have to be, both mentally and physically if I was to make it all the way across Asia – as tough as nails. If people judged that cycling a mere twenty-five miles a day qualified me as a candidate for a straitjacket, what would they make of my plans to cycle halfway across the world, averaging eighty miles a day? Inhibited by what I felt to be a very real possibility of failure, I kept my intentions largely to myself.

When I ordered the bicycle, opting for an expensive, purpose-built machine* in preference to cheaper models that wouldn't really be up to the task and might cause problems later on, there was no going back. Poring over maps in my cosy town house as the departure date loomed, arachnophobic, technophobic and plagued by a bad back, I found myself filled with trepidation and rocked by moments of chronic self-doubt. Perhaps this is only to be expected when you commit yourself to a course of action that you know will extend you to your physical and mental limits. When I experimentally lifted the fully loaded bicycle, its weight appalled me.

'He's never right, is he, darling?' said Luisa Cashmore to her husband Malcolm as they watched me set up my tiny bivvy in their garden for a trial night out a few days before I was due to set off for London. There was affection behind their mockery, but their dubious expressions indicated that the full extent of the deprivation to which I was about to commit myself was only now beginning to dawn on them. The question, albeit unspoken, was left hanging in the air between us: *Do you have any idea what you're letting yourself in for?*

No, not really. Until my departure I can only imagine.

'It's such a *shame*, isn't it?' continued Lou remorselessly at a time I was sorely in need of encouragement and reassurance.

During the night it drizzled, and Sunny Delight, the Cashmores' psychopathic marmalade cat, gave me a nasty scare by jumping from a neighbouring wall onto my back before bounding off into the bushes with what I could have sworn was a sinister chuckle. The bivvy passed the test and I remained dry, but doing too much imagining, I slept badly.

*

*For details, see appendix on page 275

Barely two hours from Calais and unable to countenance the thought of turning back, I consider abandoning the bicycle and resuming the journey on public transport. That would save some face but the prospect of sitting inside buses or trains fails to engage me; tens of thousands of backpackers travel huge distances on buses and trains every year. Having spent months researching routes and preparing myself physically – not to mention well over two thousand pounds on equipment – I *have* to cycle, damn it. The idea had been to attempt something marvellous (in the most literal sense of the term), a feat of physical endurance beyond the scope of most other people, a journey that, by testing me to my limits, might – at least for a while – repair damaged self-esteem and deliver me from a growing awareness of my mediocrity.

So much for being hard!

Bitterness begins to mingle with the self-pity already welling up inside me. Failure tastes of Perrier Water – bland and fizzing faintly on the tongue.

'That looks like hard work!' croaks a voice. The barman has noticed the loaded bicycle propped up outside and is unwittingly intruding upon private grief. At best he has a severe case of laryngitis, at worst something rather more sinister and probably terminal.

'I was on my way to India and China, but I've injured my knee. I must go back to England to see a doctor. My adventure is over,' I reply disconsolately, struggling with my rusty French.

The barman tuts sympathetically. 'There's a doctor here in the village, you know. He'll have a look at you. *Voilà! Là-bas au coin.*' He gestures to a point at the bottom of the small hill up which I've just agonisingly pedalled.

'*Merci beaucoup!*' I suppose there is nothing to be lost by following his advice, but a number of specialists recently spent months trying to rid me of my troublesome back pain without success so why should the local quack have any more luck with my knee?

The doctor is a young man who tells me that he used to be a keen cyclist himself 'until my body began to hurt everywhere.'

Maybe I'm too old for this.

After a brief examination of my knee he gives me some tablets to be taken twice a day with food, a tube of ointment to rub into the joint, and instructions to perform stretching exercises every time I stop cycling and to use lower gears in order to avoid subjecting the knee to undue stress. Then he counsels me to limit myself initially to a maximum of a hundred kilometres (sixty miles) a day. Finally, he wishes me luck. '*Massez-le!*' he urges me. '*Étirez les muscles!* In any case it is not serious because there is no swelling.'

Convinced that it's going to take considerably more than a few pills and daubs of ointment to effect a cure, I emerge from the surgery with undiminished scepticism. But by the time I lay out my sleeping bag at the end of the day in a copse just outside Cambray, the trilling of hundreds of birds and the cooing of wood-pigeons mingling with the sound of nearby traffic, the trip computer tells me that I have managed a very creditable ninety miles since leaving Ardres early in the morning. Much to my surprise (and incalculable relief) the pain had diminished as the day wore on and I found myself able to use higher gears and to increase my speed, although I was careful to change down early when climbing hills. Whether I'll be able to tackle the 4,700-metre Khunjerab Pass and the fierce winds sweeping the Taklamakan Desert remains to be seen, but staring into a glass of Perrier Water in the Café du Centre in Nordausques, I had convinced myself that I was incapable of cycling another nine miles, let alone ninety.

The only thing I remember about the barman is his voice, for I was too full of introspection and misery to notice him properly. It wasn't by any means a beautiful voice, but they were beautiful words; they may well have saved the expedition from a premature and thoroughly ignominious end.

Chapter Two
<u>Sunny Delight</u>

For all that it shouldn't have come as a surprise, the phone call announcing my redundancy arrived with much the same brutal, emasculating effect of a hard and well-aimed kick in the crotch. Initially I was too stunned to think clearly, but I should have been pleased. After all, I'd been plotting an escape route from office tedium for some time, toying with the idea of taking time out to travel. I had wanted to revel once more in the prospect of the unfamiliar instead of taking refuge from it by embedding myself in routines. I had yearned to wake up every morning to a fresh horizon and the anticipation of adventure, to marvel at new sights, sounds and smells. I had longed for the rewards of physical challenge and mental stimulation, both of which I felt had been missing from my life for too long. I had craved relief from Health and Safety regulations, ISO 9002, council tax and credit card bills, speed cameras, junk mail, double yellow lines, P60s, income tax returns, car park ticket machines that don't give change and all the other paraphernalia that distracts us from the business of living.

Escape is a common enough fantasy and for most people it remains exactly that, but with no job, partner or dependents and the coffers about to be swollen by a redundancy payment, I began to realise that I had just been handed a 'now or never' opportunity denied to those chained to the obligations and commitments that accompany careers and families. As the demolition dust cloud cleared I became exhilarated by the idea of transforming what appeared to be a negative situation into a positive one, an obstacle into an opportunity, catastrophe into catharsis. Redundancy would be the catalyst that turned daydreams into reality. I felt that I was waving a two-fingered salute at Destiny.

The relentless advance of technology has made the world seem a smaller place. Vast oceans and entire continents can be crossed in hours and overseas communication by telephone or email takes seconds. Television and radio regularly permit us to witness the earth's remotest, most inaccessible areas without having to leave the comfort of our sitting rooms. And yet, despite all the glib talk about the shrinking global village, the planet remains just as large in the literal sense as it was in the days of Magellan and Marco Polo. Maybe you have to sail or walk across it to remind yourself just how immense it is.

Or cycle. For the past five years I had been cycling to and from the office, a daily round-trip of about twenty-five miles over the undulating terrain of the Worcestershire and Shropshire countryside. From time to time I'd get wet and sometimes it was cold too, and on winter mornings I might have to deal with darkness, frost, icy roads and freezing fog, but generally I relished these daily workouts and they had made me immensely fit.

The bicycle provides us with an efficient and elegant way of getting around; it is silent, pollution-free, and faster, cheaper to run and considerably less unpredictable than a horse. A bicycle would take me to areas bypassed by buses and trains and provide the essential element of physical challenge, and although I'd be travelling slowly enough to take in the surroundings, I imagined that my speed would nevertheless be sufficient to enable me to transit countries before visas expired and cross wilderness areas before I ran out of food and water.

Television and radio filter out touch, taste and smell, those most evocative of senses, and during travel documentaries the gaze lingers upon a subject only for as long as a despotic cameraman permits. As well as enjoying an unrestricted view of my surroundings from the saddle I'd be able to hear and smell them too, and I'd experience directly the effects of heat, cold, wind, rain, sun, sandstorms and changes in terrain and road surfaces. Travelling at a comparatively gentle pace, I'd be accessible to local people, and I persuaded myself that repairs would be cheap and relatively simple.

So I reacted to redundancy by 'getting on my bike'. Literally. A former Tory minister would most definitely have approved.

*

France is a big country. One senses the increase in space as soon as one moves southeast from Calais on those long, straight, gently undulating roads. Copses and woods are dark islands adrift on a sea of wheat, and herds of cattle and sheep nibble at pasture. The traffic is lighter and towns and villages are spaced further apart than in England.

Beyond Sedan the landscape becomes one of rolling hills and secretive woods and valleys as the road enters the southern foothills of the Ardennes. I have always felt at home in France; I love the mouth-watering delicacies in the windows of the *boulangeries* and *patisseries* and I adore French cheese, wine and bread. I admire the demonstrativeness of the locals, the way perfect strangers routinely shake you by the hand and friends begin and end each encounter with *quatre bises* (two pecks on each cheek). The warm sunshine of this early June day glints off chrome, tans my forearms and brings smiles to the faces of passers-by. *'Bon appetit!'* they murmur politely as I breakfast on a couple of delicious *pains au chocolat* outside a boulangerie or lunch al fresco on a *frites merguez* in a market square. French is a musical language and the words sound like a benediction or a declaration of love. With more time on their hands and a greater fund of memories upon which to draw than the rest, pensioners approach to ask me about my route and to reminisce fondly about the cycling they themselves used to do when the flesh was a little more willing. The woman who cut my hair in a salon near Arras had been full of questions: Where are you going? How long will it take? Are you married?

A benign breeze keeps me from overheating as I cautiously negotiate the steeper inclines, wary of provoking any reaction from my knee. In contrast to the previous two days, the empty road bends and snakes its way up hills, past lush meadows and forests, past grazing cattle and cosy villages in which stone houses with rust-red tiled roofs cluster around a church. This is countryside in which I feel content; hills bring the horizons closer and there's no knowing what lies round each corner. That's just how I'd like my life to be – all variation and surprise and alternating highs and lows, the frequent chicanes and inclines concealing the view ahead. For long periods all I can hear is the hum of the tyres, the steady rhythm of my own breathing and the wind in my ears. From time to time the smell of freshly cut hay is borne to me on the breeze.

When it came to ordering equipment and deciding what to take with me, I recalled a piece of wisdom from Jerome K. Jerome's *Three Men In A Boat*:

The first list we made out had to be discarded. It was clear that the upper reaches of the Thames would not allow of the navigation of a boat sufficiently large to take the things we had set down as indispensable; so we tore the list up and looked at one another. George said: 'You know we are on the wrong track altogether. We must not think of the things we could do with, but only of the things that we can't do without.'

Although I took this excellent advice to heart, carefully evaluating each and every item in terms of weight and indispensability, I haven't yet become accustomed to the burden of a fully loaded bicycle. My body will take time to adapt to the monstrous demands I'm making of it and by the end of the day I'm tired and saddle-sore. A budget of £10 a day will mean sleeping rough whenever possible to save money, and a clump of trees just off the road provides me with the privacy I require. For the best part of two years there will be no roof over my head, no central heating, no soft mattress, and no hot bath or shower in the mornings. No fridge, no washing machine, no cooker, no toaster, no radio, no TV. No early morning cup of coffee. No Bach.

Am I insane? Perhaps this is what the journey is about: discovering the true worth of the possessions and people I'm leaving behind. Which will I miss the most and for the longest? Maybe the answers will surprise me.

The undergrowth is thick and the ground damp and lumpy and infested with slugs. A hedgehog saunters by barely four feet away, either unaware of or indifferent to my presence. There are the usual mosquitoes to keep me company but fortunately the bivvy (a glorified waterproof sack with a raised front end to provide headroom) is equipped with a net. After reclining on the Karrimat to eat supper (a crusty baguette and Camembert washed down with a litre of milk), I shave using a pocket mirror, attempting to work up a lather with shower-gel and an inadequate supply of cold water from my bottles. I could always grow a beard to save myself this grim ritual but I don't want to look too scruffy just yet; shaving maintains a semblance of cleanliness and tidiness when showers and baths are hard to come by. Unused to sleeping on a hard, uneven surface, I wake up a couple of times during the night to the sound of rustlings as the inhabitants of the wood go about their nocturnal business.

*

I've been making a habit of getting lost in French cities. Follow the *Toutes Directions* signs and you invariably get deposited on a ring road that is a *voie rapide* upon which cyclists are *interdit*. Because you (quite literally) can't afford a confrontation with the French traffic police and the risk of a fine, you follow the signs for *Centreville* and end up in the city or town centre where a jumble of signs for local amenities such as the *Salle des Sports, Piscine, Mairie* and *Gendarmerie* are of no help at all. Nobody in Metz appears to know of a route out to the main road to St Avold that will avoid the pestilential voies rapides – including the four friendly gendarmes who ask me where I'm going and what my job is in England.

My job? I no longer have one; I am redundant, superfluous, surplus to requirements, de trop. I am *free*.

As for my destination, I'm not entirely sure yet. With most of the Asian landmass prone to searing summer heat and frigid winter temperatures (and tropical areas affected by the annual arrival of the monsoons) it was immediately obvious that the departure date, schedule and direction of the journey would all depend a great deal upon climatic considerations and visa restrictions as well as my physical condition. Australia tempted me initially because it was about as far away from the United Kingdom as you could possibly get, but I have since become greatly seduced by the idea of ending the journey in Vladivostok instead. Sydney or Perth may be further away geographically but

Vladivostok, the eastern terminus of the Trans-Siberian Railway and erstwhile home of the Soviet Union's Pacific Fleet, is infinitely more remote in every other respect. The name has an appropriately 'end of the world' feel to it and until recently it was a closed city. I discovered that many people had never even heard of the place.

I tell the gendarmes that I'm cycling to India. Of that I am reasonably certain.

'*Vous devez être très courageux!*' they exclaim.

You must be very brave. I've always liked the French. In England they said I was crazy. *Never right.*

*

Brandishing a sweat-impregnated money-belt at the counter of an air-conditioned and spotlessly clean bank in the German town of Neuberg, I wonder uneasily if I pong. I am unwashed and self-conscious. My clothes are crumpled and travel-stained and my skin damp with perspiration from the morning's exertions. The staff are all freshly ironed and in clean clothes and none of them will have had to shake beetles or woodlice out of their immaculately polished shoes before putting them on. Furtively, I examine those around me for stifled exclamations, noses wrinkled in disgust or signs of nausea, but either they are all suffering from blocked sinuses or being far too polite to show their distaste.

After a pleasant ride on an empty road winding through pine-clad hills I bravely (or crazily, depending on your point of view) entered Germany at Wissembourg. Germans generally seem to have less time for me than the French, probably because I've never been able to get on with their language. I have always found its declining nouns and articles and quirky use of capital letters unnecessarily complicated, and placing the object before the verb is tantamount to placing the cart before the horse. They clearly take the Sabbath seriously, for the shops in the towns and villages of tall buildings in pastel shades of green, blue, yellow and cream were closed and the streets deserted and slumbering in the unseasonable heat. The main roads, however, were full of day-trippers stuffed into cars and on convoys of motorbikes and I gathered from the frantic beeping and gesturing of busybodies in their gleaming BMWs and Audis that using the roads when a cycle path is available is *verboten*. Nothing appears to disturb the German psyche more than to witness regulations being ignored.

*

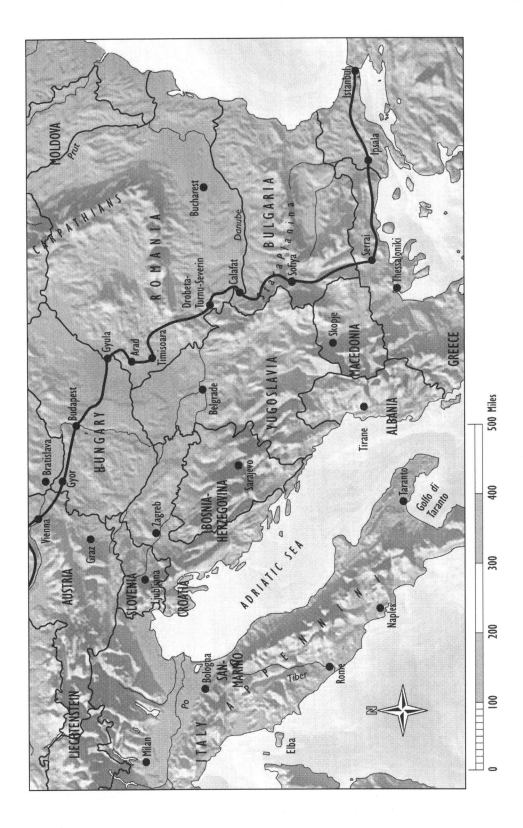

Europe figured little in my plans; I saw the first two thousand miles to Istanbul merely as an opportunity to familiarise myself with my equipment and to find answers to some pressing questions about my strength and stamina before the sterner tests ahead. Never having cycled for any distance with a loaded bicycle, I based my calculations on covering a distance of four hundred miles a week, the theory being that the greater the daily mileage, the more time I'd earn myself to rest. Austrian roads are full of bends and dips, and both the driving and the regulations are less aggressive than in Germany. Although my legs are long overdue a couple of days off I've decided to carry on clocking up the miles as long as I'm feeling healthy and strong, for my body will let me know soon enough when I need to rest. If there are to be any unscheduled delays forced by injury or illness it will be reassuring to have banked some extra miles and days, and besides, having bought myself eighteen months of freedom I shouldn't be overly concerned by timetables and duty rosters.

On the Donau Radwanderweg, a cycle path that runs alongside the Danube all the way to Vienna, I accelerate alongside the first cyclist I've seen with a bicycle similarly laden to mine and cheerfully ask him in my execrable German where he's going.

'*Ungarn!*' he grunts.

'Me too! I'm on my way to India!'

'*Viel Gluck!*' he replies, without noticeable enthusiasm.

Good luck. The German version sounds like an imprecation. Mildly chastened by this display of indifference from a fellow touring cyclist, I take the hint; some people travel alone and they prefer to keep it that way.

Unlike its more prosperous Alpine neighbour, two thirds of Hungary is less than two hundred metres above sea-level and the landscape is utterly flat, nothing but fields in all directions dotted with occasional trees. The country has an unkempt feel to it, for the roadside – particularly at lay-bys (from a number of which buxom sirens with heavily painted faces and massive thighs almost completely unconcealed by tiny skirts are beckoning to passing motorists) – is littered with plastic cups and bottles, cans, empty cigarette and condom packets, and paper napkins. Cycling is forbidden on the single-number roads, but unlike in Germany, nobody appears to care.

Two weeks and 1,243 miles after having left London, I arrive in Budapest feeling rather pleased with myself. Only one puncture so far and, contrary to some of the wilder fears expressed before my departure, I've not yet been sodomised, robbed, run over or beaten-up.

*

At the Gyula border crossing the inevitable queue of lorries is waiting to enter

Romania. I pull up alongside a Volvo from Nottingham laden with pipes to chat to the first Englishman I've encountered since leaving Calais. When I tell him what I'm doing his jaw drops.

'Rather you than me, mate!' he says.

My only previous visit to Romania was at the wheel of a similar vehicle loaded with rolls of plastic film to be used in the manufacture of laminated windscreens. Disturbed by the country's reputation for highway robbery, both by scheming peasants who faked accidents to block the road and rapacious legions of corrupt traffic police, I had felt extremely vulnerable. A heavy sense of foreboding had accompanied me until, Blighty-bound once more with a return load of tinned stew, I re-entered Hungary.

Seven years later the prospect of theft in Romania and Bulgaria continues to bother me, for I have managed to convince myself that the poverty prevalent in two of the poorest countries in Europe is unlikely to be accompanied by the traditions of hospitality and respect for the traveller that one might expect to find further east. A youthful customs official is sprawling negligently in a chair with his feet on the desk. He glances disdainfully at my dog-eared passport and tells me that it is useless because he can no longer read the front cover, and that I won't be allowed to enter Romania anyway because I'm carrying too much money. I suspect that he's after a bribe but I'm in no hurry and he's damn well not going to get one. He informs me with considerable relish that Romania have just beaten England in the European Football Championships.

'Dan Petrescu very good player!' I reply sycophantically, barely able to repress a shudder of revulsion. It is a horrid thing to have to admit and I detest kowtowing to these scumbags, but I have uttered the magic words. My adversary grins superciliously, stamps my passport and, with thinly disguised contempt, waves me through. Thus I enter Romania with the consolation of having paid only for the visa but tormented by self-loathing and with my misgivings about the country thoroughly reinforced.

The plains of Hungary extend into Western Romania, providing the richest agricultural land in the country. Early every morning peasants with crumpled, leathery faces trudge impassively along the road on their way to the fields bearing a sinister assortment of rakes, hoes, scythes and pitchforks. Farm workers are tending their livestock (usually two or three tethered cows) in the fields, many of them dozing in the pools of shade provided by the roadside trees. Ramshackle villages lining the road are full of itinerant geese, hens and ducks, and local children whistle and shout as I pass.

The most popular car in Romania is the Dachsia, based on the ancient Renault 12, but transport for the less privileged is provided by bicycles (rattling, squeaking single-geared old bone-shakers) or the humble horse and cart. The heat is ferocious and the only shade available is offered by the columns of trees lining each side of the road. With no milk or yoghurt to be had and the water from my bottles (warm and tasting of plastic) doing little to quench my thirst, I have become plagued by images of condensation-covered pint glasses brimming with lime cordial and clinking cubes of ice.

The streets of Arad's city-centre are lined with generously proportioned if slightly tatty neo-classical buildings that pre-date Ceaucescu's concrete renaissance period. Many of the communist-built monstrosities in the suburbs are either in an advanced state of decay or derelict; iron piping has haemorrhaged streaks of rust onto crumbling, mildewed concrete edifices that have become as obsolete as the ideology that spawned them. I stop to investigate a couple of food stores but all they have is bread, the ubiquitous fizz and some tired looking cakes and pastries.

*

Cars have become scarcer, giving way to the horse and cart as I head along a minor road towards the Bulgarian border. I swear as a bony youth runs out into the road to beg for a cigarette, forcing me to brake sharply. A sign just before Calafat denotes a camping site and I follow a precipitous slope down to the sandy eastern shore of the Danube. When rumbles of thunder and spots of rain drive away local swimmers and sunbathers I risk leaving the bicycle unattended for five minutes to take a cooling dip in the river, but sleep on a secluded corner of the beach is rendered all but impossible by the Romanian folk and pop songs (regularly punctuated by exultant whoops and yells) coming from what is evidently an all-night party at the nearby restaurant.

At first light I can make out the revellers sitting on a veranda overlooking the beach as I struggle to push the heavy bicycle through the soft sand up to the road. Some of my resentment evaporates as one of them rushes to my aid and another, speaking passable English, asks me where I'm from. 'Stay and eat with us!' he entreats me.

So I find myself taking a seat amongst a dozen weary hell-raisers at a long table littered with the debris of the night's carousing. An adjacent tree dapples the stained white tablecloth with light and shadow as the sun rises over the Danube. Plates loaded with meat, bread and salad are placed in front of me and I'm offered champagne and Metaxa, but mindful of the heat and the miles ahead I settle for a more sensible orange fizz instead.

My hosts have been up all night celebrating a twenty-fourth birthday and one or two of them, especially the birthday boy, are still blissfully sozzled. Seicarin, an English-speaking policeman, would love to visit England but his salary of about sixty pounds a month means that foreign holidays are a luxury he cannot afford. He feels that Romania was better off under Ceaucescu and blames his country's present ills on high-level corruption (Romanian politicians apparently seeing each four-year term in office as little more than an opportunity to line their own pockets). He also states matter-of-factly that Hitler had the right idea about the gypsies.

This apparent approval of mass extermination as a solution reeks of the very worst kind of bigotry and makes me feel distinctly uncomfortable, but I don't know enough about the subject to contradict this most affable policeman when he tells me that over 90 per cent of crime in Romania is committed by the country's estimated two million gypsies. Given that they make up only 9 per cent of the population, that's quite a feat.

*

Bulgaria's narrow Iskar valley wends its way between the tree-covered mountains and imposing pale grey cliff faces of the Stara Planina range. Finding a suitable patch of ground for a bivouac is far from easy because surfaces are either too steep or too exposed. Dog-tired after ninety-seven miles of roller-coaster cycling, I decide to make do with a stony area at the base of a cliff unsatisfactorily concealed from the road by some saplings.

I think I travel partly out of a need to be surprised and the only European country on my itinerary I haven't previously visited has been full of surprises. They began right on the border at Vidin, a short ferry ride across the Danube from Calafat, where a notice in Bulgarian Cyrillic and impeccably worded English impressed me mightily:

Ladies and Gentlemen, please write down any remarks you wish to make about the service you receive at this border, including the name and number of the official with whom you dealt, and post them in the letterbox so that the appropriate action can be taken. Thank you.

An official beckoned me to the front of the queuing cars, asked me how many days I intended to stay and had my passport stamped for me, a reception that could hardly have been more of a contrast to the welcome I received at Gyula. Much of the sparsely populated western half of Bulgaria has compared favourably with the finest areas of the Scottish Highlands, but the climate is incomparably better and the cost of living is still very cheap. I had no idea that the country was so beautiful. In every direction mountain ranges have risen, the lower slopes golden where wheat is grown, further up a layer of dark green pine and fir, and higher still, bare grey cliffs. There is nothing quite like this in Northern or Central Europe and I am convinced that the Bulgarians are sitting on a goldmine, but there is little evidence of a burgeoning tourist industry:

none of the campsites, hotels, restaurants, riding stables, bureaux de change or postcards that one would expect to find in a region apparently ideal for cycling, trekking, horse-riding, camping, canoeing and rock-climbing.

Back in Romania, Seicarin, of course, had been another surprise. Prejudiced he may have been, but the kindness shown by him and his friends had served to dispel some of my own prejudices about the poorer people of Eastern Europe... The light is failing and I'm beginning to doze off, but a nearby *clunk, clunk, clunk, swish,* repeated several times, startles me into alertness. Peering through the sparse foliage, I can make out the ample and unmistakable silhouette of a peasant woman barely ten yards away. She is energetically chopping down the porous screen of saplings providing my shelter and working her way steadily towards me.

This is one surprise I can do without; she hasn't seen me yet but at her present rate of progress discovery is imminent and, tense and naked inside my sleeping bag, I feel absurdly vulnerable. In those uneasy weeks before leaving home I had invented and rehearsed in my imagination all kinds of ridiculous predicaments, but not this one. I have absolutely no idea how she'll react – will she shriek and run off to the nearest village to fetch a posse of local thugs armed with pitchforks? Or will she decide to do something about me herself?

Clunk, clunk, clunk.

Closer now.

BRITISH CYCLIST FOUND HACKED TO DEATH IN BULGARIA

Is my adventure about to end in the most gruesome way imaginable? A grammar school and university education have left me with absolutely no idea how a naked, unarmed man ought to deal with an irascible Bulgarian peasant woman brandishing a hatchet. Surrender is out of the question because after three weeks on the road my handkerchief is no longer white and brandishing the offensive rag could easily be misinterpreted as an act of defiance. And if I have to run for it *there will be no time to put my clothes on.*

A friendly chat might defuse the encounter, but what on earth would I say? A crisp 'Good evening' followed by a disarming smile? It is highly unlikely that she'd understand English – Russian would probably be a better bet.

Dobriy Ootra then?

No. That's 'Good morning'.

Dobriy Vyecher?

Mercifully there is no need to put my tiny vocabulary of Russian to the test. With only a couple more flimsy saplings to go before discovery is inevitable, the *clunk, clunk, clunk, swish* ceases to be replaced by the more prolonged *swissssssh* of the trees being dragged to the nearby road. There follows the brisk clip-clop of a horse's hooves, becoming progressively fainter as they disappear into the gathering dusk.

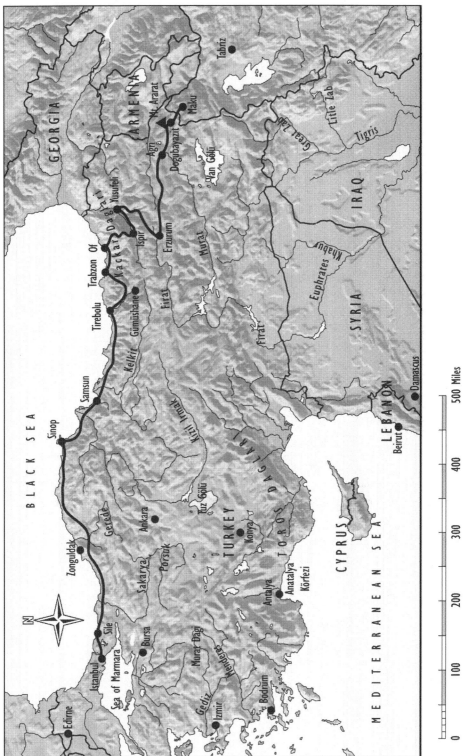

Chapter Three
Mountain Biking

Waiting to board the ferry that will take me across the Bosphorus, I am unable to rid myself of the notion that the crossing of Europe was just a training run – the hors d'oeuvre that precedes the main meal. Colossal mountain ranges and mighty deserts will henceforth straddle the route and Asia's shattered roads are grotesque caricatures of their European equivalents. The continent is scoured by dust storms, deluged by monsoons, lashed by hurricanes, shaken by earthquakes and grilled by the summer sun – and the winter air reaches temperatures that freeze the vapour inside one's nostrils. Asian countries are moreover absurdly large and tend to be administered by regimes as immoderate as the continent's topography, as cruel as its climate and as corrupt and prejudicial to human health as the parasites to be found in its water. Europe was merely an overture, announcing principal themes at the beginning of an opera.

Istanbul at the turn of the millennium is a gigantic, sprawling megalopolis of some twelve million inhabitants that straddles two continents. Legend has it that the city was founded as Byzantium in 657 BC by a colonist called Byzas, who was advised by the oracle at Delphi to locate his new colony 'opposite the blind'. Admiring the superb natural harbour of the Golden Horn on the uninhabited European shore as he sailed up the Bosphorus, Byzas (who evidently had a talent for lateral thinking and must have been phenomenally good at solving crosswords) concluded that the inhabitants of the settlement on the Asian shore at Chalcedon had to be blind and promptly founded his own colony opposite. The settlement prospered and was annexed initially by the Greeks under Alexander the Great, and eventually in 133 BC by the Romans. The city was renamed Constantinople in 330 AD when Emperor Constantine decided to transfer the capital of his empire from Rome to the shores of the Bosphorus. Despite several wars and sieges Imperial Constantinople's influence grew as Rome's declined, and it remained the capital of the Byzantine Empire until Sultan Mehmet II entered the city at the head of an Ottoman army in

1453. Churches were immediately converted into mosques and the city, renamed Istanbul, was made the capital of the Ottoman Empire. After the two-year Turkish War of Independence, during which invading Greek armies were eventually repulsed, the Ottoman Empire was abolished and a republic was formed on 29 October 1923 by Ataturk, the father of modern Turkey.

When I arrived in Istanbul eighteen years ago after hitchhiking from France, the end of Europe had seemed like the end of the world. Istanbul was the city of intrigue and danger portrayed in the best-selling book *Midnight Express* and known only to a few dedicated travellers. Although the muezzin's summons to prayer still echo metallically through loudspeakers placed high above the teeming streets on countless pencil-shaped minarets, Istanbul, like the rest of the world, has moved on. Now well and truly on the holiday map, Sultanahmet has been tamed by an invasion of backpackers and tour groups. Prices have risen, everybody seems to speak English, and the *bufes*, kebab and carpet shops have been joined by Internet cafés and bureaux de change. Trams have been installed on Divan Yolu and the big, old, petrol-guzzling American saloon cars that used to crowd the streets have been consigned to history. The Pudding Shop, now an ordinary restaurant serving unexceptional food and trading on its reputation as one of *the* early hippie haunts, was a disappointment, the atmosphere having disappeared along with the travellers' notice board where, eighteen years ago, Hendrik the Swede had left me a message.

Although Ataturk transferred the government of the new republic to Ankara – a location less vulnerable to the threat of an invasion from the sea – Istanbul nevertheless remains Turkey's largest city, her greatest port and her cultural and commercial centre. The steep narrow streets, intricate networks of alleyways, beautiful mosques, bustling bazaars, congenial climate, friendly people, excellent food, romantic views of mighty ocean-going ships at anchor on the Sea of Marmara and the fascinating juxtaposition of East and West conspire to make the city unique. I still find it an irresistible combination.

The tradesmen lugging their bulky bags onto the ferry evidently don't share my excitement at the prospect of crossing of one of the world's most evocative stretches of water. Made several times a week, year after year, this return journey must be every bit as routine for these intercontinental commuters as the daily peregrination from Charing Cross to Waterloo and back for their London counterparts.

*

After spending the night in a sloping meadow screened from the road by trees, I am woken at dawn outside Kaynarca by two dogs kicking up a tremendous din at the discovery of the tents.

'Allez, enculez!' shrieks a voice and a lithe, naked figure rushes out of the adjacent tent, stooping frequently to gather and hurl stones at them. Bearded, francophone and excitable, Eric reminds me a little of Hergé's combustible Captain Haddock and I am slightly disappointed that he didn't bellow *'Mille sabords!'* or *'Tonnerre de Brest!'* * instead.

Thoroughly awake, and anxious to make an early start before it gets too hot, I decide to get up and we eat our last breakfast together. The French couple naturally take their food seriously. Whereas I'm content to start the day with an apple or a banana, or even to skip breakfast entirely, they always have a substantial meal before setting off and insist on cooking dinner every evening. Eric, twenty-eight, followed in his father's footsteps to become a Parisian taxi driver but grew to hate the job, and Emmanuelle, a slender thirty-year-old with her dark hair cropped short, was a high-flying logistics manager who came to detest the backstabbing and office politics that accompanied her career. They ditched their jobs and left Paris in April with the intention of cycling to Madagascar to catch the first lunar eclipse of the new millennium on 21 June 2001. They yearn for a simple life in the country and talk enthusiastically of having their own hens and geese and a vegetable garden, and are thinking of running a campsite when they eventually return to France.

Content with a daily distance of around forty or fifty miles, their progress through Europe has been more leisurely than mine. They have a palatial tent which can sleep four and has an additional compartment in which to cook and eat, folding chairs, a transistor radio that only picks up Turkish stations but they invariably have it switched on anyway 'to provide atmosphere', numerous pots and pans, and even oil, salt and pepper. Emma maintains that they appreciate their home comforts, but all this indulgence comes at a price. Just before we left the campsite in Sile I experimentally lifted each of their bicycles. Emma's was comparable in weight to mine, but although Eric is smaller than me and slightly built, I was barely able to raise his loaded machine off the ground.

Having lived and worked in Leeds for six years, Emma speaks fluent English with a Yorkshire accent, but Eric's command of the language is less assured. As I became less self-conscious I started to use my French, and after spending three idyllic days cycling on empty roads amongst the cascading tree-covered mountainsides of the Black Sea Coast (taking it slowly in deference to Emma's injured right knee and rebellious stomach) we found ourselves slipping easily from one language to the other and back again.

This morning, however, our paths are to diverge. Whereas their fabulous *Entreprise Lunatique* will lead them south through Syria, Jordan, Israel, Egypt and onwards to sub-Saharan and equatorial Africa, my own, less clearly defined

*Translated in English versions of *The Adventures of Tintin* as 'Blistering barnacles!' and 'Thundering typhoons!'

journey is beckoning me east, to the Anatolian Plateau, Persia and Indochina. Alone.

'The only thing that can be said for Emma's illness is that it slowed us down and allowed me to enjoy your company for an extra two days,' I remark.

Entente cordiale is about to be replaced by splendid isolation. I have become very fond of them and parting is a painful duty to be got over with as quickly as possible. We exchange email addresses, wish each other *bon courage* and *bonne route* and urge one another to take care.

I set off more conscious of my solitude than at any time since leaving London.

*

The coast road between Kaynarca and Sinop redefines 'mountain biking' as cycling up one side of a mountain and straight back down the other. There aren't any flat bits and it is impossible to make up any speed because the descents are precipitous and winding, the surfaces a mixture of potholes, patchy tarmac and gravel. I had expected the road to be wide and teeming with holiday traffic and long-distance tourist buses, but it remains narrow and deserted and itinerant cows and donkeys outnumber vehicles. Climbing out of a valley near Ormanli at 3 mph in hot sunshine I can hear only the musical tinkle of cowbells, the monotonous chirrup of crickets and my own regular breathing.

Dogs are a menace in the mountain villages and the roads are usually either too steep or the surfaces too poor for me to outpace them. On several occasions I have had to resort to the Dog Dazer, a battery powered device that emits an ultrasonic 'beep', too high for the human ear but audible to dogs. You simply point it at the offending canine, press the button, and the animal executes a smart U-turn. At least, that's what they told me when I ordered it; on the first occasion it worked a treat and the animal pulled up and slunk away, but I believe deafness isn't uncommon in some breeds and it had no effect at all on an enormous, slavering, black hound of hell that pursued me for a considerable time, obstinately refusing to be dazed.

Fortunately the human beings in this remote area of Northern Turkey are more kindly disposed to strangers than their dogs. Few foreigners find their way to the secluded beaches, small fishing ports and reclusive villages of the Black Sea Coast, and the hospitality and generosity I have encountered along the way are ample recompense for aching muscles. Although communication problems abound, fragments of schoolboy German occasionally surface like isolated bubbles in a glass of flat beer. Thank goodness for football, which has an internationally understood language more or less of its own. The Turks are potty about the game and their knowledge is encyclopaedic. Turkey is a member of the Union of European Football Associations; her top clubs compete with Europe's elite in the Champions League, and the national team in the European Championships. Considerable interest is shown in Aston Villa because they have just signed a Turkish player, and Arsenal are often mentioned because of a recent confrontation with Galatasaray, Turkey's most successful club side.

Four men sitting on the forecourt sharing a meal at a filling station near Isanoglu invite me to join them. We eat from communal dishes using bread to scoop up the food. It is delicious fare but I have to be careful to remember to use my right hand; the left is used for wiping the backside and is considered unclean (however many times you wash it).

Separated from the baking interior by a series of mountain ranges, the Black Sea Coast is reputed to enjoy a cooler, wetter climate than the rest of Turkey. During the three days I spent with Eric and Emma we had cycled under heavy, grey skies and sheltered from downpours in village mini-markets where we were plied with tea, sweets and questions, but ever since our separation at Kaynarca the heat has been relentless. At village stores a chair is invariably brought out for me while I slake my thirst, refuel with biscuits, chocolate and fruit, and wait for the ache in my lower back to subside and the strength to return to my legs.

At one such shop halfway up a hill I find that I'm shaking like a leaf. I want milk or water, but all there is to drink is Turkish Coke so I sip saccharine fizz and nibble cheesy biscuits and a Metro chocolate bar in an attempt to restore plummeting blood sugar levels. Elderly gentlemen with unshaven, lived-in faces gesture for me to join them at their table. My offer to share the biscuits with them is politely, even deferentially, declined. Without a common language, we establish only that I'm English. The village children gather round, staring in fascination at the odd looking stranger while insatiable curiosity struggles with awe. They are smitten by the bicycle, in particular the trip computer and the dynamo. 'Woteezyornem?' ventures one of them, a little older and bolder than the rest.

After seven hours of heat and struggle on these brutal roads (not counting rest stops) I'm far too tired to make anything more than the most basic meal, never mind bother with the washing-up. Dinner consists of a simple cheese, tomato and sausage sandwich with only water to drink and I can find neither the time nor the energy to wash or shave. Lying snugly in my sleeping bag on a lofty mountaintop, peaceably waiting for the stars to break through the indigo sky, I reflect that Eric and Emma would have stripped naked and used their collapsible four-litre water carrier to have a shower. Then they'd have expertly knocked up an hors d'oeuvre of salad with vinaigrette and followed it with pasta and tomato sauce, and there would have been fruit for dessert, cups of tea and lashings of Coca-Cola – but there is so much more time and energy to spare when you are only in the saddle for three or four hours a day. It is too hot for sleep to come easily and a party is evidently in full swing in one of the valleys far below. Music, shrill, wavering and maddeningly repetitive, played by a band consisting of drums, some kind of reedy wind instrument and a megaphone-assisted baritone, wails up the mountainsides for hours.

By the time I wake up at sunrise it is already warm. I haven't had enough sleep and I sense that it is going to be another very tough day. Occasionally I envy Lukas and Martina, an attractive young Czech couple I met in Istanbul who were travelling to Australia by bus and train. By now they'll doubtless be relaxing in the Elburz mountains north of Tehran after their three-day bus ride from Istanbul. Assailed by the heady fragrance of baking asphalt and my own sweat as the sun beats down during the umpteenth long, steep climb, waving ineffectually at the flies and cursing as the wheels bounce over yet another bad patch of road, I find myself wistfully dreaming of floating effortlessly at a mile a minute inside an air-conditioned, air-suspended luxury coach, regularly refreshed by the splashes of eau de cologne offered by the attendant on all long-distance Turkish buses. To find oneself whisked over the two thousand miles of main road linking Istanbul to Tehran in just three days appears little short of miraculous in view of the fact that it has just taken me three whole days of unremitting effort to cover the 166 precipitous and bumpy miles between Isanoglu and Catalzeytin at an average speed of just over 7.5 mph.

In Doganli, a sleepy little village nestling in a cleft between mountains, I buy a litre carton of milk, a couple of bananas and a bunch of grapes from a shop and settle down on a chair on the veranda to eat, drink and rest, watching the leisurely pace of rural life and breathing in the smell of cow dung and wood-smoke. This is a side of Turkey that remains undiscovered by those who, like Lukas and Martina, elect to travel by long-distance bus. Clucking hens are scavenging around the verges and a rooster repeatedly crows in the background. A man is ambling down the single street with nine cows, some beige and some black, like chess pieces. The proprietor, who speaks some German, is telling a knot of curious onlookers that the stranger is *Inglis* and that he's on his way to *Hindustan* via Iran and Pakistan. His wife, an old woman with a kind face, frequently pauses in her activities to smile at me and insists on washing my grapes for me under the standpipe. Half a dozen men join me on the veranda, clearly with nothing better to do than exchange gossip.

'*Allahaismarladik!*' I bid them gravely, remounting the bicycle.

'*Gule gule!*' they reply, waving me off.

On the edge of the village a man is skinning a freshly slaughtered cow.

*

East of Samsun the busy road hugs the coast, passing through a successsion of ugly resort towns bristling with soulless breezeblock, brick and concrete apartment blocks, many of which are only half completed. The mountains are still there on my right, their pine-covered peaks concealed by low cloud, but they appear to have withdrawn in disgust from the contrived ugliness on the coast. The road is too narrow for the lorries and the long-distance coaches with their air-conditioned and eau-de-cologne-drenched cargoes to squeeze by with any room to spare, but waiting for a gap in the oncoming traffic before overtaking is clearly out of the question. They give me a torrid time, sounding their deafening two- and three-tone horns until, swearing, I take evasive action in the gravel and stones of the steeply cambered verge.

As I cycle further east the honking horns, flashing headlights, waving, shouting and whistling become ever more frequent. I detest being shouted at by strangers; at home this conduct is the prerogative of lunatics, drunks and immature schoolchildren. The gregarious Turks may well be expressing nothing more than friendly interest but to the more reserved English mentality such behaviour is automatically considered rude and intrusive.

Why can't they let me be? Show me some respect? For the first time in my life I am beginning thoroughly to comprehend the resentment experienced by the majority of women – despite the implied compliment – when confronted by the wolf-whistles emanating from the proverbial building site. This experience will be ruined if I can't learn to react without antagonism to minor cultural differences along the way.

*

The road from Tirebolu to Gumushane wends its way inland up a valley, following a mountain river. It is a relief to have left the din of the crowded coast road behind but the saddle-soreness that has come to trouble me at intervals ever since I left Istanbul has returned with a vengeance. Experimenting with the angle of the saddle merely moves the pressure point (and therefore the problem) either forwards to the scrotum or back towards the buttocks. The bumpy road is purgatory and I feel as though I'm sitting on shards of broken glass.

Despite the excruciating pain in my crotch I cannot fail to appreciate the natural beauty of my surroundings. Green-clad mountains rise almost sheer from the valley, with huge crags of grey rock jutting like fangs through the trees on the higher slopes. Way up on top, above the tree line, the occasional electricity pylon appears minute. Innumerable tributaries are rushing down sheer mountainsides, often as waterfalls, to join their bigger sister on her journey to the Black Sea and the air is filled with the burbling and chattering of tumbling water. The bonneted red tipper lorries that were being loaded downstream on the wider parts of the riverbed by dredgers hurtle past filled with gravel and rocks.

The tunnels that have been bored through the sheer cliff faces are unlit and so dark that I can scarcely see where I'm going, even with my lights on. Anxious to get out of these hellholes, I pedal hard, trying to plot a course as close as possible to the side of the road. The distant circle of light at the far end is taking an age to get closer and the road surface is rough and rendered invisible by the pitch-darkness. Another lorry has entered the tunnel and is thundering up from behind. It's like being in one of those ghastly nightmares in which you are trying to run away from a threatening presence but you can't get your legs to move. The noise reverberating around the confined space is starkly terrifying, apocalyptic, sounding like the approach of Doom itself; my survival depends entirely upon the efficacy of the lorry's headlights and the driver's ability to pick out my tiny rear light. *What if I hit an unseen pothole and fall off?* I feel as if I am about to be engulfed, flattened, extinguished by towering waves of sound and darkness.

At Torul I turn left towards Trabzon and the road begins to climb once more. Several loaded lorries pass by in the opposite direction, engines racing in low gear to control their descent and overheated brakes squealing. Sweat has saturated the lining of my helmet and pours down my face, stinging my eyes.

A pick-up comes to a halt in a cloud of dust and three men jump out of the cab. One of them undoes the tailgate and I realise that they are offering me a lift. I do my best to explain that although I'm grateful for their kindness, this crazy foreigner intends to cycle all the way to the top. We exchange handshakes and the van accelerates away trailing dust and fumes, the occupants doubtless shaking their heads over my eccentricity, but I have vowed to cycle the route and cycle it I will. If you can't be bothered to do something properly then why do it at all?

After two solid hours of low-gear climbing and another of those abominable tunnels, I finally reach the pass. Feeling invincible, I buy biscuits and chocolate from a shop and sit down at a table outside a café. A man leaps out of a four-wheel-drive station wagon and walks towards me, grinning widely. Wordlessly he clasps my hand. His conduct puzzles me for an instant; I can only surmise that he has seen me on the way up and is congratulating me. A boy brings me my tea, shyly asks my name and introduces himself in faltering English. He too shakes my hand and refuses payment for the tea. The Turks are generous with their admiration.

*

At the town of Of I bid a final farewell to the Black Sea. There is to be no let-up in this most unforgiving of initiations into the rigours of Asia, for barring the route inland to Ispir is the Kaçkar range of mountains and a pass of 2,600 metres. Kindly old gentlemen refreshing themselves at village teahouses examine my maps and counsel me to take an alternative route. *'Rampa!'* (mountain!) they wail, gesticulating eloquently and shaking their heads despairingly at my obstinacy.

Like so many others, they fail to understand that I have *chosen* to travel the hard way. The origins of this journey lay in a need to challenge myself – if you always take life's easiest options then how are you ever going to know what kind of stuff you're made of? I'm not so confident as to imagine that there won't one day be an obstacle which will prove too formidable an adversary for my reserves of physical and mental strength, but when that time comes I will have to discover those boundaries for myself rather than rely on guidance (however well meant) based on the limitations of other people. If I'd heeded that sort of advice I'd never have left England.

Beyond Iskedere the gradient becomes ever steeper as the road winds its way between perpendicular green walls. I take my time, stopping frequently to rest, drink, squeeze rivulets of sweat out of the saturated padding inside the helmet, and to replenish supplies at village shops. I make regular use of roadside springs, both to refill my water bottles and to cool myself down, slopping the icy water over my head, neck and arms.

Behind one of the springs is a picnic area where children are at play and a man introduces himself, speaking unexpectedly fluent English. He is a social worker by the name of Sali on a daytrip from Rize with his wife and some of the children under their care. *Kofte* (meatballs) are being barbecued and I'm presented with a vast meatball and tomato sandwich and a glass of Coke. Sali waves away my attempts to pay. Unasked, he tells me that there are a further *seventeen kilometres* of steep climbing to go before I reach the pass. Ignorance would have been preferable.

Further up I stumble into a tiny shop where, mercifully, there is a fridge in the corner. This journey is developing a habit of transforming the commonplace into the miraculous; never again will I take refrigeration for granted. I ask for a Coca-Cola. One of the two elderly men apparently in charge gestures to a chair. It is shadowy and delightfully cool inside, and we have so few words in common that we are largely untroubled by the need to make small talk. Savouring each luxurious mouthful of icy fizz, I nibble on some halva bought at a mini-market (it looks a bit like plasterboard and probably tastes like it too, but it's supposed to be nutritious). It seems scarcely credible now that in my former life I never used to think much of Coca-Cola, for during the heat and effort of the day I have come to crave the stuff with an almost narcotic intensity. The atmosphere is one of tranquil benevolence and I feel that I could quite easily go to sleep. My hosts chuckle happily when I mimic the action of sleeping, but at length we shake hands affectionately (already I feel as if they are old friends) and I return reluctantly to my battle with the forces of inertia and gravity.

Ten minutes later a car draws to a halt alongside, the driver waving his wallet at me. I realise that he's signalling that I've left my own wallet in the shop.

Shit!! I fly back down the hill, and for a second time I find myself saying good-bye to those charming, noble old men, grateful beyond words for their honesty. The wallet contained credit cards and a considerable quantity of cash in dollars. Would it have been returned to me in the same way had I left it in a bar in England? The Turkish character is full of generosity and chivalry, the automatic extension of courtesy and hospitality to a stranger a tradition that seems regrettably to have died out in the West. I'm aware that these remote mountain communities are poor even by Turkish standards, but pride and a sense of morality have clearly survived uncorrupted by the greed so prevalent in more sophisticated societies and serve to prevent people from helping themselves to something that isn't theirs. I have few scruples about leaving the bicycle unattended while I enter a shop or café because I sense instinctively that it is safe. Even so, I must be more careful in future. A part of me did indeed fall asleep in that shop.

Average speed (always assuming that I'm cycling alone and therefore at my own pace) is the most reliable barometer of physical toil. It seldom lies and today's is a paltry 6.7 mph, nearly seven hours of prodigious endeavour having yielded just forty-seven miles. I crash out under the stars on a roadside ledge, shielded from view by great piles of ballast of the sort used to anchor railway sleepers and surrounded by a vast, silent amphitheatre of mountains.

*

At first light the air at this altitude is deliciously fresh and cool, which is just as well because some of the steepest climbing is yet to come. After half an hour I down tools to drink water from a spring so exquisitely icy that it makes my head ache.

A few minutes later a lone car draws alongside me on this emptiest of roads. The trees on the slopes lower down have been replaced by short grass, boulders and scree.

'*Al-lo!*' says a voice.

'Go away!' A little ungracious admittedly, but I'm absorbed by my work and I really don't want to break my rhythm by stopping.

The car draws level once more. '*Sind sie Deutsch?*'

'*Nein!*' Nor do I want to trade banalities on the move when every breath in the thinner air at this altitude has to be fought for.

Each curve in the road tantalises me now with the possibility of release from this ordeal, but reveals only more of the same narrow, twisting asphalt, climbing ever higher.

Per Aspera Ad Astra. It is years since I last thought of my school motto. *Through Struggle To The Stars.* Never before have I been able to apply it quite so literally.

Salvation finally appears inscribed in white on a rectangular blue road sign:

OVIT DAGI GECIDI
RAKIM 2640

From my overnight position on the ledge it has taken me 1.5 hours to bludgeon out the final 5.5 miles at an average speed of only 3.5 mph. The area is remote and the pass deserted, but there is no need for teas or congratulatory handshakes here; the sense of achievement at having climbed from sea level to a pass of 8,661 feet (almost twice as high as Ben Nevis) in little more than a day is intoxicating and comes from within.

Accumulating height is like putting money in the bank. Whatever goes up must eventually come down and the subsequent freewheeling is a gloriously irresponsible spending spree, an enjoyment of the fruits of previous toil. Initially I use the brakes because the road surface isn't to be trusted, but when it improves I let her fly between sunlit mountainsides, as fast as a bird and too fast for the flies, the only sound the roaring of the wind in my ears.

*

Sensing that the weather is hotter in this parched valley than at any time since I left home, I stop at a tiny village on the narrow, deserted road that leads to Yusufeli for a much-needed cold drink. The fertile greens of the Black Sea Coast have become dehydrated browns and yellows and the mountains are barren, high-baked and crumbling. The air is as dry as the rugged landscape, which reminds me of Utah or Nevada.

My arrival scatters clucking hens and kids surround me like flies, giggling and shouting out English phrases and questions, more out of bravado than any desire for conversation or answers. At length an elderly gentleman appears, shoos off the children, and offers me the deference I've come to expect. He shakes my hand, introduces himself in German and a conversation of sorts ensues. He tells me that it is forty-two degrees Celsius and gleefully assures me that tomorrow the weather will be even hotter.

Like the circle of light at the end of one of those hellish tunnels, Yusufeli offers the promise of deliverance but never seems to get any nearer, a sure sign that I'm getting tired and fed up. The airflow is like the hot blast of a hair drier and for the first time fails to cool me down. At one point the road breaks up and I lose my gears as it bends and climbs sharply because I'm trying to swat a fly at the same time as changing down. I miss both the fly and the gears, and very nearly fall off through sheer exhaustion. 'F*****g roads!' remarks a voice that seems to belong to someone else.

I arrive in Yusufeli steaming and feeling like a baked potato after seven hours in the saddle, damp clothes clinging and sagging with the weight of absorbed sweat, skin covered in salt deposits, feet smarting and tender posterior on fire. At such times I question what I'm doing but the answer is rarely long in coming. I make straight for the first mini-market and drink a litre of chilled milk. Never has the stuff tasted so delicious. By chance there is a bicycle repair shop opposite, where the proprietor fixes my mudguard stay and refuses payment after a long session admiring the bicycle. Then to the campsite, where a blissful plunge into the fast flowing river extinguishes the fire. I could almost hear the hiss as I entered the water.

The travelling is hard and at times it has pushed me close to my limits, but exploring and redefining those limits has been immensely rewarding. Physically I've never felt better: I must have lost a stone in weight since leaving home (when I was neither overweight nor unfit), and muscles all over my body have hardened and ripple most satisfactorily under taut, deeply tanned skin. I am being forced to reassess the value of luxuries I used to take for granted and I've come to appreciate the simple pleasures of life in a way that I've rarely done before.

'Why don't you fly, Christopher?'

The recollection of that question, delivered in a tone of gentle mockery by a relentlessly pragmatic friend, never fails to elicit a smile. To travel by air would have been to miss the point entirely, and only very seldom and fleetingly do I wish that I'd opted to travel by bus and train, for you become inured to luxury – just as surely as you adapt physically and mentally to its deprivation. The astonishing size and diversity of this planet are being fully revealed to me precisely because I chose to travel in this way. Sights, sounds and smells are so much more vivid and immediate on a bicycle; my senses have remained undistracted by music, air-conditioning and cigarette smoke, and memories and impressions of a fascinating land aren't confined to fleeting glimpses through a small pane of glass.

*

Notwithstanding the intense heat, nobody in religiously conservative Eastern Turkey wears shorts. During a two-day stay in Erzurum I cover my legs in order not to stick out too much from the crowd but it is a poor disguise. In order to blend in with the locals I'd have to wear cotton trousers instead of tracksuit bottoms, an open-necked long-sleeved cotton or nylon shirt, and ideally a waistcoat and jacket plus a flat cap or skullcap. In addition to a complete change of outfit I'd have to pull out a few teeth and forget about shaving for several days.

The city's broad, tree-lined boulevards are a riot of competing restaurants, shops and stalls, the pavement kiosks (*bufes*) vying with the mini-markets for custom. Businesses offering similar products or services tend to be grouped together in Turkish cities, and at least fifty doctors and chemists are squeezed into a Hypochondriac's Alley. Many of the women are hidden behind all-enveloping chadors and veils that reveal only their eyes, and others are concealed by headscarves and long coats. I wonder how they can possibly bear the heat.

A fierce headwind makes a fool of me as I leave Erzurum. The vertical cliffs and narrow canyons of the Coruh and Oltu valleys further north have been replaced by the East Anatolian Plateau which, more fertile and ringed by distant pale-green mountains (many of them over three thousand metres high), is reminiscent of the Mongolian Steppe. I can see for miles; the sun shines on distant, emerald-green hillsides dappled with darker patches of shadow, and the gold of recently harvested rectangles alternates with the greens and browns of pasture and ploughed fields.

Eastern Anatolia is home for the majority of Turkey's neglected ten million Kurds and the villages are remarkable for their poverty. The dwellings are usually single-storey two-room mud-walled hovels with roofs of corrugated iron or dirt. Pyramids of dung bricks stacked outside are used for fuel during long and bitter winters, when temperatures can plummet to minus forty degrees Celsius. Cattle, geese and hens roam the dirt tracks in these isolated farming communities and the dogs are very large, aggressive and pale in colour. Feeling as if I've somehow blundered into a Roadrunner cartoon, I manage to outpace the first two but the next big dog is ahead of me, sniffing the air inquisitively. Aware that I haven't got enough momentum to leave it behind, I bring the bicycle to a halt and rummage in my bar-bag for the Dog Dazer. Cerberus is still looking in my direction, sizing me up. I pedal slowly forward and much to my surprise, before I've even had a chance to use the Dazer, the animal slinks away, tail between its legs. 'I'm only human, mate,' I reassure it as I cycle warily past. Maybe I smell worse than I thought.

For a main through route the E80 is gratifyingly deserted. At one point the asphalt surface ends and I ride onto a surface of loose stones and dirt. Passing vehicles, although mercifully rare, throw up a dense, choking fog of dust and I can hardly see my hand in front of my face. By the time I emerge five minutes later I am covered from head to foot in fine white powder.

Convoys of venerable lorries displaying Turkish, Iranian or Bulgarian number plates occasionally drone past. Toiling up another of Turkey's interminable hills, I can hear the sound of a heavy diesel approaching from behind. The lorry slows down as it draws level and the smiling passenger leans out of the window, holding out a cucumber. I decline because I'm not wild about cucumbers but he insists. I reach up and grab it like a runner seizing the baton in a relay race and the lorry roars off with a blast of its horn. These examples of local kindness never fail to boost morale and lend extra strength to tiring muscles, for I feel tiny on this immense plateau and under this vast sky, the wind continuing to make a mockery of my puny strength.

*

Dusty and flyblown, and just twenty miles from the Iranian border, Dogubeyazit has an unkempt, down-at-heel air about it and possesses none of the grandeur and drama of the surrounding landscape. People are thronging the dilapidated streets, urchins shouting the inevitable *Al-lo*s like parrots as I search for the campsite. Mount Ararat, reputedly the final resting-place of Noah's Ark and, at 5,137 metres, high enough to be permanently snow-capped, towers disdainfully over the manufactured squalor below.

Although the mountain is officially out of bounds to tourists and presents a difficult and dangerous climb requiring specialist knowledge and equipment, two Americans and a New Zealander staying at the campsite are intent on locating the Ark, thought to be embedded in the ice near the summit. Knowledge and equipment they have, but the mountain is in a militarily sensitive area and the authorities are stalling on the issue of the necessary permit. The discovery of the Ark will, they maintain, rubbish Darwin's theory of evolution and prove the existence of God. They believe that the Universe is only about six thousand years old instead of several million and that, far from evolving, we were created by God exactly as we are (as recorded in the Book of Genesis). They are persuasive talkers, backing up their arguments with scientific evidence, several references to the scriptures and many personal anecdotes about how God has entered their lives. Richard, a fifty-five-year-old airline pilot, has been attempting the climb every summer for the last nineteen years.

The other American, Dave Larsen, is a charismatic forty-five-year-old teacher from Pasadena. Pointing out that although species have demonstrably become extinct none have demonstrably evolved, he insists that evolution remains theory rather than scientific fact because it can neither be demonstrated nor repeated. Confident and articulate, he cites several events in his own life that he regards as positive proof of the existence of God.

Normally I would be deeply sceptical of such claims, but this is no religious crank or social misfit. On the contrary, he is highly intelligent; nobody in my view who teaches mathematics and physics can be considered anything else, and these are disciplines that moreover demand a cool appreciation of logic and an analytical brain (which is probably why I was never any good at them). Naturally drawn to people driven by passion, I find myself liking and respecting him even if I don't entirely agree with his beliefs.

He appears convinced that God has entered *my* life.

I'm not so sure; I have become rather fond of the notion that the universe is bestrode by giant, super-intelligent aliens inhabiting a different dimension and timescale to us and that God is an alien biology teacher who has created the Earth as an experiment to enable his (or her) pupils to study the extraordinary behaviour of *Homo sapiens* (in exactly the same way that we might create an environment in order to examine the behaviour of a colony of ants or the metamorphosis of caterpillars).

'If I were doing your cycling trip I'd be much happier to know that God was with me,' remonstrates Dave. 'Surely it makes sense to believe?'

'It makes excellent sense to believe, but it's not something you can *decide* to do – like making an investment or taking out an insurance policy. You either do or you don't.'

He asks if I would mind if he were to say a short prayer for me.

'Um… no, not at all.'

He closes his eyes, puts his hands together and bows his head. His words are moving rather than embarrassing and I can only envy the strength and comfort he so clearly draws from his relationship with God.

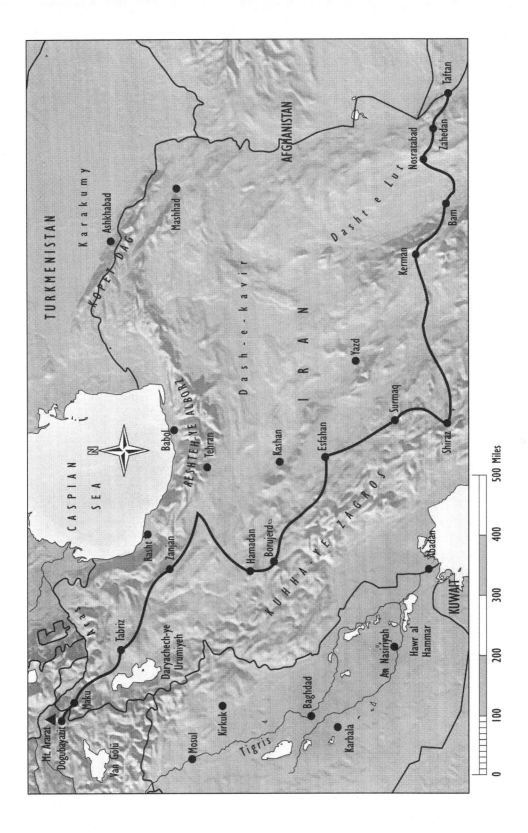

Chapter Four
'Always Right'

Turkey experienced centuries of first Greek and then Roman rule before gradually being overrun in the thirteenth, fourteenth and fifteenth centuries by the Seljuk and Ottoman Turks, who, fleeing the Mongols, imported Islam from Central Asia to Asia Minor. Although the overwhelming majority of her people are Muslim, present-day Turkey is nevertheless a secular, democratic state and it is to the West that she has turned once more. Clinging to Europe by a mere fingertip, she has applied for membership of the European Union and is a long-standing member of NATO. Western tourists are welcomed into Istanbul and Cappadocia, and they pack the resorts on her Mediterranean and Aegean coasts.

Iran, however, is a very different proposition. While Kemal Ataturk was presiding over the creation of modern Turkey, Reza Shah Pahlavi was also looking westward, aiming to transform imperial Iran into a modern, secular, westernised state with France as the model. Although the reforms he instigated were continued after his death under the auspices of his son, the latter was too impatient and possibly not quite as ruthless as his father, and crucially he underestimated the enduring importance of religion to the Iranian people. Many of the changes, which included the banning of the veil and the emancipation of women, ran directly contrary to Islamic law and few people experienced the benefits of the wealth that flooded into the country following the tripling of oil prices in 1973. The booming economy brought only corruption and growing opposition to the regime, and when supporters of the exiled Ayatollah Khomeini took to the streets Mohammed Reza Shah fled into exile, leaving a triumphant Khomeini free to return in 1979 and create an Islamic Republic governed according to the ordinances of the seventh century. So much for the Pahlavi dynasty's programmes of modernisation. It is intriguing to think that had the Shah been a little more circumspect Iran might today, like Turkey, be a modern, secular, westernised society and a member of NATO, but twenty years after the revolution the country remains in purdah, its doors slammed shut to the West.

To enter a country for the first time is to rediscover something of the magic and mysteries of childhood, and I approach each border with the same sense of happy anticipation I used to experience when opening those tiny doors on an advent calendar. With hundreds of huge lorries parked two and three deep on both sides of the road and crammed into every available space elsewhere, hot, dry and dusty Bazargan, the Iranian border town, is little more than a gigantic goods marshalling yard, but I have just stepped through the back of the wardrobe into Narnia, a parallel world full of exotic smells, tastes, colours and sounds. People behave and dress oddly and speak in mysterious tongues. They eat strange food, the design of the buildings has changed and unfamiliar makes of cars and lorries fill the streets.

Notwithstanding the warmth of the welcome I received from the little man in the Tourist Information Bureau at the border, the customary excitement is laced with apprehension as I cycle down the hill towards the town centre, for the unknown can be daunting as well as fascinating. I have just entered a theocracy run by despotic, fanatical and virulently anti-western zealots with a reputation for sponsoring anti-Zionist terrorist groups and inciting frenzied mobs to burn the American flag, and my imagination is filled with images of angry bearded men in robes and turbans and grim, shadowy women suffused with hatred for anything western. Feeling under the circumstances that I could use a little moral support, I'm anxious to catch up with the Slovenian cyclist who, according to my loquacious friend in the tourist information office, entered Iran about an hour earlier.

Herds of goats, sheep and cattle nibble at leathery, ankle-high tufts of scrub scattered about a dusty semi-desert channelling between ranges of barren mountains. At Maku the mountain ranges converge, squeezing the town into a narrow valley. Signs over shops and businesses, an incomprehensible series of dots and squiggles, serve to increase my sense of alienation and I can't find anything to eat except biscuits and sweets, but I receive plenty of friendly interest and a free tea from the proprietor of one shop.

'Robin Cook, your prime minister, is a beautiful man!' he beams.

This isn't an opinion I happen to share but beauty, as they say, is in the eye of the beholder. I cycle out of Maku reassured by the encounter and musing that the Iranians might not after all be so very different from the Turks.

Maybe Milo the Slovenian cyclist shares my unease; at any rate he appears more than happy to have company. Tall and skinny, with shoulder-length fair hair and a wispy beard, he is wearing a grey T-shirt and jeans held up with braces, and on his feet is a pair of flip-flops. His bicycle resembles something one might pick up for a tenner at a car-boot sale and the bulging fluorescent green and purple panniers appear to be held together with string, but having previously cycled across Italy, France, Germany and Switzerland, and travelled to Indonesia, Argentina and New Zealand, he is already a veteran traveller at the tender age of twenty-three. He wants to get to Australia, where he intends to find work and earn enough money to subsidise the next leg of his journey, but the rotten Australians have turned down his visa application.

At the end of the day we lay out our sleeping bags behind a stony ridge and he shows me the consulate's letter of rejection.

'It's not the Australians but irresponsible people from Eastern Europe overstaying their visas who are ultimately to blame for your difficulties,' I point out. Try as I might, I can't get him to grasp this simple fact; he is adamant that the Australians are being unreasonable. All evening he drones on interminably about visas and what everything costs. I've paid far too much for my mount because he met a German with a *titanium* bicycle costing only 1,200 deutschmarks, and he is delighted that the Pakistani visa he bought after a ten-day wait in Ankara cost a fraction of what I paid after spending a couple of hours in the Birmingham consulate.

'Do English people need visum per Argentina?' he asks me.

'I've no idea. I should think so,' I reply, wondering how someone who has led such an interesting life can possibly be so boring.

Mountains continue the next day to rise steeply on either side of a broad corridor of desert and scrub. The unexpected greenery provided by the occasional irrigated oasis appears incongruous, as if a portion of Welsh valley has been cut out and carefully pasted onto the arid hinterland. Dark-green oil tankers drone past us trailing smoke and dust. The universal car is the Paykan, an unassuming four-door saloon that I used to know as the Hillman Avenger. Although the model's production ceased in England about thirty years ago, vast quantities continue to be assembled in Iran.

The current regime has continued the renovation of the country's road network instigated by the Shah and thanks to the superb surfaces we make good time, but distances between towns and villages and other places of sustenance in a country three times the size of France are often considerable. Roadside stalls selling fruit (grapes, water melons, apples, tomatoes or pears) occasionally come to our rescue, but some commodities, such as milk, chocolate and the cakes I got used to eating in Turkey, are scarce.

We spend an age searching for bread, fresh vegetables and fruit in one village, surrounded by an ever-growing crowd of unruly urchins. When I tell one particularly repulsive child to stop tampering with my gears (I have no desire to be faced with a broken cable at this early stage) he takes his hand away and the bicycle topples over.

'For God's sake! Just leave my stuff alone!' What was left of my patience has evaporated in an explosion of anger.

'You must not get nervous!' admonishes the Bearded One, who is beginning to exasperate me almost as much as the kids.

I glare at him. 'Who's getting nervous?' I know perfectly well that he means *énervé* (angry).

At the end of the day I snuggle down into my sleeping bag in a secluded gully. I want to watch the stars appear in the sky as dusk gives way to darkness and do some thinking, but Milo is evidently keen to fill the silence.

'Do you know Iranians have to make a visum per nearly every country?'

'How fascinating!'

'When you go to Yugoslavia with truck did you make a visum?' he persists, oblivious to my sarcasm.

'No, I don't think so. If I did, I bought it at the border.' Twelve years on I remember the episode as clearly as if it were only… well, about twelve years ago.

Because the Swiss cyclist we met yesterday was wearing shorts Milo states that from tomorrow he's going to follow his example. I think he's unwise to do so; I try as far as possible to adopt local customs when travelling, not just to avoid causing offence but because I dislike attracting more attention than is strictly necessary. To that end I purchased two hideous long-sleeved striped polyester shirts – extremely uncomfortable in the heat – from a stall in Erzurum and I've started to grow a beard, not only to save precious water and the anguish of al fresco shaving, but also in the hope that with my black hair and naturally dark skin I might eventually pass as an Iranian (none of whom appear to have much time or inclination to shave).

'How many *Iranians* have you seen wearing shorts, Milo?' I ask him.

He won't budge. I think he's a fool and that he's inviting trouble but, as he so rightly says (with some heat), it's his decision. We seem to be diametrically opposed in almost everything, our exchanges ending in a series of frustrating culs-de-sac. He has no apparent sense of humour, is a poor listener and appears to have forgotten my name.

'All the English people I've met are very quiet,' he observes at length.

'Really?' I yawn.

*

The wealth that flooded into Iran following the massive hike in oil prices in 1973 led to a dramatic increase in car ownership under the Shah, and between 1970 and 1978 the number of privately-owned cars quadrupled. Because petrol is heavily subsidised by the current regime this is one of the cheapest places in the world to run a car, and the roasting streets of Tabriz – an untidy, low-rise sprawl of brick, concrete and stucco cubes dwarfed by a mountainous hinterland – are filled with fumes and the sound of horns. Roundabouts are a tricky proposition because nobody seems to be clear who has right of way –

do you give way to traffic on the roundabout or to traffic approaching from the right? Iranians are lousy drivers and it is remarkable in the circumstances how few accidents there are. The city's pavements are bustling with unshaven men wearing loose-fitting trousers and long-sleeved cotton or nylon shirts open at the neck (the tie is officially derided as a symbol of western values), and women resembling nuns in their voluminous black chadors.

According to my guidebook the only bank in the entire city that changes travellers cheques is the main branch of the Bank Melli. Stopping frequently to refer to the city plan, I eventually locate the building after cycling against the traffic flow on a one-way street. We arrive just half an hour before it closes and, probably because the staff are anxious to go home, changing money proves to be remarkably quick and painless.

Regrettably, the same cannot be said for Milo's international phone call. Emailing would probably have been cheaper and infinitely more painless than telephoning but he refuses to have anything to do with computers, so we spend a nightmare three hours in chaotic traffic and punishing heat trying to find somebody to sell him a phone card. Each time we grind to a sweaty halt to ask directions huge crowds gather to stare, but Milo (who has carried out his intention to wear shorts) is apparently blissfully unaffected by self-consciousness as well as sensitivity. Everybody we ask has a different idea of where we should go, and in the end I manage to persuade him to forget the card and phone from a hotel instead. We strike lucky at the third attempt but he complains bitterly at the price of the call, and it occurs to me that the first two establishments might well have refused him access because of his haughty insistence on wearing shorts in a country where this is tantamount to walking around in public in Y-fronts. Treat parochial customs and sensibilities with contempt and you can hardly complain if the locals don't go out of their way to accommodate you. To the Iranians he must cut either an offensive or a ludicrous figure and to me he has become an embarrassment.

*

My companion sleeps like a log. The scattered boulders are casting long shadows in the early morning sunshine and I have to shake him awake. Despite frequently asking me the time, he maintains that he can manage perfectly well without a watch and, because his bicycle isn't equipped with a trip computer, he is unable either to monitor his speed or keep any check on the distance he covers.

I have found I am unable to let go to that extent. I need targets and incentives and deadlines, and as I like to benefit from the early morning coolness I find it makes sense even to set the alarm. I am beginning to understand that I can't lead a life without any structure and that freedom for me means merely the license to set my own deadlines instead of having to submit to those imposed by others. My life remains subject to a timetable and I feel naked without a watch.

With chilled fingers we assemble and pack away our gear, the five large dogs barking menacingly at us from a nearby ridge lending unaccustomed haste to our movements. I could cheerfully murder for a filter-coffee and an alternative variety of Bach.

After an hour's steep climb in slanting sunshine and long shadows we stop, thoroughly warmed-up, on the pass near a police checkpoint for some breakfast. I open a tin of tuna and spread it on some bread, a task rendered awkward by the recent loss of my knife.

Milo is chopping raw garlic into a can of beans. 'Natural medicine!' he intones solemnly. He is a strict vegetarian and has some rather peculiar ideas about food. Apparently milk is bad for you, full of dangerous chemicals and people die from drinking too much. I find this utterly preposterous (I must have been perilously close to death on several occasions during this trip) but his dogmatism puts most matters beyond discussion.

Because I have to brake frequently to prevent myself from overtaking him on descents and he has the beating of me on the inclines, logic would suggest that my bicycle is heavier than his.

'No it isn't,' says Milo.

Reminded of a well-known Monty Python sketch, I'm tempted to ask him if he'd prefer a five-minute argument or the full half-hour, but the joke would be lost on him and I know better than to get involved in a pointless dispute with someone who has no interest in exploring alternative points of view. It is this inflexibility, bordering on arrogance, that makes his company so tiresome and I have become appalled by the notion that *Never Right* might be stuck with *Always Right* until India or beyond. Should I put his attitude down to immaturity? I can't remember ever having been that certain about anything – not even at the age of twenty-three.

'This cheese is very cheap,' he drones smugly, hacking a sliver off an unappetising pale-yellow brick he bought in Turkey ten days ago. 'One kilo for half a million Turkish lire!' He is inordinately proud that the basic road map of Iran he purchased from the Tourist Information officer at Bazargan cost him only a dollar, whereas my much larger scale Geocenter (which, delineating the contours of the land with subtle shades of green, brown, yellow, white, grey and mauve, not only tells me much more about the character of the country we're crossing but is also an object of beauty) cost me six quid from a bookshop in Kidderminster.

'Six English pounds!' he shrieks, his face a study in incredulity. *'That's nine dollars!'*

Yes, I know it is. And when I get home I intend to hang my beautiful nine-dollar map on the living room wall with my route highlighted in felt-tip pen so I can show my guests *precisely* where I met this pain-in-the-neck of a Slovenian.

He has bought some concentrated lemon juice and fiddles around for an age at roadside springs getting the mix of juice, water and sugar exactly right. We seem to spend almost as much time looking for food as we do cycling because he usually has to lumber around in search of somebody who understands English (no easy matter) so he can ask them if there is any meat in the tin of eggplants he has set his heart on. A crowd of delighted onlookers (mostly children) grows by the minute. Then, right in front of the assembled masses, the Pied Piper decides that he has to wash his feet in a nearby fountain. Desperate to leave the gawping crowds behind, I wait in the baking sunshine, fidgeting, fulminating under my breath and musing that village life in Iran must be excruciatingly dull.

Unlike in Western Europe or America, the bicycle isn't associated in developing countries with sport or recreation but with transport for those who can't afford to buy a car – and yet we must be rich because we're westerners. Farm hands, doubtless puzzled by this conundrum, whistle and holler from nearby fields in wide, irrigated valleys and I have become convinced that there is a touch of mockery in some of the *Ello Meesters* flung from the windows of passing cars. I continue to find it deeply alienating to be singled out in this way – after all, I'd never dream of shouting *Salaam Aleikom* to anybody wearing a turban or a veil on an English street; such behaviour would be considered insolent and provocative (not to mention racist).

Milo has just told me that my guidebook is a waste of money.

Ye Gods! Reflecting irritably that my companion is one of those people who knows the price of everything and the value of nothing, I embark upon a futile case for the defence. I remind him that if it hadn't been for its street map we'd never have got to the bank before it closed, and instead of sleeping out for free in the mountains south of the city we'd have been obliged to spend an expensive night in a hotel before trying our luck again today. Perhaps there is a variety of pioneering machismo associated with discovering everything for oneself but to me it seems merely stupid to disdain information if it is available, and a decent guidebook invariably saves one considerable time and trouble – not to mention expense in the long run.

Superannuated lorries, buses and mopeds envelope us in filthy clouds of carcinogenic black (or bluish-white) smoke as we do battle with a headwind and I ponder the irony of returning home bearing a legacy of supreme fitness combined with cancer of the lungs or throat. A shout from behind is the signal that Milo wants to relieve himself and he proceeds to do so in full view of the road, ostentatiously waving his discharging trouser snake at passing traffic. I prefer to find somewhere a little more private myself, particularly in a country as squeamish as Iran about displays of the flesh, and I wait for him further up the road in a highly unconvincing attempt to make out that we're travelling separately.

Chapter Five
Travelling Light

Low tables have been placed around three sides of a large room, two of which are being used as beds. A contented snoring emanates from one of them. On another a man is sitting cross-legged, eating his breakfast. Using the language section at the back of my guidebook, I order cheese, jam, bread, two eggs and tea, rolling the eggs and the cheese and jam in separate pieces of *lavash* bread, which is a little like the Indian *chapatti*. The result is a thoroughly enjoyable and sustaining vegetarian breakfast for only a dollar.

Roadside restaurants and cafés are ridiculously cheap and an ideal way to make contact with local people, who continue to appear mercifully unaffected by the anti-western rhetoric propagated by the regime. Milo, who refused to eat in cafés or restaurants because of his paranoia about being served meat, is probably tinkering at the roadside somewhere with a can of cold beans and raw garlic, a ludicrous figure in shorts breathing in lungfuls of exhaust and surrounded by gawping spectators. If I'd liked him enough I'd have accompanied him to Tehran where he has to visit the Australian Embassy, but a reluctance to fight my way into and back out of Iran's sprawling and polluted capital city instead became a useful pretext to part company. Considering that we shared an addiction to travel and were facing very similar challenges it is both surprising and a shame that we were unable to get on better. No doubt there were faults on both sides; someone with greater wisdom than the little I possess would doubtless have decided to find him amusing instead of irritating. Not once during the five days we travelled together did he ever address me by my name and our parting was unaccompanied by regret.

The traffic on the road to Hamadan is scarcer than on the highway to Tehran and the cycling is less predictable, full of bends and dips and loops as I begin a gradual ascent across a stony plateau towards a distant chain of mountains. A family in a Toyota Landcruiser stops just ahead of me and the driver gets out to present me with a bag of grapes and peaches before doing a U-turn.

How far did they go out of their way to give me this present? The trouble they took to get it to me has placed their modest gift beyond price.

A dried up riverbed winds its way between parched hills. The periodic appearance of orchards, paddies and vineyards in the otherwise desiccated landscape is explained every now and then by the chugging of a diesel powered pump, drawing water from some remote, subterranean source. I buy some more grapes from a roadside stall where I chat to three elderly men, one of whom has enormous holes in his socks.

At a small shop in Avaj, a village situated halfway up a very long, steep hill, I refresh myself with a couple of bottles of Zam-Zam, the locally manufactured orange or cola-flavoured fizz. A small crowd gradually materialises to examine the bicycle and ask me questions, and I gather that a clicking of the tongue accompanied by a shake of the head signifies approval rather than censure. Out on the road I probably remain a symbol, a bizarre representation of western eccentricity and excess, but the welcome is never less than genuine once I am revealed to people as another human being. I suspect that much of my previous inability to cope with local inquisitiveness was due to the aggravating presence of Milo.

I ask the general spokesman, a swarthy, cheerful middle-aged man badly in need of a shave and a visit to the dentists, how much further it is to the top of the hill.

'Panj (five) kilometres!' comes the reply. And then, he tells me with a gap-toothed grin, I can expect *bist* (twenty) kilometres of downhill freewheeling.

After another forty minutes of steep climbing I order a chicken kebab with rice and yoghurt at a restaurant, mixing the yoghurt into the rice to add moisture to what would otherwise have been a rather dry meal. These places are usually more suggestive of a school or a works canteen than the western concept of a restaurant, plainer and more functional with fittings consisting of plastic chairs and Formica tables laid out on a floor of black and white 'chessboard' linoleum tiling. Pictures depicting lush, conspicuously green Alpine landscapes and waterfalls (presumably representing paradise in this waterless land) are popular, and the inevitable portraits of Khomeini, the forbidding countenance Iran displays to the outside world, glower stonily down at the diners from high on the wall. With heavy, black eyebrows set beneath the high forehead of an intellectual and the dark, smouldering eyes of a fanatic, he looks cruel and puritanical.

The headmaster is watching you, boys and girls. The grim lines of that face do nothing to belie the nature of the beast crouching behind it; instead of doling out detentions this particular headmaster (accountable not to the Iranian people but to a higher authority) administered imprisonment, torture, amputation and execution in the name of God. Whatever else he may have been, Khomeini was not a tolerant or a forgiving man.

At times I can become so immersed in the physical effort of accumulating miles that I temporarily forget where I am. Occupying 636,292 square miles, Iran is roughly three times the size of France and half the size of India. Mountain ranges and strong winds render the cycling physically demanding, but the roads are rarely less than superb, the best since Germany. In early September it is still uncomfortably hot and I can't wear the appropriate clothes for fear of outraging local sensibilities.

By mid-afternoon a gale is howling across a stony, exposed plateau and passing vehicles suck me towards them. Because I got up at sunrise the eighty-mile daily target has already been reached but finding somewhere to bivouac has been difficult of late; in Europe I used to rely upon trees and bushes for concealment, but vegetation in Iran signifies an oasis and the unwelcome presence of people, livestock and dogs. Privacy is offered by the mountains, the more barren and remote the better, but when the mountains have receded into the distance there is no alternative but to improvise. After nearly seven hours in the saddle I spot some half-finished buildings that appear to offer the only concealment for miles around.

At home I was unable to lie in bed or loll in front of the TV for long without feeling guilty because there were always things to be done, but apart from making the daily entry in the diary and putting up the bivvy, there is absolutely nothing to do for the rest of the day. With Karrimat and sleeping bag laid out beneath me and the bicycle propped up against a wall, I lie on my back with the sweat drying under the afternoon sun in a kind of dazed euphoria, halfway between sleeping and waking. Four hours of glorious, guilt-free indolence to go until sundown. High on endorphins and physical contentment, I am too busy mentally digesting the day's events and route planning to succumb to boredom, although at times I feel that a good book or a little music would be a pleasant way to shorten the hot, silent afternoons. I was greatly tempted to pack my personal stereo and half a dozen CDs, but I left them behind on grounds of extra weight and their vulnerability to damage and theft.

We are defined in the material West by the careers we follow, the homes in which we live, the cars we drive, the clothes we wear, the belongings with which we choose to surround ourselves and the company we keep, but I have left almost all of these distinguishing marks behind along with the music I love. *So who am I?*

No longer surrounded by the people and possessions that used to remind me, define me and bind me, I am free to be whomsoever I like. I am travelling light in every sense – maybe I can even be myself for a while. My subconscious, however, isn't yet at peace with this new way of life, for my sleep is routinely troubled by dreams in which I'm balancing on high, rickety structures, haunted by a terrible fear of falling. Last night I dreamt that I was climbing up a fifty-foot-high grandfather clock, only for it to topple over just before I got to the top and jerk me into heart-thumping wakefulness.

*

As a representative of the discredited, decadent West I half expected to be met in Iran by emotions ranging from mild disapproval to outright hostility, but the attitude of Iranians continues to make a mockery of my earlier premonitions. The elderly proprietor of a fast-food joint on the outskirts of Hamadan wants to know, amongst other things, if I'm married. I find it easiest to answer this particular question in the affirmative; a 'no' requires too much explanation and they usually end up feeling sorry for me, which I find rather chastening. It is considered pretty disastrous here if you aren't married and don't have children by the age of thirty (never mind forty) and their genuinely expressed sympathy makes me feel like a failure – notwithstanding the discovery that I rather like some aspects of being single. Having the freedom to make this journey is but one example.

He opens a notebook half-filled with neat, handwritten Farsi at a fresh page and gives me a pen. Not really knowing what he wants, and quite certain that he won't understand a word of it anyway, I write down my name and email address, the date and brief details of my route. When I ask him for the bill, he refuses to let me pay. He is quite adamant, so what can I do but shake his hand and thank him?

When I buy a tomato and a cucumber near the end of the day in Goukar the boy behind the till refuses to take any money for them, so yet again I have to replace my wallet unopened. Even the police are human. Normally I cycle straight through the many checkpoints, but a couple of officers wave me to a halt near Borujerd. I understand the word *kuda?* (where?) because it is the same in Russian, and the two questions that recur above all others are 'where are you from?' and 'where are you going?' so I tell them. When they ask me with the help of sign language where I sleep I mutter something about hotels and restaurants because I have a feeling that sleeping rough and camping in the open are officially forbidden. They nod trustingly. It is a good-natured encounter and as soon as their curiosity is satisfied I get their permission to continue.

Breakfast in a small café near Miyandast consists of two bowls of porridge pleasantly flavoured with cinnamon followed by goat's cheese wrapped in lavash bread, all washed down with three glasses of sugary tea. After eight days on the road since leaving Dogubeyazit I am sorely in need of a shower and the opportunity to wash the dust of desert bivouacs and the soot exhaled by passing vehicles from my clothes. My shirt is crusty with salt and general grime, my trousers are covered in dust and oil – at some stage I must have caught them against the chain – and the embryonic beard makes me look like an escaped convict, but Mahmoud the proprietor and his acolytes don't seem to mind. Sporting villainous looking beards of their own, they watch affably as I set about the business of satisfying a massive appetite. Mahmoud (who bears a passing resemblance to Cut-throat Jake in the Captain Pugwash books) leafs through my guidebook and reverently kisses the photograph of the Shah.

Khomeini's portrait, however, receives a sacrilegious thumbs-down. When Khomeini returned from exile in 1979 there were only thirty-five million people in Iran, but the population has since all but doubled. Almost seventy per cent of the current population is under thirty, and their attitudes are often very different from those held by their parents twenty years ago. Generally I prefer not to discuss political or religious matters during encounters with local people and they are rarely mentioned anyway, but Mahmoud's gesture was the first evidence I've seen that the regime may have lost touch with the people it claims to represent. Ironically, many consider it guilty of the very corruption that brought down the Shah and swept it to power, and in the presidential election of May 1997 Mohammad Khatami, a moderate, pragmatic clergyman, won an unprecedented seventy per cent of the electorate's votes on a platform advocating greater personal freedom. The real power in Iran rests not with the president, however, but with the Supreme Leader of the Republic, Ayatollah Ali Khamenei, a hardliner elected by a council of religious leaders. More than three years after the election conservatives and reformers remain locked in a struggle for supremacy and the pace of change is slow.

Lorries have been trundling past on the dual carriageway between Dorud-Azna and Esfahan. Chained onto their flatbed trailers are great slabs and blocks of marble quarried from the mountains. A dark-green Mercedes lorry sounds its horn and the co-driver leans out of the window to give me a wave; I spoke to him in a restaurant yesterday. I am burning up energy at a frightening rate and the immense distances that exist between eating and watering holes mean that I tend to fuel up whenever I can rather than when I want to. Over their *chelo morgh* (chicken with rice) or kebabs, drivers smile or wave at me in roadside restaurants, indicating by sign language that they passed me earlier. Most of them must have done so many times and I have had to decline several offers of a lift.

'Mersi, khost mazé bud!' (Thank you, it was delicious!) I murmur on paying the bill.

*

Friday, the Muslim day of rest, starts slowly in Esfahan. The traffic on the Chahar Bagh Abbassi is thin, the pavements are deserted and the metal shutters covering shop fronts remain down. I walk along a broad avenue between beige stucco facades down to the river, but Iran is suffering from its worst drought in thirty years and, like all the other rivers I've seen in the country so far, the Zayande is dry. By the time I've crossed to the opposite bank by way of one of the narrow seventeenth-century bridges for which the city is famous, the heat has become oppressive. I have come to appreciate that the trees planted in parks, on pavements and along the promenades in these hot cities have a functional as well as a decorative purpose.

Imam Khomeini Square, presided over from one end by the immense blue-tiled portals and patterned turquoise domes of the spectacular Masjed-e Imam mosque, consists of wide, paved walkways running between well-tended gardens. The area is enclosed on all sides by a bazaar, rows of vaulted arches providing shade over passageways serving shops in which carpets, handicrafts, souvenirs, tools, fruit and spices are displayed.

Newspapers, cinema and TV remain under rigid state control but computers and satellite dishes are threatening to lift the veil with which the mullahs have sought to 'protect' the Iranian people. In Iraj's carpet shop a single computer is connected to the Internet. The line is often busy, the computer is in great demand from other travellers, and in a country where everything else is absurdly cheap, emailing is expensive at over £2 an hour. Since one of the priorities of a totalitarian regime has to be to control the public's access to information it comes as something of a surprise that surfing the Internet is permitted at all in Iran. Although Internet sites considered unsuitable by the Government are apparently blocked, effective monitoring of the vast worldwide web must be a near impossible task. The Internet's high cost currently places it beyond the reach of most Iranians, but as soon as it becomes more widely available prices will surely follow the pattern elsewhere and fall.

Western travellers assemble every evening in the courtyard of the Amir Kabir Hotel to exchange travellers' tales and ponder the mystery of what the locals do with their spare time. No-one has seen any discos, swimming pools, sports halls, pubs or clubs. The authorities are opposed to chess, card games and backgammon, and gambling is prohibited. Hopefully the Iranians have no need to bolster their self-confidence by getting drunk, for the consumption, possession, production and sale of alcohol are all serious crimes and the country's many vineyards are dedicated to the production of grapes and raisins instead of wine. In the West the availability of alcohol and the presence of music are inextricably linked to the idea of 'having a good time' (a party without either would be inconceivable) and if there had been beers in Esfahan no doubt we would have drunk them. The only stuff available, however, is vile-tasting imported alcohol-free lager, and Khomeini considered western pop music decadent and unworthy of an Islamic Republic. Six months after the revolution he stated in a broadcast on Iran Radio: 'An Islamic regime must be serious in every aspect of life. There is no fun in Islam. There can be no fun or enjoyment in whatever is serious.' Nevertheless picnics appear to be popular and there are cinemas, but few foreign films are considered suitable (probably too much fun) and the locally produced films that survive the censor are presumably bland, uncontroversial and – above all – serious.

One evening I climb a narrow stairway to a teahouse overlooking Imam Khomeini Square to watch the sun set over the remarkable mosque. With lanterns hanging from the vaulted roofs, carpets decorating the walls and a hint of conspiracy in the air, teahouses – in which locals gather to drink tea, smoke their water pipes and exchange gossip – are the Iranian equivalent of a pub. As the only seats available on the open balcony are facing away from the square I have to twist quite awkwardly to get a view of the mosque, a structure that – for me at any rate – invites veneration of the architects and craftsmen responsible for its sumptuous design and construction rather than homage to the Almighty.

All my interactions in Iran having hitherto been with men, I am not a little astonished when the two black shapes seated opposite sit down next to me. One of them, speaking fluent English, explains that they are being pestered by a local man and would be grateful if I'd allow them my protection. This, I fear, is a little like requesting a drug-addict to take charge of a pharmacy, for despite her concealing black shroud I can see that she is quite beautiful. Her name is Bahar, which she informs me means 'spring'. She asks me where I'm from, offers me a cake, and tells me in a low voice that she would love to leave Iran and is studying German with the intention of one day emigrating to Germany where she has 'a friend'. I am instantly jealous. Her companion, Azar-Noosh, is quieter, plainer and less self-assured. We swap addresses and telephone numbers and Bahar asks me to ring her tomorrow. The day after she is going to Tehran for a few days.

Khomeini referred to the Shah's forcible banning of the veil as 'one of the darkest moments in the history of Islam'. Women, obliged to imprison their bodies, personalities and individuality in public behind the all-enveloping chador or raincoat and headscarf, are banned from participating in several sports and it is illegal for them even to ride a bicycle. If they wish to swim in a public place then they have to do so fully clothed. Polygamy is once again permitted and they can be married as early as the age of nine. Mixed dancing, public displays of heterosexual affection and fraternisation with foreigners are all actively discouraged by the Komitehs, groups of government appointed stooges charged with the enforcement of the Islamic code. Although Bahar understandably detests it, I have come to find the chador rather alluring; it lends the opposite sex an aura of remoteness and mystery – particularly when a sleeve is drawn back to reveal a slender wrist or a flash of jewellery, or a hem is momentarily lifted to reveal a tantalising glimpse of jeans and high heels or the forbidden fruit of a well-turned ankle and painted toenails. According to the regulations the hair must be completely hidden, but the more rebellious women defiantly wear their hoods or scarves set well back on their heads, reminding me of the kids at school who used to challenge 'the system' by wearing non-regulation red socks or their ties knotted loosely beneath an unbuttoned collar. Like those kids, the women are exploring the limits of their freedom and my heart goes out to them.

The next day I take a deep breath and ring Bahar from the hotel, but she can't come out because she has a German lesson and she won't be back from Tehran for another three days.

'What are your plans?' she asks, sounding far too cool and self-possessed for my liking.

I can't make any until I get my visa extension on Wednesday. Perhaps I'll ring her on Thursday, when she returns from Tehran? Awkwardly, I say good-bye.

What did I expect? To learn more about the intriguing shadowy world inhabited by Iranian women, certainly. Anything more? Her attitude towards me yesterday had been very inviting but many Iranians, cut off for so long from the outside world, are merely intrigued by foreigners. Confident, intelligent and stunningly attractive, she will never be short of suitors and of course there's that blasted German, but why insist on giving me her phone number if she didn't want me to use it? I replace the receiver feeling confused and wishing that I shared her sangfroid.

I spend a couple of hours in the hotel's courtyard with the bicycle, checking it over and oiling it. The early afternoon heat renders the slightest expenditure of energy exhausting and the pavements and streets are quiet. It is siesta time and Esfahan is dozing in the sunshine – even the moneychangers that loiter near Imam Khomeini Square disappear at this time of the day. I have purchased some strips of foam rubber from a shop stocked with old car seats to replace the bubble-wrap I've been using with limited success since Dogubeyazit to combat saddle-soreness, and while I'm taping them to the saddle a German called Ralf saunters over with an air of professional interest. Another lone cyclist, he left Hanover at the beginning of May and he too is heading for Pakistan.

Citing the recent kidnappings of three western travellers, the Foreign Office's website 'strongly advises' against overland travel through South East Iran and Baluchistan, but with Taliban-ruled Afghanistan out of bounds there is no alternative road east. Although I have vowed to cycle as much of the route as I can, cyclists must be particularly vulnerable to attack and I'm not at all keen on the idea of being kidnapped. People usually bring trouble upon themselves;

were the three travellers abducted only because they were unfortunate enough to be in the wrong place at the wrong time, or because they were acting naively or stupidly? A vision of my father, haggard with worry, trying to raise enough ransom money to save the worthless hide of a son who ignored warnings given for his own good, brings me out in a cold sweat.

Ralf, however, is determined to cycle the whole way and suggests that we do the dangerous stretch between Kerman and Quetta together. He reassures me that he met a Japanese cyclist in Turkey who had cycled the route in the opposite direction without any problems and points out – with some justification – that institutions such as the Foreign Office have to 'cover their asses'.

Still undecided whether to continue by bicycle or to opt for discretion and the bus (but reasoning that if we get kidnapped I could always tell my father that it was 'this German bloke's' fault), I agree to postpone a final decision until we rendezvous in Kerman. One's entire life is a series of calculated risks and I'd like to learn more about the degree and the nature of the hazards facing us in Baluchistan before finally making up my mind.

Chapter Six
Zam-Zam, Cockroaches and *Moby Dick*

I had been hoping that the detour to Shiraz and the Zagros Mountains might bring something different – a glimpse of snow-capped peaks, perhaps, or verdant valleys moistened by snowmelt – but during the four days it takes to cycle the three hundred miles from Esfahan to Shiraz I find myself experiencing a sense of deja vu. The heat, the dust, the headwinds, the steep hills, the mountain passes, the dusty villages of tiny mud-brick houses and the spectacular landscapes of desert and mountains have been constant companions ever since Bazargan.

The wind is like a living thing, capricious and temperamental and downright bloody-minded at times, determined to prevent me from getting to where I want to; I've won every battle so far, but the war is never over. Passing drivers continue to toot their horns and wave, and some lorries are scarcely any faster than the bicycle on the steeper hills. One co-driver appeared to be yelling encouragement, leaning out of his window and exhorting me to get to the top as if I was the favourite horse in a race. Geriatric Mercedes buses displaying portraits of the Imams and slogans of varying degrees of piety such as 'Beautiful Bus', 'Mohammed', 'Mash'Allah' (God Is Wonderful) and 'My God' – I suspect that in the latter case something has been lost in the translation – roar past vomiting black clouds of undigested diesel from their exhausts and with the panels enclosing their rear-mounted engines propped open to prevent overheating. My own cooling system frequently threatens to boil over, the sweat stinging my eyes as I power my way up to another pass under a fierce sun. At night I sleep fitfully, partly due to the difficulties of breathing through a nose blocked by the dust and exhaust fumes inhaled during the day, and partly because the full moon is bright enough to cast shadows across the desert.

Whenever the cycling itself loses a little of its magic people obligingly step in to entertain me during rest stops. While I'm propping the bicycle up outside a restaurant in a nondescript village called Surmaq a thickset man beams at me from his white pick-up and asks me where I'm from. Nothing unusual in that, but his English is better than most and he claims to have friends in Norwich. If

I follow the pick-up he will take me to a better establishment down the road.

A luxury coach is parked outside the restaurant of his choice.

'I think these people also are English,' murmurs my friend, stepping through the door and indicating the packed tables within. Then, without any warning, he places a proprietary arm across my shoulders and bellows: 'THIS MAN HAS COME FROM ENGLAND ON HIS BICYCLE!'

It is as if he has just lobbed a rock into a pond. Ripples of astonishment emanate from the assembled diners, most of whom are elderly. All eyes are turned in our direction. The presence of about fifty British OAPs in this outback village is every bit as extraordinary to me as the sudden apparition of an English cyclist must be to them. It is some time before I can tuck into my congealing chelo morgh because several people have come up to our table to ask me about my journey. A number of them insist on taking my photograph and very kindly offer to send me copies. A lady asks me solicitously if there is anything I need (but sadly no-one there uses my preferred brand of toothpaste), another presents me with a tin of extra-strong mints, and they all wonder at the Herculean nature of my achievement and marvel at the distance I still have to cover – and I simply *must* write a book about it! They are touring the country by coach and I ask them a trifle wistfully if anyone would like to swap their nice comfortable seat for my saddle, but there are no takers.

Having already covered a respectable sixty miles I decide to accept Sasan's invitation to spend the night with him at his home in Abadeh. He used to be Iran's champion cyclist and would have competed in the 1980 Olympic Games if the revolution hadn't intervened. He has a farm near Surmaq where he grows wheat and grapes, and he would like to own cattle too. He is renting a small apartment until his new house is built and his wife is the first Iranian woman I've seen not to wear the headscarf. They assure me that Iranians are free to wear and to do pretty much whatever they like within the privacy of their own homes and that they even drink wine.

*

Mindful of my rendezvous with Ralf (who is cycling a more direct route via Yazd) in Kerman, I leave Shiraz after only a day, cycling out of the city past the airport on a busy dual carriageway. Beyond the city limits are several roadside stalls selling pomegranates, and near Pol-e Fasa is further evidence of Iran's drought: pale sand and glistening white salt-flats are all that's left of a dried-up lake.

By the time I stop just outside Estehban there are over a hundred miles on the trip computer and I'm running on empty, but I am unable to find anywhere to sleep. The road is bisecting a wide, fertile plain and the barren escarpments and concealing contours of the mountains, although visible, are beyond reach. The fields are full of farm hands, children and herds of goats, and the roadsides are lined with people waiting for lifts or buses home. A stony ridge provides shelter from the road, but farm hands are still moving around amongst the nearby fig trees. As I stand there, perspiring and irresolute, a pickup trailing dust joins the road from a nearby dirt track and scrunches to a halt alongside.

'Can I be of service?' asks the driver.

'I am looking for somewhere to sleep,' I reply, hoping that he'll somehow solve my problem for me.

He remains silent, however, so I ask him if I can sleep in one of the fields. He replies in the affirmative and I wheel the bicycle off the road and prop it up under a fig tree.

A few minutes later three men approach while I'm reclining on the Karrimat eating grapes.

Shit! I did so want to be left in peace. I ask permission to spend the night on their land, but the eldest, a gaunt, white-haired man of around sixty, signals that I'm to sleep in his house. Hurriedly I repack the bicycle and follow them, dragging it with difficulty over the loose soil.

The old man's name is Zhozai and his two lieutenants are called Akbar and Assad. Zhozai's wife, two daughters and a grandchild are waiting for him at home. We exchange pleasantries with the help of the guidebook's language section (which is invariably a great ice-breaker) and then we eat. It is simple fare: bread and goat's cheese with walnuts, cucumber and melon, and the inevitable glasses of tea. I play devil's advocate, testing the political climate by pointing in turn at the pictures in the guidebook of the Shah, Khomeini, Khamenei and Khatami and asking them if each potentate is *huub* (good).

No to the Shah, yes to the others. Out in the rural backwoods people are conservative in their attitudes and there appears to be less urge for change than in the cities; Sasan too was anti-Shah. Their loyalty is understandable: because the regime has returned land that used to be owned feudally by rich and powerful families to the peasants and has invested heavily in the rural infrastructure, extending and improving roads and increasing the availability of electricity and drinking water, fewer people are migrating to the cities in search of a better life.

Zhozai and his family are devout Muslims. At one point I'm slightly puzzled to see the old man standing erect and muttering, apparently to himself. Comprehension dawns when he suddenly kneels and touches his forehead to the ground, repeating the action twice. The mother and two daughters are always well hidden by their chadors and they refuse to be photographed; the chador is *huub*. As always, religion is most deep-rooted amongst the poor and the uneducated and these are the people who would have been most alienated by the Shah's ill-fated attempts to drag Iran headlong into the twentieth century.

Assad and Akbar return home at dusk, leaving Zhozai and me to sleep outside on the veranda whilst the women disappear into the house. The air is warm and the silence awesome, the Zagros Mountains a deeper, looming blackness against the charcoal, star-filled night sky.

At dawn Zhozai lights a fire and boils water for tea. After breakfast (scrambled eggs with lavash bread) I present Fatima – the baby's mother – with a selection of foreign coins as a souvenir and refill my water bottles. Time to go. I thank Zhozai for his hospitality and shake him by the hand, but when I extend my hand to Fatima she recoils in horror and I realise that I have committed a classic faux pas; *any* contact of the flesh between strangers of the opposite sex is evidently forbidden in these ultra-conservative areas of Iran and I have probably just offered my host's daughter the equivalent of a French kiss. Holding hands as a demonstration of heterosexual affection is frowned upon even in the more liberal atmosphere prevailing within the cities, but for adults of the *same* sex to stroll hand in hand has none of the implications that such behaviour would elicit in the West and is a common sight throughout Iran – albeit one that I took a while to get used to.

*

I wake up in the desert outside Hoseinabad after another beastly dream involving deep stairwells, broken banisters and vertigo with an obscure sensation that something is wrong.

The mountains have been left behind and for the past two days the road has been crossing a remote landscape of scrub and flat, shimmering desert. There have been few villages, even fewer restaurants, the occasional isolated black tent inhabited by Qashqai nomads, very little traffic, plenty of mirages and not a vestige of shade.

I squat and a torrent of diarrhoea splatters onto the gravely surface. The simple routine of getting dressed is desperately hard work, and so great is the temptation to go back to sleep that I crawl back into my sleeping bag fully clothed. With no shade and limited supplies of food and water, however, this is no place to be ill and twenty minutes later I force myself to get up.

After little more than an hour's cycling I stop, panting and sweating, in the inadequate shade provided by a small, thorny tree to rest and nibble half-heartedly at an apple. For the first time in my adult life a colonic valve abruptly opens without permission, deluging my cycling shorts (which I'm wearing beneath my trousers). I wheel the bicycle off the road, prop it up against some boulders, and do my best to clean myself up with tissues and water, very grateful that there is nobody around in this isolated place to witness my humiliation.

By the time I stop an hour later at a roadside kiosk to drink a couple of bottles of Zam-Zam my head is swimming. When I ask the vendor if I can sleep for a couple of hours in the inviting rectangle of shade behind the kiosk, doing my best to explain that I'm ill, he points to a brick building behind the kiosk and tells me that I can rest inside.

The single-storey building comprises a spacious hallway, a room containing a bed, a screen and several pharmaceutical products in a glass cabinet, a kitchen, toilets (thank goodness), and two large, empty rooms upon the floors of which a number of mats and cushions have been laid out. I lay down my sleeping bag and fall asleep instantly under a poster of Gary Neville, the Manchester United defender.

I spend the rest of the day and all night in that room, drifting between the blackest, most profound oblivion, strange, almost hallucinogenic dreams, and a sort of dazed semi-consciousness in which my head seems to have detached itself and is floating somewhere above my body, which is burning hot.

Another flood of diarrhoea in the morning leaves me feeling as weak as a kitten. I try to eat a little of the breakfast I'm offered although, even after twenty-four hours without food, I'm not hungry. When I ask about the first-aid room my host explains that his job is to deal with any accidents or emergencies on this isolated section of road. Like so many others I've met in Iran, he'd love to live and work in England, but I have to tell him that he has little chance of realising his dream.

Although I'm less than a day's ride away from Kerman, cycling remains out of the question. My appointment with Ralf having been scheduled for midday tomorrow, I have run out of time to recuperate; there is no alternative but to concede defeat and take the bus. Assisted by the owner of the kiosk and the first-aid man, I flag it down. The bicycle is hauled aboard through the rear doors and placed in front of the back seats, and I am ushered to a seat of honour right at the front. To my astonishment the blind man who was waiting with me at the roadside starts to sing in a high, quavering voice while the attendant shuffles down the aisle collecting money. A little later he alights in a remote patch of desert, presumably to sing for his supper on another bus.

The landscape sliding past the window, although austerely beautiful, is harsh and forbidding, and I reflect that to tackle this stretch I really would have had to be 100 per cent fit. The mountains have returned, causing the road to rise and fall in irregular cadences, and opportunities for rest or refreshment would have been scarce.

The two young men seated immediately behind me have established that I'm English.

'Liverpool?' hypothesises one of them. European football appears regularly on Iranian TV and Iranians are almost as fanatical about the game as the Turks.

'Charlton Atheletic!' postulates his friend. Iran is full of Charlton fans because this unfashionable club possesses the signature of Karim Bagheri, the first Iranian player to ply his trade in the Premiership.

'Tottenham Hotspur!' I counter, without joy.

'Tottenham very beautiful!' says an appreciative voice on my left.

I can only conclude that he's never seen them play. The attendant, a cocky youth whom I'm convinced has overcharged me, plies me with glasses of tea and pistachio nuts (which I find inedible). When he hands the bicycle down to me outside the bus station in Kerman he brazenly asks me for a tip and, too weak and sick to argue, I hand him another five thousand rials.

Feeling utterly unequal to the business of finding a hotel, I study the guidebook's street map, trying in vain to get my bearings. A group of men whiling the afternoon away on a park bench beckon to me. I wheel the bike over and ask for directions to the Hotel Ommid. A tall man with a thick mane of salt-and-pepper hair and the obligatory stubble mounts a bicycle and announces that he'll take me there himself.

The Ommid is full. So is the second hotel we try. A bicycle tour of the city's hotels is positively the last thing I need under the circumstances, but my benefactor takes me home to have lunch with his delightful family. His wife teaches English at a local school and they have three handsome sons of seventeen, twelve and ten, and a daughter who, even at the tender age of fifteen, is already smoulderingly beautiful. It is a happy house, full of affectionate teasing and laughter and I feel sure that Khomeini would have disapproved. My guardian angel, who is called Khosrol, phones some hotels and at length finds one with a room available. He has gone to the most extraordinary lengths on my behalf and, recalling Zhozai and the first-aid man, I reflect that whenever I have been most in need of it help has been provided with unassuming generosity. At forty thousand rials a night the room isn't as cheap as some, but an en suite toilet and a shower are included and the cockroaches are on the house.

While drinking Zam-Zam in a café the following day I experience a sudden surge of nausea. Desperate to avoid the humiliation of chundering all over the tables and floor, I stumble outside. Khosrol leads me to a deserted spot where I can puke into some flowerbeds without drawing too much attention to myself, but the nausea fades away in the fresh air. Although I'd almost certainly have benefited from it, I've never been able to make myself sick.

Describing the incident to Ralf, I explain that although I've just laid one phobia to rest by adopting the Asian custom of wiping my bottom with water and my hand (far more efficient than smearing it with dry tissue), I can't yet bring myself to stick my fingers down my throat.

'Use your other hand,' he suggests helpfully.

Ralf ('my friends call me Ralf but *you* can call me Bob') is that rarest of phenomena: a German who can't take anything seriously. Maybe he picked up his anarchic sense of humour along with his fluent American English in the United States, where he spent a year working as a waiter in a German restaurant at Disneyland in Florida. He went on to spend a further two years travelling around the States and ever since has spent as much of his time on the road and as little of it working as possible (to the obvious disgust of his workaholic, self-made father). He lives rent-free in an apartment belonging to the latter and does the occasional menial factory job only for long enough to fund his next trip abroad. He has cycled to the North Cape, driven via Poland to Minsk, Moscow and St Petersburg before returning to Germany via the Baltic States, and has journeyed extensively in South East Asia, South America and the Caribbean. Whenever he's not working or travelling a typical day at home in Pattensen involves getting up late, eating, reading football magazines, playing computer games and watching TV, preferably football.

'I can spend days like that, hardly ever going out of the house,' he drawls in a fluent hybrid that incongruously mingles the vowels of Lower Saxony and the Midwest. 'Time just flies and I never get bored. Eighty per cent of the four million unemployed people in Germany suffer from depression because they are desperate to work, so why can't they concentrate on finding *them* jobs and leave lazy bastards like me alone?'

Fortunately he is prepared to wait in Kerman until I've made a complete recovery from my stomach problems. It has occurred to me that the tactic of travelling together is scarcely going to be any more effective against a group of Kalashnikov-wielding brigands than going it alone, but a student in Shiraz told me that although the road from Kerman to the Pakistan border was dangerous and that tourists had indeed been abducted in the area, the last one was snatched about a year ago. I have concluded that (as long as I obey certain fundamental rules) being kidnapped will be considerably less likely than being run over.

Khosrol seems to be very fond of me but I can't imagine why. I must be lousy company. He comes into my hotel room and perches on the spare bed. We had arranged to eat out but I find myself beset by stomach cramps and quite unable to countenance the idea of food, so we order tea instead and he helps himself to some of my biscuits. He says that I am like a brother to him and is convinced that we have lived together in a previous life. Last night he gave me a beautiful rosary, hand-made out of bone.

He is short of money because of the work being carried out on his new house. Feeling as if it is not only being turned inside out and periodically emptied but also wrung by powerful hands, my stomach is still giving me hell and I feel clammy and sick.

'Which do you think is more important?' I ask him. 'Your money or your health?'

'Sank you, sank you!' he beams, inconsequentially planting a grizzly kiss on my forehead.

Much as I like him, it is a relief when he finally gets up to leave. I can't cope with conversation; all I want to do is visit the toilet one more time and sink into oblivion.

*

When on my third day in Kerman my stomach accepted a meal of meaty chunks with rice, yoghurt and salad without the usual rumblings of discontent, I began to feel that at last I might be on the mend. After four days convalescing in the city I'm anxious to leave behind my squalid room, the evil-smelling toilets, the cockroaches and the copy of *Moby Dick* bequeathed to me by Toby (a rather cerebral Oxford University postgraduate I bumped into initially in Esfahan and then in Shiraz). I have told Ralf that we can plan our departure for tomorrow, and I stock up for the journey ahead with apples, pears and grapes from a nearby fruit stall.

I have arranged to meet Ralf at a restaurant at midday, but when at half past twelve he still hasn't arrived I order a meal – if he can't be bothered to turn up on time, why should I afford him the courtesy of waiting? By the time I've finished eating, having deliberately taken my time, there is still no sign of the maverick Kraut and irritation is gradually giving way to concern. The staff on the reception desk at his hotel inform me that he's not in his room so he can't be that sick and some of the concern evaporates. *Bloody Germans! So unreliable!*

Unlike Ralf, Khosrol shows up at the appointed time and we take a taxi to his single-storey house in a recently built suburb. The builders are still there, hard at work, and he tells me that the modifications should be completed tomorrow. His charming family are in boisterous form and I find myself parrying the girlfriend question and why I've never married with the usual platitudes and half-truths. It is difficult to explain the western concept of cohabiting because it is unknown in Iran, and on one occasion I feel obliged to point out that the United Kingdom isn't an Islamic Republic. Khosrol manages to obtain the phone number of Ralf's hotel and a few seconds later I'm speaking to him.

'Oh, man!' he groans. 'I've got what you had – I've been vomiting and shitting all night!' He is puzzled by the hotel staff's information that he was out when I called. 'I've not left my room all day, but I suppose you could say I was "out" in one sense,' he says ruefully.

'So no chance of leaving tomorrow then?'

'Absolutely not! Maybe Sunday – *insh'allah.*'

Khosrol and his family also maintain that I will only leave Kerman *insh'allah* (God willing) and there does indeed seem to be some sinister force at work preventing us from leaving the city.

*

Woken at half past five by the morning sun filtering through the glass skylight, I watch a huge cockroach easing its bulk through a crack in the ceiling. On Fridays there is even less to do in Kerman than usual because most shops and businesses are closed, so I decide to go and see a film in one of the cinemas. Since it is the most formulaic action movie imaginable, rendering any dialogue or commentary largely superfluous, a lack of Farsi isn't really a disadvantage. I walk along the hot, empty streets to Ralf's hotel reflecting that although nudity is immoral the regime's censors evidently have no problem with gory violence. Maybe the delay is all for the best: although it is nearly October the energy-sapping early afternoon heat is still barely tolerable.

The door of Room 2 is ajar, revealing a jumble of clothes and belongings scattered untidily on every available surface and in particular the floor. The bicycle propped against a bed confirms that I've got the right place. Ralf's inert figure is on the other bed. He doesn't stir when I call his name, but within a few seconds his subconscious appears to sense an alien presence nearby and he sits up.

'Hey, Dude!' He dredges up a wan smile.

'Do you *always* leave your door wide-open?' I ask him, aghast at the potential consequences of this lapse in security.

'Er, no. Not usually. I guess I was beyond caring last night.'

The room is both larger and cheaper than mine. A revolving fan hanging from the ceiling is gently stirring the warm air.

'Your place sucks!' he observes with his usual directness.

'I know it isn't up to much but it does have an en suite bathroom, which I found indispensable in my condition. And the people there are nice enough.'

He grins. 'Meaning that they aren't *complete* assholes? I love that expression!' Although he has improved since yesterday, he is still feeling weak and isn't up to eating anything. 'This is the fifth time I've been sick in the five months since I left,' he complains. 'Four times stomach and once with the flu.'

This compares with my three times in four months. Although the five-week crossing of Europe served to instil confidence and prepare me for the greater physical challenges ahead, it failed to prepare my stomach, and the wretched afternoon I spent holed up in my hostel in Istanbul alternately squatting and vomiting was all too symptomatic of my arrival on the threshold of Asia. The worst of such attacks is the weakness they leave behind and I counted myself fortunate that I fell ill at a place where I was able recuperate in comfort instead of on the road in the middle of nowhere (a fate that has since befallen me twice in Iran). Ralf has a theory that the cycling drains our bodies to such an extent that there is no energy left with which to fend off bugs and diseases, but I believe that most of the illnesses that afflict westerners here do so because our bodies haven't yet developed any immunity to the more evil strains of bacilli to be found rampaging around Asia. Opportunistic microbes multiply in the developing world along with violations of human rights.

Toby warned me in his dry, intellectual way that Herman Melville has 'a somewhat tangential style', but having ploughed through half of *Moby Dick* I've found that although the chunky paperback is ideal for crushing cockroaches, its contents are, well, frankly Toby old chap, *boring*. Something about this dour, long-winded epic recalls *Paradise Lost* (a set text that caused me much unhappiness at school) with Melville's diabolical albino whale assuming the role of Milton's Satan. Sorely in need of something more entertaining, I return to my hotel armed with Ralf's copy of *Dirk Gently's Holistic Detective Agency* by Douglas Adams and spend the rest of the afternoon reading it in my depressing room. The time passes tolerably quickly and for a while I'm oblivious to the legions of marching cockroaches and the stench emanating from next door. Having an en suite toilet is a distinctly mixed blessing now that my intestines have made a full recovery from their recent paralysis.

The following morning, after much deliberation, Ralf pronounces himself fit enough to totter to the nearest snack bar for a Zam-Zam. He changes out of his shorts into his slacks, revealing a pair of underpants so utterly shredded that I question the purpose of wearing them at all. They look as if they've been torn apart by a pack of dogs or raked by several bursts of machine-gun fire.

'These are my *best* ones,' he says complacently. 'You should see the others! I don't have a single pair of underpants without holes in them.'

'My last girlfriend made me throw out any socks or pants as soon as she spotted a single hole.'

'Now I understand why she's your *ex*-girlfriend – too lazy to mend them!'

I am beginning to suspect my companion of harbouring misogynistic tendencies. We make our way, painfully slowly, to the same snack bar in which I found myself on the verge of throwing up a few days ago. Smirking kids shout '*El-lo*' at us and pebbles are lobbed in our direction.

'It's nice to know that we're not the only ones really bored by this dump,' says Ralf moodily.

'Yes, but *we* don't go around giggling and shouting *Salaam Aleikom* at everyone.'

'You can probably cope better with the boredom if you're really stupid though,' he replies caustically. 'Since coming to this country I've talked to some of the stupidest people on the planet.'

We are both vexed by the delay. The lowest points on this enterprise have usually occurred when I've felt unable, for whatever reason, to move on. Similar feelings of boredom and frustration were engendered during the week I had to spend waiting for the arrival of new tubes and tyres at a mosquito-infested campsite in the Greek resort of Nea Karvali. Ralf has had enough of the Developing World, and in particular, Islam. He shares none of my affection for Turkey and had a dreadful time at the hands of stone-throwing Kurds in the southeast. Two days ago a walkie-talkie toting policeman arrived in his hotel's reception area where he happened to be lounging around in a pair of shorts and peremptorily told him to dress properly.

'Can you believe it?' he exclaims indignantly. 'It's like being in a big kindergarten!' He intends to cycle to Lahore as quickly as possible and then fly to Australia.

After a visit to an ice cream parlour he abruptly announces that he needs to lie down.

By early evening I've finished the Douglas Adams. Only Herman Melville left (and by Page 243 he still hasn't got to the point). More chicken and rice at the restaurant across the road. It's Saturday night and I fall asleep yearning for *Match of the Day* and cheese on toast.

*

On Sunday morning I kill a couple more fat cockroaches with *Moby Dick* and the friendly man in reception shows me a centre-spread picture of Michael Owen in a glossy Iranian sports magazine. I pay for another two nights and explain to him that I won't be able to leave until my sick friend at the Asadi Hotel has recovered.

'Guest House Asadi?' he exclaims, throwing up his hands in horror. 'Not good! Very dirty!'

I find Ralf lying on his bed at the aforementioned establishment listlessly reading one of his books for the fifth time. He cannot see himself able to leave until Tuesday – *insh'allah*.

After a lunch of *abgusht* (a stew consisting of chunks of beef or mutton, lentils and potatoes with bread) at a café, we take tea in the atmospheric *Chaykhune-ye Vakil,* the subterranean teahouse and restaurant in the centre of the bazaar.

'Those idiots are beginning to annoy me,' says Ralf, glancing balefully at the inevitable photographs of the Islamic Republic's holy trinity, Khatami, Khomeini and Khamenei.

'If we stay here for much longer we'll qualify for Iranian nationality and you could run for the position of Supreme Leader yourself.'

'That'd be an idea! I'd make the sale and consumption of alcohol and drugs compulsory, ban the chador and make the men wear shorts at all times.'

'Even in the winter?'

'Especially in the winter.'

'You could start by banning all children between the ages of five and fifteen.'

He nods enthusiastically. 'And instead of Khomeini there'd be pictures of Franz Beckenbauer on every wall, and German football on TV.'

We wander back through the bazaar amongst displays of spices, pomegranates, grapes, melons, chickens, beef, nuts, beans, tomatoes, soap, shampoo, toothpaste, moisturising cream, watches, jewellery, leather belts, wallets, T-shirts, trousers, sewing machines, cutlery, dinner sets, kettles, samovars, carpets, cloth, audio and hi-fi. On the way to our favourite ice cream parlour I have my umpteenth near-death experience crossing a street; I have become convinced that Iranian drivers are homicidal and speed up as soon as they see that you're about to step out from the kerb.

'I've been in this country for six weeks and one day... and counting,' says Ralf despairingly as we sit at a table hunched over our ice creams. 'God, I'd be fed up if I were a woman here. The men look so... *primitive*. Hidden women and primitive men... ruled by a bunch of corrupt, hypocritical old bastards who bugger off to Bahrain every few days to drink, gamble and f**k. They have doubles to take their places while they're away, of course.'

'Hmm... maybe you're right! In any event I don't think mixing religion with politics and economics works – religion should be a matter of personal choice, not government policy.'

'Ah, but those guys are clever,' says Ralf, a speculative finger deeply embedded in one of his nostrils. 'Any criticism of them counts as a blasphemy against God.'

Chapter Seven
Savouring Moments

Early on Tuesday 3 October we wobble tentatively down Imam Khomeini Street from the Asadi Guesthouse before turning left at the roundabout onto Shahab Street, where we discover that a bracket on Ralf's luggage rack has broken and it occurs to me that we may be destined to remain in Kerman forever. A Heath-Robinson bodge with a bungee strap salvages the situation, however, and after a final pause to obtain petrol for my stove from a filling station on the outskirts of the city, we head out into the desert.

Perhaps because we've spent so much time trapped in the city, the harsh Iranian scenery appears more than usually appealing. Rugged mountains, looming khaki in the foreground or towering grey in the distance, rear up from the dusty desert floor, displaying dramatic contrasts of light and shadow in the clear morning sunlight. Bandits aren't the only hazard to be encountered in Iran's south-eastern province of Sistan va Baluchistan; a report under the headline 'Wild Boars Spark Panic' in the English language *Iran News* caught my eye when I was in Shiraz. Driven crazy with thirst by the unprecedented drought, the boars are apparently rushing into towns and villages in a desperate search for water, disseminating panic amongst residents. Henceforth we will have to guard our water bottles as well as our wallets.

'Shall we sing something?' shouts Ralf from behind.

'What have you got in mind?'

'How about the English national anthem?'

'OK. Take it away then!'

'I don't know the words.'

'All right, I'll sing it and you can hum along.'

We belt out *God Save the Queen* and I suggest that in the interests of protocol we really ought to perform the German national anthem too.

'I don't know the words for that one either!'

'Doesn't it start with *Deutschland, Deutschland uber alles*?'

'Not any more! After the last war somebody decided that those words were no longer "appropriate".'

So we hum the German national anthem and, because we're Good Europeans, the *Marseillaise* as well, but before long we are compelled to save our breath because the road has been climbing steadily. After a rest in a lay-by where two friendly lorry drivers share their tea with us, we reach a pass and a glorious spell of storming downhill cycling follows, with panoramic views of mountains and desert laid out before us beneath a steely sky. I am Gandalf in Tolkien's *The Lord Of The Rings,* riding his peerless steed Shadowfax to the rescue of the besieged city of Minas Tirith.

During a further pause for refreshment at a roadside café a man asks Ralf if he is Japanese.

'A mistake anyone could have made,' I remark. My companion is fair of complexion and stands at six foot two in battered size twelve trainers still speckled with the faint, dried out remnants of the bouts of squitters that afflicted him in Kerman.

'Most people either take me for a Japanese or a Jamaican,' he replies imperturbably.

The sky has darkened and a headwind springs up as we resume cycling. We are obliged to put on our waterproofs when spots of rain multiply to become a downpour. When the rain eventually eases off a glorious rainbow inscribes a dramatic parabola against a glowering, pewter sky.

Whereas I favour sleeping in the open, Ralf has expressed a strong preference for shelter in the form of an abandoned building or one of the many culverts that run beneath the road. Despite having previously sworn that I'd never sleep under the road unless I was truly desperate, I find myself laying out my sleeping bag in one of these concrete bunkers. It is spacious, provides concealment from fellow beings, shelter from wind and rain, and it is surprisingly quiet, layers of concrete and bitumen muffling the sound of the occasional car or lorry passing only a few feet above us.

'*Strangers in the night! Two lonely people...*' Ralf's hideous baritone echoes unpleasantly off the concrete walls and ceiling as I set up the stove. Distant pairs of headlights can be occasionally be seen moving stealthily across the desert like will-o'-the-wisps. Smugglers? Characters engaged in more nefarious activities might also find these useful places in which to conceal themselves. Or a police patrol? Either way, we are relieved when they head off in a different direction and disappear.

*

Two forty-six-year-old bachelors, an Austrian and a Swiss, have arrived by bicycle at Ali Amiri's Legal Guesthouse in Bam. Alois and Urs set out independently but joined forces in Turkey. Urs, whose aim is to cycle via India and South East Asia to New Zealand, hardly ever opens his mouth so it is difficult initially to know exactly what to make of him, but Alois makes the rest of us look like dilettantes. This remarkable character started travelling independently at the age of fifteen and reckons to have visited about 150 of the 200-odd countries in the world. Cycling around South America, he had to contend with hundred-day headwinds in Patagonia and armed robbery in Columbia. At the age of forty he ran the Vienna marathon in a very respectable two hours twenty-seven minutes. An accomplished mountaineer, he has walked from the Khyber Pass to Darjeeling, and he has canoed the Amazon, where he slept in his canoe amongst crocodiles and swarms of mosquitoes and took his morning swim with the piranhas.

'How come you didn't get eaten alive?' we ask him disbelievingly.

'Because piranhas aren't dangerous unless there's blood in the water,' he replies casually. 'You just have to be careful not to cut yourself. And the crocodiles couldn't jump over the sides of the canoe.'

The second part of this statement doesn't quite ring true because I happen to know that crocodiles can and do jump; a young croc leapt at me while I was touring a crocodile farm in Zimbabwe, and despite the fact that it wasn't fully-grown and there had been a stout wire-mesh fence between us, the incident had been distinctly unnerving. It must have been a really big canoe – or maybe the crocodiles just weren't hungry. He intends to cycle on through Pakistan, India, South-East Asia and China. Then he'll fly to California and cycle across the States, completing his circumnavigation of the globe by flying across the Atlantic and cycling back home across Europe to Austria. Between journeys he teaches German and skiing. A real-life, Austrian version of Indiana Jones, he is unfailingly optimistic and gregarious and one of those rare people who radiates energy and confidence. It is impossible not to loathe him.

Consumed by envy, Ralf and I find ourselves discussing the Austrian Phenomenon at a restaurant. 'Alois is probably good in bed too,' says Ralf sardonically, tucking into his kebab. 'I can imagine the piranhas warning each other: "Careful boys! It's Alois taking his morning dip – for God's sake don't cut yourselves!"' Radiating lethargy and cynicism, he could hardly be more unlike the dynamic Austrian superman.

'*Instinct* must have told the crocodiles that Alois was in that canoe and that they'd get their heads ripped-off if they attacked him,' I conjecture spitefully. 'If these men and women were allowed to eat together do you suppose we'd get one of those spontaneous orgies of sexual depravity which are always breaking out between courses at restaurants in England and Germany?'

The segregation of male and female diners by a curtain is probably just an extension of the custom of separate toilets and changing rooms which we accept without question in the West, but along with the obsessive public concealment of the flesh and body contours it reinforces my impression that in Iran such laws exist because the opposite sexes can't be trusted to keep their hands off each other and have to be isolated, like naughty children.

*

A crowing rooster is answered by barking and howling dogs, and the muezzin at the local mosque joins the chorus soon afterwards, making the hour before dawn in Bam one of the noisiest times of the entire day. Barely audible above the general din, the alarm on my wristwatch cheeps superfluously and Ralf responds with a deafening fart.

'More tea, vicar?' I enquire automatically, having rather painstakingly explained this oldest of English jokes to him.

He yawns and stretches. 'You know, I wouldn't mind being a vicar.'

'The fact that you don't believe in God might be a slight snag.'

Ralf maintains that he doesn't believe in God, but I beg to disagree. How can he deny the existence of God whilst believing in a system of reincarnation that punishes the guilty and rewards the innocent? We debated matters theological at an Internet office in Kerman where his brutally frank – and possibly sacrilegious – announcement that he had no wife, no job and didn't believe in God astounded and appalled the staff (who, unusually, happened to speak excellent English and for whom the existence of God was, of course, beyond question).

'There's always a snag with every job I go for,' he says happily. 'Usually it's motivation.'

The series of oasis villages and the palm trees which line the route beyond Bam eventually give way to flat, open desert, the surface a blend of sand and stones. An awkward crosswind springs up, hindering our progress. *When the going gets tough, the tough get going.* The phrase repeats itself over and over inside my head like a mantra.

'Hungry?' Ralf flings the word over his shoulder as we struggle past the bloated carcass of a donkey.

After two more hours of bludgeoning our way into the wind, wallowing like ships in a heavy sea and taking it in turns to slipstream each other, we pause for a rest, leaning the bicycles against one of the green and white road signs indicating in both Farsi and Latin script that Shurgaz, the next village, is fifteen kilometres away.

'I wonder how many people back at home have ever had to go without their mahogany toilet seats, "soft, strong and incredibly long" toilet rolls, mirrors, towel rails, air-fresheners and bidets,' I muse after a brief excursion into the desert armed only with a water bottle.

'Faggots!' snarls Ralf, who has never been able to adopt the Asian method and elects to tidy up instead with pages torn from an issue of *Kicker*, the German football magazine. He takes the lead again, but is clearly struggling against the wind.

Come on, Ralf, fight it! You can use anger productively by distilling it into energy; I overtake him, directing my fury against the gale and transferring it to the cranks. *Rage against the dying of the light!*

Shurgaz consists merely of a police barracks and checkpoint marooned in countless acres of sand and scrub. Not yet back to full strength, Ralf can manage no more so we strike camp amongst the sand dunes.

In the morning we breakfast on biscuits, an apple and the rest of the feta cheese. Ralf can be heard muttering that my Prussian obsession with clocks and early starts would persuade any casual passer-by (were such a thing likely in this inhospitable desert) that *I* was the German and *he* was the Englishman. Before we joined forces in Kerman he used to sleep until either the heat or the flies would wake him up in a pool of sweat at around eleven o'clock and then, having wasted the best part of the day, he'd end it by cycling in the dark.

My stocks of food are running low and my companion, apart from some grapes, has run out of provisions entirely. The thought of the substantial meal we are going to have at a restaurant in Kahurag, the next town marked on my map, spurs us onwards into the gale, but like Shurgaz, Kahurag proves to be nothing more than sand dunes and a police checkpoint. It is a crushing disappointment. Pasta is all I have left and we have to eat, so I set up the stove. We shovel down plain pasta with olive oil, and a compassionate lorry driver donates tea and a watermelon. The watermelon is unripe and tastes a little odd, but we are in no position to be fussy.

'If Nosratabad turns out to be just another checkpoint we'll have to eat a policeman,' says Ralf, the blue and white silk VFL Bochum football scarf tied over his shaven head to prevent sunburn lending him a faintly piratical air.

'We could always tuck into Urs.' I bite into a crunchy, bright-green segment of watermelon. 'Alois will probably be along soon, towing him with a rope.'

'Austria has produced some remarkable people for such a small country.'

'Alois, Schwarzenegger, Hitler, Mozart...'

'I'd put Alois somewhere between Schwarzenegger and Hitler. Mozart doesn't really fit in.'

Signs frequently warn motorists to beware roaming camels but the only animals to be seen are lying in varying stages of decomposition at the roadside, victims either of the drought or an accident. Several police pick-ups have been cruising past in both directions with machine guns mounted in the back, evidence of the seriousness with which the regime treats drug smuggling from the nearby Afghan and Pakistani borders. My estimate that it will take us three hours to get to Nosratabad and food soon proves to be wildly optimistic, for I hadn't counted on twenty-five miles of unwelcome ascent into an arid mountain landscape of austere, craggy beauty. With no end of the climb in sight we collapse at the end of a tunnel and, frantic with hunger, check through all our panniers for forgotten scraps of food. Ralf eventually unearths a pitifully small bag of nuts and raisins.

Nosratabad is a dusty nonentity of a village full of evil brats who chuck stones at us. There is little in the few shops and, unaware of his danger (for cannibalism has never seemed so attractive), the truculent old bastard in charge of the only restaurant in town refuses to cook us a meal. Ralf abruptly loses his temper, bellowing in classic parade-ground style that we want eggs and bread (both of which are clearly available) *AND WE WANT THEM NOW*. A rant is so much more potent when delivered in a German accent and two meals are grudgingly served.

Breakfast after another night in a culvert consists of a tin of cold baked beans each. Cycling behind Ralf has become particularly unpleasant and I find myself wondering irritably why he has to stop pedalling every time he lets rip with one of his thunderous farts. Threatened with asphyxiation and having nearly collided with his back wheel on a number of occasions, I overtake, glaring at him.

He grins back sheepishly.

After two exhausting hours of cycling into another headwind we shelter in a culvert near a police checkpoint and I cook the rest of the pasta. An interested puppy settles down a few feet away to watch as we mix in a couple of cans of an unspecified vegetable stew. It gratefully accepts the biscuits Ralf lobs at it but refuses to come any closer.

I mention that my last girlfriend has two Dobermans. 'Lovely dogs! The smaller, nippier one is called Porsche and the bigger one Mercedes.'

'No kidding? She sounds like a crazy bitch – no wonder you got rid of her!'

I don't think I've ever in my life come across anyone quite so cynical about the opposite sex. Our conversations have ranged effortlessly from the fantastic through the mundane to the bizarre and taken regular diversions down little-used side-roads to explore the obscene and the taboo. As well as sharing our dreams and our fears and analysing our inhibitions, we have discussed Beethoven, Jurgen Klinsmann, God, Steffi Graf and Alois; we have explored Aldi, Adolf, *Anschluss*, Austria, Alois (again), allergies and alliteration; and we have pondered political correctness, Pakistanis, potholes, punctures, pimples, past participles – Ralf is a keen student of the English language – and piles. Yet he has never mentioned the women who have shared his life. There must be a reason for his cynicism and I wonder if at some point in his dark and mysterious past he has had a Bad Experience, but if so he has never shown any inclination to talk about it and I know better than to press him. Many years ago the only woman with whom I've ever wanted to spend the rest of my life decided that she'd be better off without me and for the next five years I had remained bitter, very single and utterly disinclined to discuss the matter; for a considerable time I had foolishly allowed resentment to distort my perception of the entire female population. Watching him continue his attempts to reel in the puppy, I conclude that Ralf relates better to dogs than women. They are certainly less complex.

'Maybe you were a dog in a previous incarnation,' I suggest.

'I must have been a very *well-behaved* dog to be reborn as a German – the highest possible life-form – and to live in a country that pays such generous unemployment benefit.'

'You'll be back as a dog in the *next* incarnation, though.'

'More likely a flea on the dog's back!'

'You'll end up as a maggot wriggling on a pile of poo if you don't do the dishes more often,' I admonish him, rinsing the greasy plates and saucepans in cold water. He rarely helps with the cooking and never does any washing up.

'You know you said you're allergic to cats?' he says reasonably. 'Well, *I'm* allergic to work.'

*

Every male in Zahedan is clad in the baggy trousers and a long, loose shirt called a *Shalwar Qamiz*, an outfit rarely seen in the rest of Iran and indicative perhaps of our proximity to the Pakistan border. Although the guidebook is disparaging about the city (population 410,000), we agree that the ice cream parlour is right up there with the very best and at least as good as the one in Kerman. So maybe Zahedan is a little short of mosques, museums and monuments, but we cyclists tend to assess a place first and foremost on the quality and quantity of its restaurants and cafés; lost calories have to be replaced by the daily consumption of prodigious amounts of food and drink.

We tackle breakfast in the hotel's canteen with the Turbocharged Austrian – who appears to be one of those people whose sole purpose on this earth is to demonstrate that you aren't quite as remarkable as you thought you were – and his silent Swiss henchman. They took only two days to cycle from Bam (as opposed to our three). 'Yesterday we did a hundred miles of cycling uphill into a bad wind,' says Alois.

I'm beginning to find his ability to trump everything we do faintly irritating. *Bad wind? Try slipstreaming Ralf, mate. Then you'll learn something about the nature of bad wind.*'

'That guy had a great sense of humour, you know,' remarks the latter, apparently transfixed by the full-length picture of Ayatollah Khomeini adorning the wall opposite.

'I understand he did a really good cabaret act,' I reply, wondering just where this conversation is heading. I can't imagine a more mirthless face. It is inconceivable to me that this stern, patriarchal figure ever smiled, let alone laughed or cracked a joke – or made love to his wife. *There is no fun in Islam.* He looks dyspeptic and disillusioned.

'The trouble is that everybody took his ideas seriously,' continues Ralf. 'He only meant them to be a joke.'

The discussion turns to the European Union's boycott of Austria following the far right Freedom Party's recent surge to power in that country. According to Alois, France and Belgium were the instigators of the boycott and the rest, with the exception of the UK and Bavaria, followed their lead. As a result he has refused to speak to French people in their own language. I describe how France's illegal extension of the ban on the import of British beef led me to boycott French apples, cheese and wine. I have nothing but contempt for a foreign policy which appears to be based upon the premise that the rules only apply to everyone else, and at times I suspect that France's posturing and petulance are the behaviour of a nation with a chip on its shoulder, fretting at its diminishing influence in a world increasingly dominated by the American culture and the English language. Although Urs, being Swiss, remains appropriately non-aligned, there is suddenly a strong anti-French feeling at the table.

'We should form an Anglo-Austrian alliance against the French!' I suggest.

'Let's start a war!' exclaims the German, reverting abruptly to the national stereotype.

Following an abortive visit to the Indian consulate (where I had virtually to prise Ralf off the sofa in the reception area), a barber shaves off my hideous beard.

'Before, you looked like the survivor of a shipwreck; now you look like one of those mad Nazi scientists who carried out "experiments" in the concentration camp laboratories,' comments Ralf.

During an afternoon spent lounging in the hotel room we discuss the idea of cycling the length of the Americas from Alaska to Tierra del Fuego (Alois, of course, has already done it), but I still see the journey I'm making as a one-off. I am clinging to the hope that it will change me in some way, enabling me to return home with new ideas, different priorities, more maturity, wider horizons and greater self-confidence. It might even make me more like Alois.

Ralf, who has declared that he has no intention of ever 'settling down', is sceptical: 'Within three months of getting home you'll be back to how you were before you left. You'll have to re-adapt just to fit in.'

'Not necessarily,' I argue. '"Fitting in" has never been one of my priorities and other people can think whatever they like as far as I'm concerned. It's *my* life, not theirs, and I've only got one chance to make the most of it. When "the end is near" I want to be able to say in the words of the song that I did it *My Way*.'

'I don't like giving in to that sort of pressure either, but I usually find that I have to compromise; I don't want to make life unnecessarily difficult for myself.'

The paths of eccentricity are never easy to follow; because they are too small and seldom trodden to be marked on any map you have to navigate by instinct, and sometimes you have to hack away at the brambles and stinging-nettles of peer mistrust and incomprehension as you go, for we live in a society that encourages conformity.

At school I was considered unorthodox because my parents never felt the need for a television and consequently I was the only one in the class ignorant of the exploits of *Joe Ninety*, *Thunderbirds*, *The Six-Million-Dollar Man* and *Blake's Seven*. For a while I pretended I knew what my companions were talking about, but eventually I grew up and stopped pretending. At university my fellow undergraduates found themselves holiday jobs stacking supermarket shelves in order to fund their social activities during term-time, but I boycotted the campus bars so that I could enjoy three months of heady freedom thumbing my way around Europe every summer. Whereas my contemporaries embarked upon sensible careers in teaching, banking, law and medicine, I fulfilled a childhood ambition and surprised a lot of people by becoming a lorry driver. I went on to work, eat and sleep all over the Continent in lorries and for several years I continued to surprise people. Eventually I gave up long-distance driving because I wanted a social life and time to write; I began to cycle prodigious distances each day to and from the office (thereby subjecting myself to more astonishment) while everyone else drove.

Although at intervals the brambles and nettles grew thick and I got scratched and stung, they never really deterred me because I had been motivated by passion. But then the doubts multiplied as the rejection slips began to pile up and my relationship came under increasing strain. Stuck in a job that failed to excite and mired in a relationship that no longer felt right, the desire for change became overwhelming. Redundancy hadn't been the cause of that change; it had merely facilitated it. I set off on this journey to escape the routine of the nine-to-five treadmill and rediscover something of my erstwhile assurance and sense of direction.

Ralf, on the other hand, positively relishes routines and has no objection at all to doing the same thing day after day – but only as long as he doesn't have to do it. A natural rebel, travel frees *him* from the horror of Obligations.

The following morning we tackle a huge hotel breakfast of bread, three fried eggs each, butter and jam. Of Alois and Urs there is no sign.

'I bet they've already gone.'

'They're probably aiming to get to Nok Kundi today,' mumbles Ralf indistinctly, his mouth full of fried egg.

'They're crazy – that would be about 230 kilometres in one day!'

'It would just about be possible.'

'Only if they have ideal conditions. And Alois never mentioned skipping breakfast last night.'

'That's his way. He likes to *surprise* people.'

Maybe I have a little more in common with Alois than I thought.

Fugitives respectively from Routine and Obligations, we set off towards Mirjave and the Pakistan border feeling outclassed. Ralf is a slow starter, but with the wind at our backs and the road gently descending as it bisects an area of scrub and desert squeezed between ranges of crumpled khaki mountains, we gradually pick up speed.

Turbaned figures are driving camel trains alongside the road in the opposite direction. Earlier in the year two Swedish cyclists had their tent raked by automatic gunfire while camping out at night somewhere in this area. The Swedes survived but their bicycles were wrecked and their journey ended in a premature return to Sweden.

After three hours of steady progress we lunch in a culvert on bread and feta cheese. Ralf then leisurely consumes three bananas and moves on to graze unhurriedly on a large bag of nuts and raisins.

'Come on, Windhorse! Let's burn rubber!' I know that he's experiencing an endorphin rush, high on the euphoria that follows a long, hard ride, but anxious to cover as much mileage as possible while the wind remains behind us, I am beginning to fidget.

'I'm savouring the moment!' he mumbles, crunching bovinely.

That's the trouble with these endorphin junkies: once they stop it is terribly difficult to get them moving again, and although I enjoy my endorphins as much as the next man, I prefer to get the hard work over and done with before I feel ready to relax and enjoy my high.

'We've got great conditions, so let's make use of them while they last!' I persist.

'Give me five!'

By the time we finally hit the road the wind has changed direction and I curse him for his inertia.

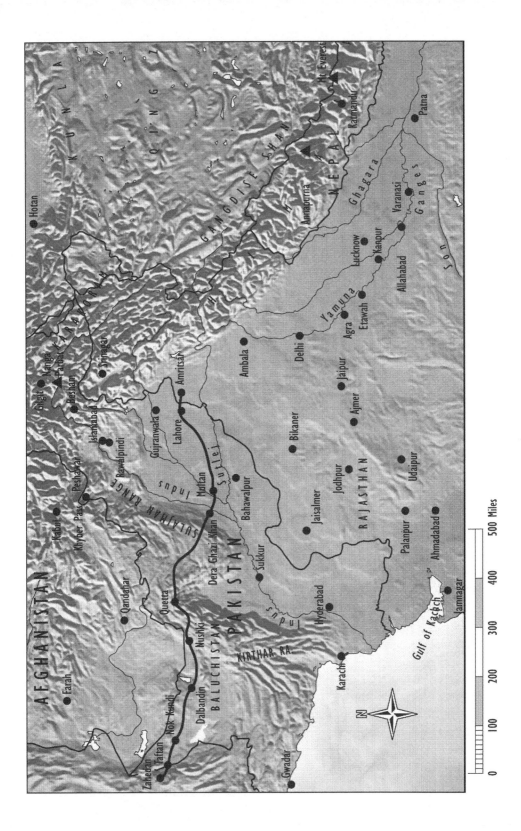

Chapter Eight
Bandit Country

Pakistan is an acronym consisting of Punjab, Afghania (the North-West Frontier Province), Kashmir, Indus-Sind and Baluchistan. The country's bloody birth in 1947 resulted from a fear that the Muslim minority would find itself the subject of discrimination in an independent, Hindu-dominated India (notwithstanding the fact that Hindus, Muslims and Sikhs had coexisted on the subcontinent in relative peace for centuries). Two-fifths of the subcontinent's Muslims nevertheless chose to remain in India and, although they form less than an eighth of India's vast population, there are now, ironically, more Muslims in India than in Pakistan (which, after Indonesia, is the world's second most populous Muslim country). For the fourth time in Pakistan's brief fifty-three-year existence the elected government was ousted in 1999 by the army and the country remains under military rule.

I still approach each border expecting it to be the precursor of some dramatic topographical or climatic change, but I'm invariably disappointed and the Mirjave–Taftan border is no exception; Taftan is a dusty, undistinguished jumble of single-storey brick and stucco connected by dirt roads and surrounded by desert. The moneychangers are almost as thick as the flies and, after some hard bargaining, we change fifty dollars each. Whereas the party of half a dozen Japanese backpackers (Japanese tourists being almost as ubiquitous as Japanese cars and hi-fi) and the lone German waiting disconsolately for the overnight bus will arrive in Quetta sometime tomorrow having seen little or nothing of Baluchistan and its inhabitants, the same 450-mile journey (assuming we aren't abducted or shot) will take us all of six days, during which we will surely become well acquainted with both. We cycle off on one of the dirt tracks until it joins the main road to Quetta, the only stretch of tarmac in town.

Relaxing with a proprietorial air in front of the government run PTDC Hotel next to a large green and white Pakistani flag are none other than Alois and Urs, who arrived at noon. Four European cyclists stroll into downtown Taftan in the warm twilight, searching in vain for a source of entertainment.

The streets are throbbing to the sound of generators and thronging with men and goats, but where are the women? Whereas Iran covers up its women the Islamic Republic of Pakistan appears to secrete them away somewhere. Ralf propounds an interesting but slightly far-fetched theory that 99.8 per cent of Pakistan's population is in fact made up of men and there *are* virtually no women.

*

The asphalt road out of Taftan is narrow and unmarked, and after weeks of cycling on Iran's superb roads, the surface feels rough. We cycle into the early morning sun forgetting at first that traffic in Pakistan drives on the left, but as barely half a dozen vehicles pass us in the first hour, it hardly matters. The desert is a flat moonscape of stones and rocks upon sand, grey over ochre. From time to time saffron dunes surge up like waves, some of them encroaching on the road surface.

Baluchistan shares with the North-West Frontier Province a reputation for lawlessness. Covering an area of roughly 214,000 square miles, this inhospitable land of mountains and desert is larger than the United Kingdom but is home to a mere six million people, an ethnic stew of Baluch, Brahui and Pashtuns seasoned with a few intrepid settlers from other areas of Pakistan and refugees from the fighting in neighbouring Afghanistan.

A police pick-up draws alongside and signals for us to stop, and we are politely interviewed in English. Where are we from? Have we cycled all the way from there? Are we not worried by the possibility of a road accident or robbery? No? Then good luck! Several heavily armed men are sprawled around a machine gun mounted in the back; the Afghan border is somewhere on the other side of the mountain range on our left and this area, sometimes referred to as the Golden Crescent, is drug smuggling and bandit territory. An email from an Australian traveller I met in Istanbul passed on the following encouraging advice from his brother:

As for the touring English fellah he's pretty brave (or stupid) taking his bike through Pakistan. Is he going to cycle through Baluchistan????? It is fucking dangerous there – our bus got stranded in the middle of the night there and the guys from Karachi were shitting themselves – surely that must be saying something!

Heartwarming stuff.

However if he is lucky enough to see some nomads on the move it will all be worthwhile – an unforgettable sight especially at daybreak in a broken down bus! He absolutely has to go to Peshawar it is amazing – the bazaars are like none he'll ever see and is he going up the Karakoram Highway? I'm so jealous if he is. Lahore is pretty cool but a bit fetid and stinky but great mosques and temples and there's always the cricket I suppose. If he is not vegetarian while he is in Quetta he should find someone to eat out with and go try Chicken Kari it is to die for. Swat valley is also beautiful. If he is a smoker he will die and go to heaven if you get my drift – free at Rawalpindi in certain guesthouses I believe.

There are three cardinal rules to follow, at least until we get to Quetta: never leave the main highway, never travel after dark, and never camp out in the open (as the Swedes did).

During a refreshment stop I glance surreptitiously at my companion. *Brave or stupid?*

Gazing vacantly into the middle distance, he appears to be Communing With His Inner-Self and signally fails to provide the reassurance I'm seeking. 'Any bandits will get to Alois and Urs first,' he remarks with satisfaction. 'We'll probably come across their dead bodies lying by the roadside – the *bandits'* bodies I mean of course.'

' – Mutilated beyond recognition and with their own Kalashnikovs rammed up their arses.'

'I can just imagine Urs sitting back and leaving Alois to get on with it: "Come on Alois, there's work to be done!" Then, after a couple of minutes: "OK, you can stop now! Alois! Hey!! Alois!! Stop!! ENOUGH!!"'

After three hours, barely thirty miles away from Nok Kundi, Ralf decides that he wants to eat some pasta. The wind has changed direction and is beginning make a nuisance of itself, so we stop near an isolated radio station and set up our kitchen behind a wall. We have been observed: a few minutes later one of the workers at the station is shaking our hands and asking us our names.

'Chris.'

'Forgotten,' says Ralf curtly.

'Be careful,' I warn him. 'It's all very well telling that taxi driver in Bam that we're married and that I'm expecting your child, but this is different. Some of these people understand English a little better and might object to your facetiousness.'

Nok Kundi is a little like Taftan but smaller and, if anything, even more unprepossessing. In the absence of hotels we are shown to a room in an empty building on the edge of town where I de-coke my stove whilst the Red Baron, periodically muttering spine-chilling imprecations in his hideous native tongue, mends a puncture.

'What does *schadenfreude* mean?' I ask him, apropos of nothing in particular.

He ponders for a moment. 'I think it means me laughing my ass off if a woman told you she'd rather have a sex change than go on a date with somebody who looks like he's been overlooked at the Nuremberg trials.' He eyes me judiciously. 'You'd have stood a better chance with women in the Germany of, say, 1936.'

As in Taftan there is no electricity. The stench from the toilet down the corridor is nauseating and dense clouds of flies are a persistent nuisance until they mysteriously disappear at sundown. (What *happens* to flies after dusk? Where do they go?) After eating a repulsive meal consisting of strings and nuggets of gristle submerged in an oily sauce accompanied by rice and chapattis at a roadside eatery we opt, burping apprehensively, to lay our sleeping bags down in the yard outside the building where it is cooler and we are no longer troubled by the horror emanating from the toilet.

*

A diesel generator coughs into noisy life in the pre-dawn darkness and the sound is met by a chorus of barking dogs and braying donkeys; Nok Kundi is waking up to a new day. I watch the stars fade away as the sky gradually lightens.

The road from Nok Kundi to Dalbandin must be the best in Pakistan. Constructed by Iranians (according to a notice on the edge of town), it is a surface upon which to glide effortlessly in top gear, but after half an hour we encounter another headwind and any thoughts of top gear and effortless gliding have to be abandoned. Nearly three hours later my back is aching from the strain and the balls of my feet are smarting from contact with the pedals.

Although dunes occasionally rise above the plain in voluptuous golden curves, the desert has remained predominantly flat, grey and stony with occasional glimpses of sand showing beneath the pebble surface like shafts of sunlight through curtains. It is a thing of beauty, of subtle, and occasionally dramatic, changes of complexion. Jagged grey mountains rise in the distance. There is something wonderfully compelling about true desolation. The silence when we stop and listen instead of talking or eating is awesome: no birds, no traffic, no people. Even the wind makes little noise because there are no trees or grass or bushes to catch it. It is still hot enough in mid-October to make us grateful that we weren't out here in July, when cycling would have been unthinkable.

The next day a local cyclist passing by in the opposite direction near Dalbandin takes aim and expertly directs his gobbet of spit into my face. To hit a moving target with such accuracy must have taken a lot of practice. I can't imagine why he did it. It is the first clear manifestation of hostility I've encountered.

The landscape has become one of pure, undulating sand dunes. This, we agree, nodding sagely at each other, is *proper* desert. I swerve to avoid a pothole (since Dalbandin the baking asphalt ribbon has become narrow and fissured), hit a pile of sand, and for the first time since that rainy afternoon in Calais, I fall off. Fortunately the landing is a soft one, but I have become concerned by my stomach, which is again displaying signs of discontent and has replaced back and crotch as the weakest link in my constitution.

During a rest stop Ralf clumsily kicks over one of his water bottles and I have to give him some of my precious supplies. Then his bicycle falls over.

He glances at it indifferently. 'These things happen,' he says mildly.

'You'd have starved to death or died of thirst by now if it wasn't for my pasta and water,' I reply sanctimoniously. 'I'm sure *Alois* never drops his water bottles or his bike.'

'I've put up with more shit in the past three minutes than Alois has during his entire trip.'

'In his entire lifetime I should think.'

'He has had problems though. Remember that time he nearly strangled a kid in Eastern Turkey who tried to steal his equipment?'

'The difference is that *your* problems are almost always self-inflicted.'

When the road takes an abrupt turn to the right and begins to head directly towards a towering mountain range I express concern. It has been another day of battling with the wind and I feel none too good; the diarrhoea has returned and the sun is uncomfortably hot.

'According to your map we don't cross any more mountains today,' Ralf points out.

'Then I'll have to sue Nelles Maps.'

'Three million dollars for mental cruelty! Trouble is they'd probably sue you to the tune of *ten* million for stupidity.'

'If I hired *you* as my lawyer they'd have an open and shut case.'

The road curves round again to the left to run alongside the mountains and, relieved that litigation won't after all be necessary, we sit down in the dust outside a roadside shack, sipping Coca-Cola and idly watching the road.

'They are pretty big on Toyota pick-ups here,' I observe.

'They drive them out into the desert every night loaded with crates of beer and women and have "Tailgate Parties".'

A retired French couple on their way to Nepal stop their caravanette on a deserted stretch of road for a chat and to offer us water. The sun, shining like a vast un-dipped headlight, is trying to burn a hole through my neck and there is no shade. I feel weak and dizzy and horribly envious of their two-litre engine, CD player, refrigerator, and bunks. If they hadn't been so delightful we'd probably have mugged them. By the time we check in at the rest house in Padag after enduring a hundred miles of intense heat and bullying headwinds since leaving Yakmach at daybreak, I feel far from well.

'I might just shag one of those goats later,' says Ralf ruminatively as we sip lemonade in a café. Along with *inertia* and *vicarious* (which he thought meant 'pertaining to vicars' until I put him right), the word *shag* is a recent addition to his English vocabulary and he is rather proud of it.

'I haven't the energy for a shag. Not even if Claudia Schiffer herself were to *beg* me for one.'

'I wouldn't touch that bitch,' says Ralf fastidiously. 'Not now that she's been *contaminated* by David Copperfield "The Celebrated Illusionist".'

*

Beyond Padag the road runs alongside a range of frowning black mountains that cast long, finger-shaped shadows across the desert, now glimmering palely in the clear early morning light. Then more flat, stony desert eventually reverts to dunes. On several occasions we spy camels, and occasionally goats too. The conditions are close to ideal, with no wind or mountain ranges to cross but, weakened by another stomach bug, I can find no power on the hills. It is a minor consolation that Urs, somewhere ahead of us, is suffering too.

We cycle past a number of brick kilns surrounded by neatly stacked rows of bricks that are being loaded by hand into tractor-drawn trailers. Whenever we pass through an oasis children scream 'pen, pen, pen!' and large all-male crowds, every individual clad in the shalwar qamiz, gather to study the infidels during refreshment stops.

'Isn't there anything on TV?' Ralf asks the onlookers irascibly, but he receives only nonplussed stares by way of a response.

I've become so used to being stared at that I scarcely notice them any more, so when on one occasion I broke wind loudly and absent-mindedly I was startled to be greeted by stifled laughter and suppressed giggles. Flatulence is a horrid, antisocial habit that I think displays a certain contempt for those around you and in normal company I'm far more discreet – but I had forgotten that we had an audience and Ralf cannot be described by any stretch of the imagination as 'normal company'. When you're in the middle of a desert in the company of an antisocial, iconoclastic, nihilistic *freak*, an oxymoron in human form who by his own admission would rather fornicate with a goat than one of the world's most beautiful women, the finer points of etiquette appear somewhat irrelevant.

*

The mountain scenery beyond Nushki is spectacular and some of the ascents are long and very steep but the power has miraculously returned to my legs; today it is Ralf's turn to feel under the weather. At a checkpoint we are offered the usual handshakes and courtesy by the military before being ushered into a room to enter our details into a ledger. The tea is lukewarm and we discreetly pour it away when nobody is looking.

A lone diesel locomotive with *PAKISTAN RAILWAYS* painted on it in large letters chugs slowly past on the nearby railway line against a background of perpendicular sandstone cliffs. It is a moment to savour as the implications belatedly sink in.

I've cycled all the way to Pakistan.

That's over six thousand miles from home. Whatever the physical and mental struggles to come I no longer fear the prospect of ignominy, even if I have to return home tomorrow.

Whereas I savour moments, Ralf savours hours (or even entire days given half the chance). Getting the High Priest of Inertia rolling when he's feeling below par is even more difficult than usual. He has developed the art of making a bottle of Coke and a bag of Bombay Mix last for an eternity while I fret about the lengthening shadows, the wind direction and the miles we still have to cover.

*

Jinnah Road in Quetta is crammed with bicycle repair shops, fruit stalls, fast-food stalls, restaurants, cafés, tailors, international couriers, motorcycle dealers, hotels, film sellers and developers, chemists, bookshops, and carpet sellers. Crowded buses crawl by, touting for custom, the conductors yelling out the destinations. The teeming, uneven pavements of this sprawling city are patrolled by beggars, many of them women concealed from head to toe in the *burqa,* a single blue-grey shroud-like garment which I associate with the Taliban regime across the border in nearby Afghanistan. They may indeed be Afghan refugees. With only a grill-like opening through which they can peer, they have been transformed into shadowy, ghostly figures.

I use the three days in Quetta to hand-wash my filthy clothes, lubricate and check the bicycle, read and send emails, and above all, to rest and eat. All four of us have been ill at various times during the past few days and have lost weight, and we need to rebuild our strength before leaving. My stomach is still wobbly and I cannot face fried or greasy food, which almost entirely rules out the local cuisine. Ralf looks even more unprepossessingly gaunt and bony than usual, Urs looks knackered and Alois for once looks every one of his forty-six years. Our favourite eatery is the Café China in Mission Road, where we stuff ourselves every evening amongst Quetta's elite with huge bowls of noodle and wanton soup and plates piled high with chopsuey and chowmein.

To my lasting delight, books written in English are readily available for the first time since I left the UK. One afternoon I triumphantly purchase a dog-eared paperback copy of *Maddon's Rock* by Hammond Innes from a pavement stall.

Ralf has acquired something called *Blind Ambition*.

'Typically American!' is Alois' scornful verdict.

'I couldn't find any *Austrian* books,' retorts Ralf sarcastically.

'Did they write any?' I ask.

'Yes, one – *Mein Kampf.* '

After leaving the Café China for the last time we squeeze into an auto rickshaw for the journey back to the hotel, where we trade email addresses. Alois is remaining in Quetta for an extra day and Urs, troubled by an injured knee, will be making a lone detour via Sukkur to avoid the worst of the mountains.

Ralf and I are leaving in the morning. I was in favour of remaining together until our paths finally separate at Lahore, but Ralf, who guards his independence so jealously that it might almost be mistaken for misanthropy, has expressed a preference for a little solitary cycling. It appears that he has had enough not only of Muslim fundamentalism and food poisoning, but of me too.

'We're bound to meet up on the way,' he says as we shake hands. He is itching to get to an airport and onto a plane to Thailand or Australia.

'Insh'allah!' I reply.

Solidarity in the face of hunger, headwinds, exhaustion and sickness, and the observation of and participation in each other's struggles to engage locals and to make sense of the Islamic culture have permitted a rare degree of mutual sympathy and understanding to develop between us over the past three weeks. Although in many respects we are undoubtedly very different animals, conversation and the exchange of ideas flowed with an effortlessness and absence of tension that I usually find difficult to sustain.

He nods, grinning. *'Insh'allah!'*

Chapter Nine
Engine Trouble

The road from Quetta to Loralai bisects a wide desert corridor that channels its way between multi-faceted mountain ranges. At the end of a village it forks; either route will apparently take me to Loralai but people urge me to take the right-hand fork because it is a short cut. With their cheerful assurances that the surface is metalled still ringing in my ears, the asphalt ends after three miles to be replaced by a moonscape of dust and rocks and wok-shaped craters. I consider turning back and wringing the necks of the bastards, but I loathe backtracking and I've already had to retrace my steps once today: I missed the turning in Kuchlagh, cycling an energy-sapping ten miles towards the Afghan border at Chaman before realising my mistake.

After more than half an hour spent bumping along in low gear the decision to persevere is rewarded by a return of the asphalt – although it is badly potholed. Narrow and empty, the road climbs steadily towards more craggy mountain ranges, the sterility of the rocky landscape occasionally relieved by the unexpected greenery of irrigated orchards.

A nocturnal bivouac in the desert is followed by two hours of cycling dangerously fast on perforated asphalt into a blinding early morning sun before I finally rejoin the main road at Loralai. Convoys of Japanese pick-ups apparently operating as unofficial taxis slalom by with people crammed into the back. The road is narrow and I have to squeeze past oncoming lorries. From some drivers I get a grin and a blast of the horn (which I acknowledge with a wave), but a few knuckle-heads appear to find it amusing to force me off the road by driving straight towards me and, in a hair-raising game of cat-and-mouse, pulling away at the last minute.

I have become increasingly unsure of my reception in the populated oasis areas. Some bystanders beg me to stop and take tea with them, but a fellow-cyclist coming from the other direction bellows suddenly and incoherently as if trying deliberately to startle me, and a man driving an approaching pick-up leans out and lands a punch on my shoulder. Shrieking children rush from the fields and orchards or mud-brick buildings aligning the road. A boy tries to set his dog on me but the dog, although very large, is fortunately of a pacifist disposition and shows no interest whatsoever. Another takes aim with a stick, and when I instinctively duck there are peals of satanic laughter and stones bounce on the road surface behind me.

It is therefore with a measure of relief that I finally leave Baluchistan and enter the Punjab at Rakni. The Sulaiman Range of mountains, running from north to south for hundreds of miles, is a final formidable physical barrier barring the road east to India. Fuelled by a breakfast of bananas and milk, I am grateful for the coolness of the morning air as I tackle a series of multiple hairpin bends. Frequently I have to wait on the stony verge to let a lorry past, for the road has remained absurdly narrow. The traffic is almost exclusively made up of freight, modern Japanese Hinos, Isuzus and Nissans outnumbering the bonneted Bedfords, a vintage British design that dates back to the fifties. The lorries are, without exception, gaudily decorated to the nth degree; the towering wooden bodywork leans forward over the cabs like the stern of a sixteenth-century galleon and every surface, right down to the burnished bumpers and wheel hubs, is a riot of patterns, motifs, reflectors and slogans in Urdu and idiosyncratic English. The jingling of hundreds of ornamental chains and medallions hanging from front and rear bumpers often precedes the sound of labouring engines, and the delicious odour emanating from payloads consisting of crates of apples harvested from the orchards of Baluchistan mingles with the wafts of hashish issuing from open windows and the harsh reek of exhaust. Terrible logjams ensue whenever an ascending line of lorries meets a descending convoy, and the drivers are obliged to inch their vehicles, lurching and swaying alarmingly under their heavy loads, past each other with one set of wheels on the rocky verge.

The interminable climb to the pass at Fort Munro is more than matched by a spectacular descent through countless switchbacks. Groups of goats, cows and donkeys are wandering at the roadside and I fly past several lorries inching down the slope in low gear. As the road at last bottoms out, the scenery changes to one of flat, sandy desert, without any mountains to break the monotony. There are people out there, God help them, skinny, scarecrow figures breaking rocks with sledgehammers in this suffocating heat. Innumerable conveyor-belts are decanting stones into clanking machines that vomit out a fine white powder, dumping it into cone-shaped piles. It is a dusty, choking, red-hot inferno, and I can't help thinking of penal colonies. Acres of the desert and a workforce probably numbering thousands are exploited in this way.

*

Rubbish is being swept into piles and burned at the side of the road as I find my way out of Dera Ghazi Khan at daybreak, weaving in and out of the throngs of pedestrians, camels, goats and oxen, and the donkey and horse-drawn carts that compete with auto rickshaws to provide a taxi service. The presence of water has wrought a remarkable transformation in the terrain east of the city; the empty deserts, boulder-strewn wastes and wide, mountainous amphitheatres of Iran and Baluchistan have been replaced by a level, fertile landscape of fields and trees irrigated by the mighty Indus. Some of the fields are awash. Donkeys and horses are moving along at a brisk trot, pulling carts almost entirely concealed by sheaves of cotton, and teams of oxen lumber stoically between the shafts at a more sedate pace. Animals here have to work for a living and there is no sentimentality or affection to be seen. Whilst most beasts look reasonably well cared for, others, with their ribs clearly visible, appear undernourished and sticks are routinely used on creatures struggling under the weight of their burdens. It must be uncomfortably hot for them later on in the day and I can't imagine how they manage in the summer. If they can't be put to practical use animals appear to be regarded as pests; people in the developing world can rarely afford the luxury of pets. In Turkey and Iran dogs were employed either to guard property or herd sheep, but in Pakistan I have hardly seen any at all. One exception is the skinny mutt with a sore on its back wandering forlornly in the dust while I'm refreshing myself with a Pepsi outside a roadside shack. If it wasn't for a fear of catching rabies I'd have called it over and fussed it, but the reactions of the locals are to curse and fling objects at it whenever it barks or dares to get too close.

Like the animals, the gangs of workers resurfacing National Highway 5 with picks and shovels seem willing, patient, and mutely resigned to their fate. Beyond Multan the road becomes a dual carriageway. Motorists appear to use whichever carriageway takes their fancy, frequently darting across the central reservation and warning oncoming traffic of their presence by flashing their headlights and sounding their horns.

Although there hasn't been a breath of wind and the roads have remained flat and their surfaces greatly improved, the ride from Dera Ghazi Khan to Lahore is proving in its own way to be every bit as exhausting as anything I encountered on the Black Sea Coast where, remorseless though the demands of the terrain were, I was able to draw immense satisfaction from my physical prowess. Amongst the cotton fields of the Punjab the battle has to be fought against a weakness pervading my body; I've acquired a sore throat, a persistent, dry cough, a heavy cold and an unquenchable thirst. I am too hot at night to sleep properly and I still can't get on with the food. I left Iran eagerly anticipating my first curry since leaving home but I have found the usual offerings of fatty fragments of gristle and bone or lentils swimming in oily sauce quite inedible and there is very little in the way of alternatives.

Napoleon once famously stated that an army marches on its stomach and much the same applies to a cyclist; if I can't eat I'm in trouble. I attempt to inject some energy into leaden limbs by forcing down a banana, having to accompany it with mouthfuls of Pepsi because for some reason I am unable to summon any saliva. My head is full of snot but it is too time-consuming and disruptive to my rhythm to stop and retrieve my slimy handkerchief from the bar bag every time I need to blow my nose – I have long since learnt instead to hold one nostril closed, lean outwards, blow sharply, and allow gravity and the airstream to do the rest. On the windswept plateaus of Iran, before I'd perfected the technique, there were some rather gruesome accidents (particularly during high-viscosity discharges); the trick is to ensure that the wind is blowing in the right direction first.

The oppressive heat and humidity, lack of sleep and inevitable loss of weight due to a non-existent appetite and a poor diet have combined to render me listless and irritable. Every mile cycled seems to last for an eternity, and whenever I stop to drink bottle after bottle of cold fizz or mango juice, or to eat, I am drenched in sweat. Then, with energy levels and stamina way down, I have to deal with the people. With 59 per cent of Pakistan's 140 million-strong population squeezed into the Punjab, encounters with my fellow humans have become much more frequent than they were in Baluchistan.

Some way back from the verge are trees and a wall. As soon as the coast is reasonably clear I sneak off the road, discreetly prop the bicycle up behind a tree, sit down with my back against the wall and, with a sigh of weary satisfaction, open a tin of pineapples. Within a minute, however, an eagle-eyed passer-by has spotted me and walks over to investigate. He is rapidly joined by two others. Number Three speaks some English. *How are you? Where are you going? What is your good name? What is your country? What is your profession?* Two inquisitive cyclists amble over to add four more staring eyes to the group. They are entirely oblivious to any hints that I might want to enjoy my meal in peace, and in my fragile state the interrogation feels like a verbal equivalent of rape.

Why can't you leave me alone? shrieks an inner voice. I suspect that the concept of privacy is so alien to these people that the word doesn't even exist in Urdu.

*

Barely forty miles away from Lahore, I stop at a large filling station. Next to the parking area are a couple of roadside inns and a mosque. The infection from the sore throat has moved down to my chest and every cough brings forth a shining green jewel of phlegm, but I am still, somehow, squeezing out the miles – ninety-six of them today. Having been unable to find anywhere else to sleep, I get permission at one of the inns to occupy a *charpoy* (rope bed). A worker from the nearby milk factory speaks some English and many of his questions are quite perceptive, demanding a modicum of reflection and more than the usual monosyllabic answers. What countries have I seen? Am I not afraid, travelling alone? (Only once so far have I been truly afraid, on the highway into Istanbul when I thought I was about to die, but that had nothing to do with being alone.) Why am I doing this? (Now that *is* a good question!) And what do I think of the Pakistani people? I have to be careful about how I answer that last one, for it is difficult to be charitable or even fair when you are exhausted and ill. At length my inquisitor disappears to the local mosque to pray and I lie down on the charpoy, but I am unable to sleep until the television, which is showing a cricket match at top volume, is switched off at about midnight.

*

Some coincidences are so remarkable that they hint at destiny and I felt that the staging of a one-day cricket international between England and Pakistan in Lahore only a day after my arrival in the city might almost have been arranged for my personal benefit. How then could I not buy a ticket?

When play begins at twelve there are still some empty seats, but these fill rapidly. Lahore's Qaddafi Stadium, named after that great and noble philosopher, philanthropist and leader of men, Colonel Qaddafi of Libya, is a modern and impressive amphitheatre. The enclosures are named after famous Pakistani players of the past, such as Zaheer Abbas, Imran Khan and Javed Miandad.

Trescothick looks bang in form and sets about the Pakistani opening bowlers with evident relish. Stewart takes longer to get his eye in, but is just beginning to tick along nicely when he heaves at a ball from one of the spinners, misses it, and is stumped. Nassar Hussain continues to play the junior partner to Trescothick, who rapidly passes fifty and looks set for a really big score. However he miscues a simple catch to mid-on and goes for 68. With only two wickets sacrificed and over a hundred runs on the board, England are still in a solid position, but Trescothick's dismissal proves to be the turning point of the match. The players fail to capitalise on their good start by allowing the Pakistani spinners to tie them down, and the wickets tumble as they look to increase the scoring rate. They are dismissed for 211 in the forty-ninth over, leaving Pakistan a comfortable target that they reach with ease in front of a jubilant crowd. There is dancing in the aisles, plastic water bottles are thrown, and the yellow paper placards bearing a red '4' or '6' (provided by Shell and placed on every seat so that they can be brandished at appropriate moments) are folded into paper darts and flung. With England being put to the sword, I consider this behaviour to be in distinctly poor taste. How many trees had to be cut down to allow forty thousand cretins to throw their darts? And what are they going to do with all that rubbish? A multinational corporation like Shell really ought to be more environmentally responsible.

A haze of pollution hangs over the five million inhabitants of Lahore, most of whom will probably never have heard of environmental responsibility. The city resounds to the buzzing of thousands of auto rickshaws. Cramped, noisy and with no suspension to speak of, they can turn on a sixpence and squeeze through gaps you think aren't there. Fortunately there are plenty of handles upon which to cling during the frequent, unexpected and violent changes of speed and direction. The driver needs every one of his five mirrors, and I am amazed at the apparent absence of road rage in traffic conditions that would turn the average English driver into a gibbering wreck within seconds. Often three vehicles will head simultaneously for a gap into which only two will fit, and an accident is averted only when one driver loses his nerve and pulls back at the last possible second. The entire Pakistani Highway Code can be summed up very succinctly in just four words: *He Who Dares Wins*, and it is better for your peace of mind that you don't pay too much attention to what is going on around you. Astonishingly, the system seems to work, but only because *every* driver in Pakistan is a road-hog and this is the accepted way to drive.

Some of the grandeur of the imposing British-built buildings on The Mall has faded. Facades of peeling stucco and flaking paint give many of them a distinctly second-hand look. There are few straight lines elsewhere in the city. Walls either lean in or out. Sections are either missing or have broken away. No town council would get away with these pavements in the litigious climate of the developed world: surfaces are uneven, paving slabs tilt and gaping holes threaten to swallow the unwary. Trees and parks are oases in a desert of asphalt and low-rise concrete, brick and stucco. Cricket in Pakistan is a religion, and on every available patch of grass a match is in progress. The game is played on every level, from people dressed immaculately in whites playing on a properly marked-out pitch to a bunch of urchins using an upturned bucket for stumps. This grass-roots passion for the game doesn't exist in England, so it is little wonder that the national team is so regularly thrashed by the likes of Pakistan, India and the West Indies. Climate, so much more conducive to playing cricket than in England, must be an additional factor.

After searching the budget hotels around the railway station in vain for a sign of Ralf (it would have been pleasant to savour a few more moments together) I head back to The Mall in pursuit of sustenance and find it at the Pizza Hut, a piece of America dumped in the middle of Lahore. Rap (a word that in my opinion should always be prefaced by a 'c') is being churned out by the loudspeakers and oily waiters address customers in a way that makes you realise that nothing they say is spontaneous. *Your 'Size Does Matter' will be seven and a half minutes, sir,* and *Is everything all right for you, sir?* are clearly phrases which have been painstakingly rehearsed from some dreadful corporate customer-care bible. I'd rather have spontaneity, even in the form of interminable questions.

Halfway through an edible but expensive pizza a grinning Alois unexpectedly appears. I am delighted as well as surprised to see him. He orders himself a meal and we compare notes about the cycling since Quetta. My appetite is still not what it was and I am eating more out of a sense of duty than with my erstwhile pleasure but Alois (who exudes the same relentless and mildly offensive jauntiness of a radio disc-jockey) has been restored to full health and considered it 'excellent cycling' between Quetta and Lahore. This is his last day in Pakistan; tomorrow he will continue his circumnavigation of the globe by cycling into India.

*

Sensing that my strength is gradually returning, I decide to spend a day being a tourist, wandering for over an hour amongst the sandstone and marble collection of palaces, halls, mosques, museums and gardens inside the Fort before crossing the busy Circular Road to Iqbal Park and the Minar-e-Pakistan, a triumphal sixty-metre-high concrete structure that faintly recalls the shape of the Eiffel Tower. When I sit down on some nearby steps to admire the view of the Fort and the Badshahi Mosque, four men promptly sit down opposite and one of them asks me which country I'm from.

'England.'

'What city?'

'Birmingham.'

'How old are you?'

'Forty.'

'You are very young!'

'No, I'm very old!'

'Are you married?'

'No.'

General astonishment and much shaking of heads. 'Why?'

Evidently you have to have a pretty powerful reason to be single beyond the age of twenty-five, but apart from the obvious defence that I've not yet found the right woman, I haven't got one. I am tempted to make a facetious reply along the lines of *I haven't been able to find anybody good enough for me*, but the joke would undoubtedly be lost on them.

'Because I enjoy my freedom,' I say instead.

Their expressions indicate that they don't quite know what to make of this. 'What do you think of Pakistani people?' continues their spokesman, giving up the struggle.

I shrug. 'They're fine!' How can I answer in any other way without taking the risk of offending my audience?

'Are you a Christian?'

'Yes.' (As in Iran it is taken for granted that I believe in God and I'm not inclined to disillusion them).

'Protestant or Catholic?'

'Protestant.'

'What do you think of Muslim people?'

The questions are relentless. As religion has no significant part to play in my life I don't tend to identify or assess other people by their choice of worship. There is only one answer I can give.

'I like them!'

It has been a meaningless exchange and they depart little wiser for their interrogation. Granted, I didn't try very hard to enlighten them but, unlike the milk-factory worker, they didn't ask the right questions.

The Internet cafés are full of young Pakistani males. Deprived by Islamic law of a more natural, wholesome access to the opposite sex, many of them are eagerly surfing through the porn sites. Some of the fetishes and fantasies enacted on the computer screens are going to give these sexually naïve young men some pretty twisted ideas about women in general and western women in particular. However you attempt to repress it, the sexual urge will always find a way to express itself (not only in the viewing or acquisition of pornography, but quite possibly also in covert homosexual, or even bestial acts). It is as indomitable as Hydra, the monster of Greek mythology: cut off one of its heads and another will rear up to take its place.

I am sharing my hotel room with several ants. While I'm washing my clothes in the sink a mouse peeks inquisitively at me before darting away, unable to hold my gaze. Whenever I use the washbasin the floor floods but, perversely, there is only a dribble of cold water to be had from the shower. The sheets on the bed are grey with ancient grime and I find the absence of cockroaches puzzling. Perhaps they haven't heard of the place yet, but I've acquired *Jane Eyre* with which to welcome them if necessary. The rooms in the plusher Amer Hotel next door are far too expensive but the friendly restaurant staff can knock up an excellent, thoroughly British breakfast of scrambled egg, toast and marmalade and a pot of highly drinkable tea, all for less than a pound. In a four-week-old copy of *The Sunday Times* purchased at considerable expense from Falletti's Hotel in Egerton Road I read avidly about Milosevic's fall from power, the latest controversy in the battle for the right to run the National Lottery, and Keegan's resignation following that abysmal 1-0 home defeat by Germany – all the more humiliating when you are informed of the result while in the company of a gloating, football-mad Kraut. If there had been any doubt remaining in my mind about the true meaning of *schadenfreude*, it finally vanished in Quetta.

*

At the Indian High Commission in the Foreign Enclave I pay 2,200 rupees for a six-month visa. Islamabad, the modern city that has replaced Karachi as Pakistan's capital, reminds me a little of that English vision of utopia, Milton Keynes – with sunshine. The urban landscape exudes a sense of space and order that I associate more with Europe or the USA than the Indian subcontinent. Numbered sectors – G4, F6 etc – are connected by a grid of broad boulevards and dual carriageways also identified by number rather than name – Fifth Avenue, Sixth Avenue, and so on. There are no oxen-, donkey- or horse-drawn carts, and instead of auto rickshaws there are black and yellow Suzuki taxis. Recently mown and rubbish-free areas of grass and well-tended trees border pothole-free roads and streets. Even the air is clean. Shops and businesses sell computers, cell phones, information technology and real estate. Rectangular, concrete office blocks host airline offices, travel agencies, banks and authorised moneychangers. Islamabad is the seat of government and many of the organs of administration have their central offices in the city too.

Early the following morning a taxi driver takes me to the ultra-modern bus depot of Daewoo Express in Rawalpindi and demands 400 rupees, exactly four times the fare I was expecting.

'Oh, come off it!' I protest. 'I've been taken to Rawalpindi for 100 rupees.'

'But you say you want air-con bus. I take you to non air-con bus for 90 rupees.'

The vulture gave me no warning of the price difference. I bargain him down to 350 rupees and pay with bad grace, kicking myself for failing to determine the fare before getting in. Another gullible tourist has just been fleeced; angrily slamming the passenger door shut, I tell myself that I should have known better. Indeed I *had* known better but I'd decided to trust him just as I had trusted the other, more honest taxi drivers who charged me only 100 rupees for journeys of similar distance. Leaving my wallet behind in a shop in Turkey might have been taking things a little too far, but if you don't give people the opportunity to be honest how are you ever going to know if they are or not? Trust can be very rewarding but it is a high-risk strategy, and I literally can't afford to gamble too often.

At 290 rupees the bus ticket is another shock – double what I've been used to paying – but it isn't long before I realise that this is a very superior bus service. The driver, dressed in uniform instead of the usual Shalwar Qamiz pyjama suit, looks like an airline pilot. A pretty, uniformed, and clearly emancipated stewardess (a world away from the women of Baluchistan) gives a pre-departure address in which she welcomes the passengers aboard in Urdu and English 'in the name of the mighty Allah, all powerful and all merciful.' The similarity to air travel doesn't end there. A television screen at the front of the bus is showing a movie and we are all given earplugs. We are offered plastic cups of Pepsi en route and a little lunch pack consisting of a sandwich and a piece of cake. Having finished *Jane Eyre*, I pass my time aboard reading Erskine Childers' *The Riddle of the Sands,* trying not to think of all the money I have just spent, and wondering how on earth I'm going to get back onto the bicycle after so much pampering.

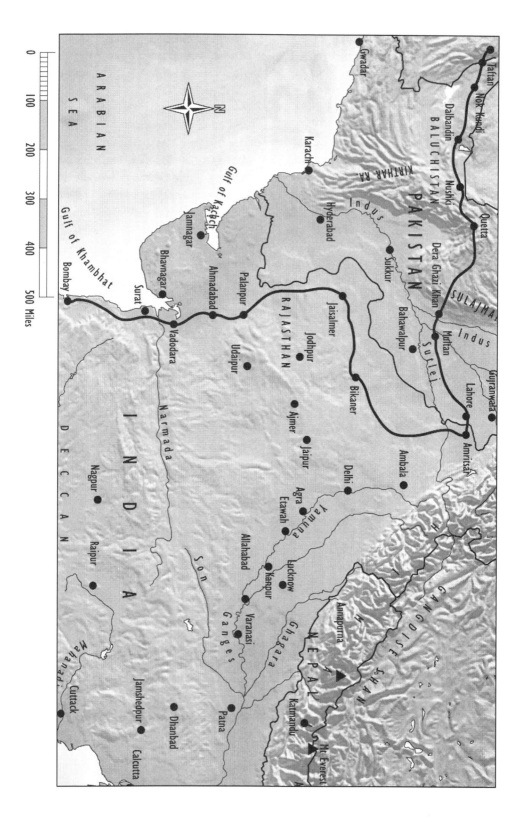

Part Two: Tour de India

You're on your bike for the whole day, six or seven hours, in all kinds of weather and conditions, over cobblestones and gravel, in mud and wind and rain, and even hail, and you do not give into pain. Everything hurts. Your back hurts, your feet hurt, your hands hurt, your neck hurts, your legs hurt, and of course, your butt hurts.

Lance Armstrong (seven times winner of the Tour de France) in his autobiography 'It's Not About The Bike'.

Chapter Ten
Accident-prone Drivers

'Punjab' is a word meaning 'five rivers'. The Sutlej, Beas, Ravi, Chenab and Jhelum ran with blood during the genocidal fury that followed the painful and bloody amputation of Pakistan in 1947. Between half a million and a million people were slaughtered and an estimated seventeen million fled in both directions across a new frontier that separated Muslim from Hindu. A kingdom in its own right until the British annexed it in 1849 and regarded by the Sikhs as their homeland, the Punjab was cut in two.

There are some eighteen million Sikhs in India. The faith was founded in 1499 by Nanak, the first of the ten Gurus. Nabind, the tenth Guru, inaugurated the *khalsa*, a brotherhood of warriors who abide by a strict moral code that includes abstention from alcohol, tobacco and drugs and whose quest is for *dharmayudha* (righteousness). He ordered his disciples to keep their hair and beards uncut to symbolise saintliness, to carry a comb to keep the unshorn hair tidy, to wear *kaccha* (loose underpants) to represent modesty, to encircle the wrist with an iron bangle to indicate humility, and to equip themselves with a dagger or sword to signal their readiness to defend their cause (a right recognised by the Indian Constitution). All Sikh men wear a turban and bear the surname of Singh (which means 'lion') to betoken their rejection of the caste system, but in practice caste is as fundamental to the Sikh way of life as it is in the rest of India – as indeed are alcohol, tobacco and drugs.

With 400 kg of gleaming gold leaf covering its outer walls and domes, the Golden Temple in Amritsar is the Sikhs' holiest shrine. After depositing my boots and socks at a kiosk I walk barefoot through an archway beneath a clock tower into a shallow pool and out the other side into an immense, airy quadrangle of tall, marble buildings. Connected by a causeway known as the Gurus' Bridge, the temple stands at the centre of the rectangular pool of water from which the city takes its name (*Amritsar* meaning 'Pool Of Nectar'). When in 1984 Mrs Ghandi reacted to the temple's occupation by armed extremists demanding a separate Sikh homeland by controversially sending in the tanks of the Indian army, she signed her own death warrant. The buildings were damaged during the subsequent shelling and she was assassinated by her Sikh bodyguards in retribution for the desecration of their place of worship. More than three thousand people were killed during the subsequent Hindu–Sikh riots.

I stroll along the walkways that enclose the pool pondering the distinction between cult and religion and enjoying the smooth hardness of the cool marble flagstones beneath my feet and the sensation of fresh air between my toes. Of the destruction of 1984 there remains no trace. The morning sun dazzles from a deep blue sky, casting a reflection of gleaming gold and brilliant white marble upon the surface of the 'pool of immortality and bliss', in which several pilgrims are washing away their sins. Worshippers stoop reverently to touch their foreheads on the threshold of the temple before entering. Rows of people sitting cross-legged on the floor within are listening raptly to three musicians, two playing accordions and singing whilst a third taps a light, rhythmic tattoo upon the drums. Loudspeakers broadcast the soothing and curiously hypnotic music throughout the complex. The Granth Sahib, the holy book containing the teachings of the ten Sikh gurus in more than six thousand verses and hymns, lies before them upon a dais, covered by a shroud.

In the crowded streets beyond this oasis of serenity the senses are overwhelmed by a kaleidoscopic whirl of sights, sounds and smells. Motor and pedal rickshaws, scooters, mopeds, bicycles, pedestrians and cars compete for space on the streets. Mangy dogs are scavenging in piles of rubbish and energetic puppies engaging one another in juvenile trials of strength. Bicycle and scooter repair shops, travel agents, money changers, general stores, pavement purveyors of false teeth and other gruesome wares, hotels, restaurants, food stalls, clothes shops, panel beaters, shoe shops, PCOs (public call offices), sweet shops and banks are all fanatically advertised by colourful billboards and banners and squeezed so tightly together that it is impossible to take everything in, even at walking pace. The tinkling of countless bicycle bells mingles with the angry buzzing and impatient beeping of motor scooters and auto rickshaws, and the disagreeable smells of sun-baked urine and rotting piles of rubbish mingle with the exhaust fumes. A man is urinating unselfconsciously against a wall.

Thousands of parading school children are adding to the traffic chaos on Queen's Road. First come rank upon rank of boys, freshly scrubbed and smartly dressed in school uniform. Some are playing musical instruments or chanting and others holding banners aloft proclaiming the name of their school. They are followed by marching girls, their dazzling smiles and predominantly white outfits contrasting with their glowing, dark skin and gleaming, jet-black tresses, usually arranged in long plaits.

Outside my hotel is a grog shop, and next to that a bar. A man is selling 'special' lassi (yoghurt with added cannabis) from a stall and a family of pigs is rooting in the rubbish at the side of the road. Back in my room I drink a Kingfisher beer, my first alcoholic beverage since leaving Turkey several weeks ago.

Good-bye at last to Islam and God Bless India.

*

Whereas the migration of travellers from Europe to India, Southeast Asia, Indonesia and Australia has become a little too commonplace to my way of thinking, the challenge of the ice-bound Karakoram and Pamir mountain ranges, the intimidating vastness of China and the remote Russian Far-East combines elements of originality and eccentricity that I find irresistible. The latter route will moreover vindicate absolutely the decision to travel by bicycle, for foreign registered motor vehicles are prohibited from entering China and having already demonstrated that a determined freak on a bicycle can travel anywhere that people in an expensive four-wheel drive or on a powerful motorbike can, I have discovered an overpowering urge to thumb my nose at them by accessing areas they can't.

The time for equivocation finally ran out when I reached Amritsar, but my mind was already made up: instead of cycling east to Calcutta and flying on to Bangkok I will spend the winter months attempting to do fuller justice to India before returning to Pakistan in April, where I will ride the Karakoram Highway north to cross the stratospheric Khunjerab Pass and plunge into the uncompromising mountain and desert landscapes of Chinese Turkestan.

The lush, fertile landscape south of Amritsar is a mirror image of the scenery on the other side of the border. *FEEDER FOR RAJASTHAN* proclaims a notice alongside a canal. *GROW CROPS REQUIRING LESS WATER* it urges. Farmers the world over will surely cultivate whatever the market demands and the soil and climate permit. I cycle past cotton and sugarcane plantations and people working in the fields with shovels and scythes. Bicycles, pedal rickshaws, bullock carts, tractors and lorries outnumber cars. Many of the basic, single-gear bicycles are adapted to carry the most extraordinary loads; several are buried under sugarcane and others are laden with big metal churns, but the strangest load I saw was on two bicycles carrying open wicker trays full of live chickens. With direction signs in English having become scarce beyond Kot Kapura I am faced with the tricky task of trying to memorise the Punjabi script for Abohar and Ganganagar. Adding to my navigational problems is the matter of pronunciation when asking the way; Abohar is actually pronounced 'Ubwar'.

I stop at a *dhaba* or roadside café near Ganganagar. Most of these places are very basic, with painted wooden tables and benches and a few charpoy beds set out on an uneven floor of compacted earth beneath a canopy of wooden rafters supporting layers of thatch or coconut matting. Water is stored in four huge earthenware pots and steaming saucepans are standing on a roaring gas stove. In the corner a man is moulding dough into chapattis, and a satisfied belch rumbles out of the gloom somewhere behind me as I sit in the shadowy interior pondering my order.

Two lorry drivers amble over, leaving the mates (who are little more than boys) to check pressures by thumping the tyres with steel rods. Indian lorries are generally burnt orange in colour and bear signs indicating the states in which they are licensed to operate, or in some cases *National Permit* or *All India Permit*. They all have *Horn Please* (meaning, I think, 'Sound Horn Before Overtaking') written on the back. Two manufacturers, Tata and Ashok Leyland, seem to have the market sewn up and I wonder how it is that the Japanese have penetrated the Pakistani market so thoroughly whilst failing so completely to have any impact in India. Something to do with import tariffs no doubt.

One of the three men sitting at a nearby table engages me in conversation. What is my opinion of India? I reply that I've only been in the country for three days, which I judge to be insufficient time to form an opinion on such a vast and complex subject. His English is poor and he doesn't understand, but he insists on buying me a beer in spite of my protests that alcohol and cycling don't mix. His face is too close to mine when he talks and I find him rather overbearing. When I get up to pay he insists that I am his guest and that he will pay the bill. I suspect that he is slightly drunk. All he wants from me is English coins but I don't have any left so I give him coins from France, Hungary and Iran instead.

'You are a great man!' he declares, giving me a bear hug.

The sugarcane and cotton plantations continue into Rajasthan as far as Suratgar, after which the road bisects a rolling landscape of sand dunes covered by scrub and scattered trees. Oxen have been superseded by camels and the traffic is becoming scarcer, villages further apart, the soil sandier, and the high cloud which obligingly filtered the sun in the Punjab has disappeared entirely. Half of the vehicles on the road are owned by the army and I pass dozens of military barracks and depots, for it is in the deserts of Rajasthan that India plays her war games and does her nuclear testing. After three wars, in 1948, 1965 and 1971, antagonism between India and Pakistan remains high and troop concentrations in both countries are greatest either side of the border, a wound which has festered for over fifty years and continues to haemorrhage in Kashmir.

It strikes me that war invariably appears to be prosecuted between or within those countries whose populations can least afford it. Does conflict stem from poverty or poverty from conflict? I suspect that once set in motion the cycle is self-perpetuating. War is an expensive business and the maintenance of Pakistan's 620,000-strong army accounts for about 30 per cent of the government's spending. Education receives less than a tenth as much (even though almost half of the nation's 140 million citizens are under the age of fifteen) and the economy is a shambles. In India less than half of the children between the ages of six and fourteen receive any formal education at all and the national literacy rate is one of the lowest in the world. Trade between the two countries remains negligible.

The distant *thump-thump* of artillery is all too symptomatic of the wasted billions that might otherwise have been channelled to reduce hardship and improve living standards in both India and Pakistan. Travel has taught me that human beings the world over have far more in common with each other than matters upon which to disagree, and that despite the bigotry and incendiary rhetoric of self-serving political and religious leaders, people generally get on with each other if left to do so. Is a small, mountainous, land-locked state really worth the sacrifice made by the millions in both countries who cannot read or write and who live out their entire lives trapped in penury?

When two children squabble over a toy because neither can bear the thought of sharing it with the other, the simplest solution is usually to remove the focus of resentment by confiscating the toy. If the protagonists were compelled to withdraw (with the United Nations enacting the role of angry parent) and Kashmir were restored the autonomy it enjoyed prior to Partition as a Princely State, India and Pakistan might then concern themselves with matters economic rather than military and Kashmir could be left to become a neutral tourist paradise, a sort of subcontinental Switzerland – or at the very least another Nepal. Government money should be invested in the enrichment instead of the elimination of lives; a similarly skewed sense of priorities eventually bankrupted the Soviet Union.

*

The owner of a dhaba near Lunkaransa is rare in that he has cultivated a paunch of considerable size; one doesn't see many fat Indians. He proudly shows me a row of saucepans half-full of various enticing sauces and then says that I can't have any. Perhaps he's saving it all for himself.

In Turkey the food was a little too expensive to allow me to eat really well; in Iran it was cheap but lacked variety and was sometimes difficult to find; in Pakistan it was inedible and I wondered at times if I'd ever be able to look a curry in the face again; but India, coming immediately after the gastronomic horrors of Pakistan, is the land of milk and honey. The food is cheap, readily available and invariably delicious. Even at the most basic dhabas Indian food, served on metal trays and plates, isn't swimming in grease and the dishes of vegetable curry, dal, raita, parathas and chapattis taste wonderful, and because I've been eating well my strength has returned to something like normal levels.

The reluctant chef is eventually persuaded to rustle up a plate of dal and a couple of chapattis while a male crowd collects around the bicycle, fascinated by the gears, the trip computer and the odd-looking pedals (they have never come across cleats before and there is much puzzlement until I lift my feet to show them the metal inserts bolted to the soles of my boots). At times I can no longer see the damn thing because the bodies are packed so tightly around it, but my reaction has become one of resignation. After all, if a Rajput warrior were to ride his camel or a Tamil *mahout* to steer his elephant down the Kidderminster Road and tether the animal outside the Welch Gate Diner while he refreshed himself within there'd be a similarly goggle-eyed response and I'd be amongst the first to ask 'which country?'

Someone asks me if my water bottles contain oil for the brakes.

'No, water for the engine!' I reply. People are earnestly counting the gears, but I do wish that they wouldn't tug on the levers.

A bonneted lorry is parked a few yards away. The driver's mate hitches up his dhoti and climbs onto the front bumper to inspect the engine (momentarily revealing to the world that he's not wearing any underpants).

A man in Row Z asks if the bicycle can do 50 kph.

In a moment of madness I once clocked 60 mph (98 kph) near a place called Stanford Bridge, but it is rare indeed to find a gradient sufficiently steep and straight and smooth to permit such speeds. A bicycle will go just as fast as you, gravity and the road surface will allow it to. It's a silly question, but I nod gravely and he looks awed.

*

Bikaner is the usual Indian frenzy of crowds and traffic milling around complacent cows, some lying down in the middle of the road. Correctly identifying the presence of food, one of these ladies dribbles and snuffles inquisitively over my panniers as I pause to consult the street plan in my guidebook. Then I find myself locked in a desperate struggle to fend off Her Serene Holiness' determined attempts to digest the guidebook's contents in the most literal way. It's a little like wrestling with a bulldozer. A boy is showing interest in the bicycle so, still breathless from my exertions with the cow, I decide that I might as well take advantage of the situation by asking him for directions to the Evergreen Hotel.

'What is your name?' he counters obliquely.

'Chris.'

'Which country?'

'England.'

'What is your hobby?'

'Torturing small boys.'

'Mine is collecting coins.'

I have to tell him several times that I don't have any English coins.

Eventually the penny (so to speak) drops. 'Give me Indian coins!' is his parting shot.

Beyond Bikaner the rolling dunes have disappeared. Camels and goats can be seen grazing upon thorny trees (the latter standing on their hind legs to get at the lower branches) and there are patches of grass, although it is short and sparse. Whereas yesterday there was only sand, there is soil, piles of hay and ploughed fields. The traffic is limited to a few lorries, the occasional bus, infrequent minibuses, the venerable Hindustan Ambassador cars (replicas of the 1950s Morris Oxford), and camels pulling single-axle carts. From time to time gazelles career across the road and bound into the flat distance with extraordinary speed and grace, and a long-tailed grey monkey lopes across the road on all fours. Vultures plucking at one of the many bloodied corpses lying at the side of the road flap their wings and hiss resentfully at my approach and I hold my breath as I pass; the stench of putrefying flesh is far from pleasant. In the villages the inevitable cows wander unconcernedly down the middle of the road, and unlike in Iran and Pakistan, there are plenty of dogs, usually asleep in the shade. They live off scraps and scavenge and evidently manage well enough not to hunt cyclists.

The Rajputs were a warlike people and garrisoned their towns. Built on a small hill, the turrets and battlements of the spectacular honey-coloured citadel of Jaisalmer tower above the plain and can be seen for miles. Centuries ago the city's position on the spice route connecting India and Central Asia brought it great wealth, but the rise in shipping and the development of the port of Bombay resulted in its gradual decline as a centre of trade and Partition eventually sealed it off from the rest of Asia. Owing to its strategic location close to the Pakistan border Jaisalmer has reinvented itself as a military base, but the tourist trade provides the bulk of its income.

Some of the narrow streets within the massive thirty-foot-high sandstone walls are so steep that I have to dismount and push the heavy bicycle, the metal cleats on my boots finding little purchase on the cobblestones. A man gives the bicycle a helping shove and I smile my thanks; the Indians are so obliging. At the top of the hill I enter an entrancing network of tiny, paved lanes and alleyways winding between massive stone buildings with jutting balconies. Jain and Hindu temples, palaces and the exquisitely carved facades of the traditional Rajput mansions called *havelis* (originally the property of wealthy merchants) rub shoulders in narrow alleys with Internet cafés, foreign-exchange offices, souvenir shops, travel agents advertising camel safaris, rooftop restaurants, and guest houses and hotels with names like *Desert View, Jaisal Palace* and *Fort View*.

A most un-Indian peace reigns, for the shady streets and walkways are too narrow to permit motor traffic and the cars and auto rickshaws are confined to the town that has sprung up below to encircle the citadel's gigantic walls. On several occasions I have to squeeze past salivating cows, and men wearing sandals and dressed in the usual cotton trousers and long-sleeved nylon or cotton shirts respectfully greet me with 'Good morning' or 'Hello sir' or '*Namaste*' and ask if I'd like to hire a rickshaw or visit their shops; or they offer emailing facilities or the use of a phone or accommodation in a room with a view of the surrounding desert.

On a balcony overlooking the small square I feast on toast, poached egg, baked beans and grated cheese, washing it all down with a filter coffee, the thoroughly English breakfast about which I have been dreaming for the past five months. Although I adore Indian food and believe that sampling local fare is an essential and (usually) very enjoyable part of travelling, a diet consisting uniquely of omelettes for breakfast and various curries for the rest of the day can become a little repetitive.

Down below a small crowd has assembled to admire a sleek, German-registered motorbike. When the scavenging groups of cows, goats and dogs have eaten their fill the Untouchables converge to scoop what remains of the swept-up piles of rubbish into a pick-up, into the back of which an enterprising cow is attempting unsuccessfully to clamber. I find it surprising that these mobile incinerators find enough scraps upon which to live, but they don't look underfed and obviously thrive on cardboard and paper.

*

The first two hours of the day are the best. The dawn air is chilly, raising the hairs on my bare forearms as the sun appears as a flaming red ball over the fields to the left. Several grey monkeys with long tails and lugubrious expressions lope across the road in front of me and bound into the trees with casual, astonishing athleticism. Vehicles hoot, not a polite *pip* but a full-blown blast on their multi-toned horns. I ought to hang a sign on the back of the bicycle saying *No Horn Thank You*. Or *Quiet Please!* Or even *Ssshhh!* Auto rickshaws and motor scooters draw alongside, their occupants subjecting me to a prolonged, silent scrutiny before accelerating away. People inhabiting isolated settlements consisting of circular mud dwellings with dome-shaped thatched roofs stand at the side of the road and stare. Some flap their hands, indicating that they want me to stop. Others call out unintelligibly, or simply raise their hands in a silent salute. Children tending flocks of sheep or goats shout and scream, hysterical with excitement. When one of a group of women dressed in white says 'Hello' I am so surprised that I nearly fall off the bicycle, but recover my composure just in time to return the greeting. Until then the women have stared, but not once have they waved or addressed me.

A dense screen of trees casts long shadows across the road well into mid-morning. Following the long night's rest I feel refreshed and full of vigour as I cross from Rajasthan into Gujarat, the stomach bugs, colds, sore throats, chest infections and general weakness I experienced in Pakistan a rapidly fading memory. Although it has responded and shaped itself to the task in a way that has exceeded my wildest expectations and laid to rest my principal fear that it just wouldn't be up to the job, my body has nevertheless developed some ingenious ways of ensuring that I don't push it too hard. As it gets hotter later on in the day the aches and pains announce themselves. The discomfort accumulating in the lower right-hand side of my back, a developing soreness in my crotch area and a smarting in my left foot where the shoe contacts the pedal conspire to ensure regular roadside halts for rest and refreshment, during which the bicycle becomes engulfed by a crowd of people prodding the saddle, yanking the brake and gear levers, puzzling over the pedals and gears, and experimentally pressing the buttons on the trip computer.

The Hotel Cappal on the Ahmadabad Road in Palanpur is rather posh and a room costs more than I normally like to pay, but I feel like indulging myself. Waiters rush to help me with my bags and I wonder how much baksheesh is expected. The room boasts a twenty-four-channel cable television upon which I can watch *BBC World*, a telephone with which to summon room service and a toilet that is the last word in sophistication: when you've finished your business you turn a tap on the wall and a thin but powerful jet of water fires straight up your anus. To direct, simply move your buttocks a fraction on the toilet seat, and to vary the water pressure turn the tap. No need for paper and no need to soil your hands. If these toilets were introduced in the West trees would be saved, litter reduced and standards of hygiene considerably advanced.

*

An Indian's journey through life is dictated by caste. Society is divided into four castes, the *Brahmins* or priestly caste at the top, followed by the *Kshatriyas* (nobles and warriors), the *Vaishyas* or *Banyas* (farmers and traders) and finally the *Sudras*, the manual workers. The *Dalits* or Untouchables, those who undertake the tasks that no others are willing to perform – for example cleaning lavatories, washing clothes, working in tanneries (leather is unclean) and tending cremation grounds – are without caste. Foreigners are likewise excluded from the caste system.

More deeply entrenched than the English class system at its zenith, this hierarchy is rigidly reinforced by religion. Each caste has a set of religious and social obligations to fulfil, known as its *dharma*. The Brahmins must study the Vedic texts (scriptures) and pass them on to successive generations; the Kshatriyas have to immerse themselves in weaponry and the art of government; the Vaishyas pursue careers in agriculture or commerce; and the Sudras are destined to serve the other castes. Those born into a lowly caste must accept their destiny, and their reward for doing so will be reincarnation into a higher caste. Those who behave inappropriately, however, will be punished in the next life by being reborn as an animal or an insect.

The western objective of self-improvement is discouraged, for the Hindu's place in society is determined by his – or her – *karma* (conduct or action) in a *previous* incarnation. By fulfilling their obligations and accepting their inherited condition people hope to ascend to more favourable circumstances in the *next* life, and so on through each incarnation until eventually they achieve *moksha* – liberation from the cycle of rebirth. The system encourages apathy and inertia amongst hoi polloi (for one is rewarded not by initiative, enterprise, talent or hard work but by acquiescence) whilst conveniently maintaining the status quo for the wealthy and powerful elite.

I have detected a similar hierarchy on the road. Lorries and buses are at the apex of the pyramid, followed by cars and vans. Auto rickshaws and scooters occupy the third tier, with bicycles and pedal rickshaws right down at the base of the pecking order, for only the pedestrian caste defers to a cyclist. I think that those who feared for my safety before I left were filled with romantic visions of robbery, violence, kidnapping or even murder by brigands (and snakes alone kill twenty thousand people a year in India) but by far the greatest threat of injury or extinction probably comes from a more prosaic source: Indian road-death statistics are amongst the worst in the world.

The verges of the busy road connecting Palanpur and Ahmadabad are littered with accidents and breakdowns. The clamour is deafening, for like the emergency services using their sirens at home, motorists sound their horns incessantly to warn lower castes to make way. On hearing the ugly blare of approaching horns local cyclists immediately leave the road in droves, scattering like wildebeest ambushed by a lion and only rejoining it after the car, lorry or bus has passed. If I can only likewise accept my humble position as a cyclist I might get to be a bus driver in the next incarnation, but layers of habit learned and developed over a lifetime cannot easily be peeled away within a few weeks. Brought up with a more democratic version of the Highway Code, I cannot bring myself to follow their example, and instead of adopting a sensible policy of self-preservation I cling obstinately to the road, foolishly trying to instil in these yobbos some British etiquette. Cyclists use their own bells or klaxons almost continuously in built-up areas because if members of the pedestrian sub-caste don't hear you coming they generally assume that you're not there, but as my bicycle is equipped with neither bell nor beeper I have to resort to shouting – usually an anguished '*NO!*' as somebody blithely steps out in front of me.

The bus drivers (who might have learned their trade from a manual written by Mister Toad) are probably the most reckless of all, and with a full complement of passengers to endanger their irresponsibility is magnified in my eyes by a factor of about forty. They have a particularly infuriating tendency to slam on the brakes (no indicators or brake lights, naturally) immediately after overtaking to pick up or drop off passengers, leaving you with no room to pass on the outside. As a cyclist you are forced either to head for a narrow gap on the inside (running the risk of colliding with alighting passengers or crashing headlong into an opening door) or to stop behind and wait, seething at the wasted energy.

The lorries are poorly maintained and overloading routinely raises their centres of gravity, rendering them dangerously unstable. Many of the drivers are untrained and exhausted, their actions uncoordinated by alcohol and their minds anaesthetized by *bhang* (hashish). Several cut in dangerously after squeezing past with inches to spare, deafening me with blasts from their multi-toned horns. Each time I have to take evasive action to avoid a head-on collision with an oncoming Tata or Ashok Leyland executing an ill-timed overtaking manoeuvre, I eloquently spread out my right arm, palm upwards *(where am I supposed to go, mate?)* before either braking hard or leaving the road at the last possible moment and relieving my feelings by swearing. One of the most rewarding experiences in India is to witness one of these behemoths bearing down upon a cow that has wandered into the road. The horn blasts are met with lofty indifference and the lorry (or bus) is forced to screech to a halt, the cows clearly aware that they are divine and quite invulnerable.

Unlike the cows, however, I am neither divine nor invulnerable. Clinging to a deeply entrenched belief that a bicycle has just as much right to be on the road as a truck or a bus or a car is not only pointless but might well get me killed. It fills me with futile rage too. Momentum on a bicycle is easily lost and hard to regain and the frustration I experience when forced to brake – whether by overtaking lorries, buses cutting in and stopping suddenly in front of me, auto rickshaws executing ill-timed U-turns, the incredible propensity of pedestrians and my fellow cyclists of simply getting in the way, or by the multitude of speed retarding strips at the entry and exit points of level crossings, bridges and towns – is mentally tiring and tends to put me in a foul mood.

The Gujarati authorities are campaigning for greater road safety with signs in English such as *SAFETY COMES IN CANS: I CAN, YOU CAN, WE CAN* and *THIS IS A HIGHWAY, NOT A RUNWAY.* What effect, if any, these cryptic messages have is debatable; the literacy rate in Gujarat is only 61 per cent, and how many of those people are able to read or understand English? I can only assume that the signs are repeated elsewhere in Hindi or Gujarati.

'W****r!' I roar at the driver through his open window when an overtaking bus cuts dangerously in front of a lorry to avoid a head-on collision with an oncoming car and then promptly screeches to a halt to regurgitate a passenger.

Why can't they wait? Believing that life is a priceless opportunity of limited duration that comes our way just once and not several times (and I'd like to be given the chance to cram as much experience as possible into mine), I share none of the apparent indifference of Indians – for whom earthly life is a matter of little importance – whenever I witness an example of dangerous and stupid driving. The signs *TAKE YOUR TIME NOT YOUR LIFE* at the roadside south of Rajapur miss the point; if someone considers their life worthless enough to warrant committing suicide in the cause of punctuality then that's entirely their prerogative, but the poor wretches coming the other way on a blind bend might just have a different scale of priorities.

*

Between Mahesana and Gandhinagar a badly needed dual carriageway is being built. Graceful hour-glass figures in colourful saris, condemned by the iniquitous caste system to their brutal way of life, are stooping to clear the soil under-bed of the new road by placing stones in shallow, wok-shaped wicker trays and carrying them away on their heads. It must be the most dreadful thing of all to exist without hope; however bad things get and however cynical I may appear at times, I have never lost the belief that it lies within my own power to transform my life for the better – which I think probably defines me as an optimist. The only source of comfort to these women, however, must be the notion that they will eventually escape their condition in another life. I think religions that promote the concept of life after death devalue and diminish the significance of life *before* death and that many Indians appear to have all too little reason to live and far too much incentive to die.

At each red light in Ahmadabad, a sprawling and polluted city of four million souls, I wait in a flotilla of mopeds, scooters and auto rickshaws all revving their puny two-stroke engines and enveloping me in a noxious cloud of blue-grey smoke. Because there isn't a single direction sign in English I learn something of the frustration of being illiterate, and some of the auto-rickshaw drivers appear never to have heard of Bombay or Mumbai. Slow-moving and slow-witted cyclists, pedestrians, dogs, cows and camels drawing carts regularly obstruct the way ahead. Buses stop without warning in the middle of the road to decant passengers who thus run the risk of being run over as soon as they disembark, and then, when I am already committed to passing them, they suddenly accelerate away, leaving me stranded in the middle of the road and thinking nostalgically of those plaintive little notices *Please Let Buses Pull Out!* on the rear of buses at home. In India the idea that one might be in a position to prevent a bus from doing *anything* has acquired a sort of quaint, otherworldly charm.

Between Ahmadabad and Bombay the NH8 becomes one of the busiest and most dangerous racetracks in India. The desire to make progress is tempered by concern for the bicycle; the surface is breaking up badly in places, forcing me to swerve round holes and bounce over ripples and slovenly repairs which rise a good inch above the surrounding asphalt. A breakdown on a narrow bridge near Navsari has caused a huge backlog of lorries to build up, but I work my way to the front of the chaos by cycling along the verge, dodging the gobbets of phlegm and spit ejected through nearside windows by the drivers' mates.

ACCIDENT-PRONE AREA! DRIVE SLOWLY! importune roadside signs on winding sections of road.

How can an *area* be accident-prone? Accident-prone *drivers*, surely!

To wage a one-man crusade to reform Indian driving habits is arrogant and dangerous folly, for I will never change India; I can only hope that India might change me – *before* I come to a sticky end on one of her roads. More eloquent than any of the cautionary road signs (but evidently just as ignored) are the scores of wrecked vehicles abandoned at the roadside.

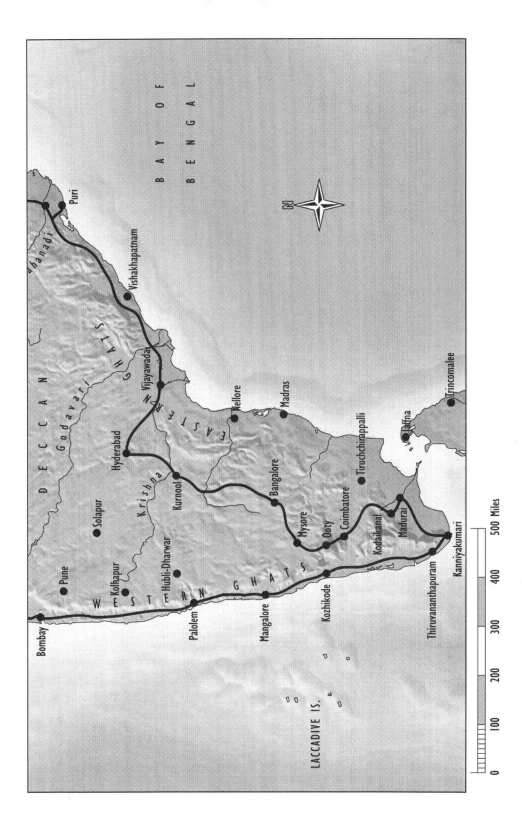

Chapter Eleven
'Foot Odour' and 'Special' Tea

Cycling past miles of pavement dwellings built out of wood, canvas, plastic sheeting and corrugated iron, past naked children playing at the roadside and long lines of lorries waiting to enter the nearby docks, I find a way out of India's greatest city. Like Calcutta, Bombay is a magnet for India's poverty-stricken rural dwellers. Roughly half of the city's fifteen million residents live in shantytowns, and the total population is expected to rise to around twenty-eight million by the year 2015. Three days was insufficient time to discover the city's soul but accommodation was too expensive to permit a longer stay.

The NH17, which follows the coast south from Bombay all the way down to Cochin, is a far nicer road than the frantic ant-run that leads north to Ahmadabad. The surface is better, the traffic considerably lighter, and the scenery more interesting as it climbs and twists into the dense rainforests of the Western Ghats, the tropical chain of mountains that runs parallel to India's west coast for a thousand miles. Every year in June pregnant monsoon clouds approaching from the Indian Ocean are forced upwards by these mountains to condense in the cooler stratosphere, deluging the Ghats and replenishing the Mahanadi, the Godavari, the Krishna and the Kaveri. These rivers and their tributaries quench the thirst of central and southern India, providing vital nourishment for plant, animal and human life during their progress east to the Bay of Bengal. Over twenty-nine feet of rain falls annually in some areas.

A buffalo is lying dead at the roadside, rigor mortis extending its legs stiffly out in front of it. Two men with a goat wedged between them buzz past on a moped trailing blue smoke and a man is enigmatically pushing a sewing machine bolted onto a trolley in the opposite direction. What is his good name? Where is he going? What is his profession? What is his salary? I should have stopped to ask him – had he spoken English the answers might have been fascinating. Slender women in luminous saris are trotting briskly along the verge supporting improbably large and heavy looking bundles of firewood or urns of water on their heads, shapely buttocks wiggling enticingly beneath silk wrappings.

The sun shines, a thousand tropical birds tweet and trill, and two oxen pulling a cart lumber past as, pleasantly stoned on endorphins, I sit down in the dust at the roadside in the shade of a giant banyan tree trailing creepers to refuel with some sugary Indian snacks, propping up my back against one of the panniers. Although the threat from other road users remains, my confidence has increased immeasurably since those early, uncertain days in Europe. As long as the bicycle is running trouble-free and I'm fit and healthy, I now feel that I have little to fear from natural obstacles, whether headwinds, mountain ranges, thunderstorms or deserts. The bicycle, mechanically simple but a nasty, fiddly piece of apparatus to someone as ham-fisted with a spanner as I am, has required only a few minor adjustments and periodic checking and lubricating. Apart from a rash of punctures in Eastern Europe it has given little trouble thus far, although the chain and gear cluster will surely have to be replaced soon.

Tiny figures can be seen halfway up a mountainside, working on the land. The relentless requirements of a burgeoning population have reduced the area of undisturbed rainforest covering the Western Ghats from an estimated sixty-two thousand square miles at the twentieth century's inception to just five thousand at its conclusion. Vast areas have been cleared for eucalyptus, tea, coffee, cardamom and cashew plantations, plus road building, mining and hydroelectric projects. Fewer trees are left to soak up the rainfall and the plundering of India's forests is a major cause of flooding.

*

The place names in Goa reflect the state's four and a half centuries as a Portuguese enclave until it was liberated by India as recently as 1961. On the road leading south from Mapusa I feel unaccountably weary and unable to establish any kind of rhythm, despite excellent health, regular intakes of fuel and a good night's sleep. Maybe my body needs rest, but I think that on this occasion the reason for my fatigue is psychological; on the face of it I have an easy day's cycling to Palolem, and because I have fewer miles to cover than usual I have persuaded myself that they will be easy miles. Far from it: they are hot, mountainous and bumpy miles. I cycle thirstily past whitewashed Roman Catholic churches, shimmering paddy fields, waving palms and roadside billboards advertising Kingfisher, Directors Special and San Miguel beers. My adrenalin levels haven't risen to the occasion and without the necessary mental adjustment I just don't feel 'up for it'.

Palolem is full of backpackers and dread-locked hippy types clad in sarongs. Local businesses have sprung up to cater for western tastes and requirements, but despite the proliferation of Internet cafés, restaurants, hotels, Public Call

Offices and stalls selling toilet rolls, clothes, second-hand books, handicrafts and souvenirs, the village has retained some of its Indian feel. The beach, a wide arc of golden sand fringed with palms and low, forested hills, is idyllic. I peel off my sweat-stained clothes and jog past a couple of narrow fishing boats drawn up on the sand before plunging into the welcoming sea.

*

Corrugated asphalt constantly rises and falls in a series of short, sharp undulations as I continue southwards into Karnataka following four days of indolence on the beaches of Goa. A drinks stop at a restaurant in Kampta is memorable for the following exchange:

WAITER: Foot odour?
ME: I beg your pardon?
WAITER: You have foot odour?
ME (playing for time): I'm sorry, I don't understand.
This is getting embarrassing! Is he about to offer me talcum powder or a fresh pair of socks? I know my feet are sweaty and might pong a little when I take off my boots at the end of the day (after all, this is the tropics) but surely they aren't so offensive that he can smell them with my boots still on?
WAITER (impassively): Some people first take drinks and then odour foot.
ME (mightily relieved): Oh! No, I'm not hungry. Just thirsty, thank you!

The journey south has been accompanied by a gradual increase in heat and humidity and even the morning freshness has disappeared. Bridges cross broad, shining stretches of water on their way down from the Western Ghats to the Arabian Sea. It is inadvisable to contemplate the scenery because as soon as I lift my eyes from the road it can be guaranteed that the bicycle will fall into a pothole. I toil sweatily past Indian Oil, Bharat Petroleum and HP (Hindustan Petroleum) filling stations, broken down and overturned trucks and buses, palm trees, coconut groves, teams of oxen and brown, sinewy, scantily-clad men knee-deep in water and mud ploughing paddies, deserted beaches and lush, rainforest covered hills. Past temples, mosques, churches, bicycle repair shops, general stores, restaurants, dhabas, tyre retreaders, hairdressers, bus stands, auto rickshaw and taxi ranks, brightly painted walls advertising Yellow Pages or L&T Cement, past *'allo's* and *'hi's* and *'what is your name's* and *'where are you going's* and shrieks and whistles.

Under the cumulative onslaught of tropical heat, crowds, shrieking horns, abominable driving and sheer tiredness, my temper can become fragile towards the end of a long day. Maybe I should stop earlier and content myself with fifty-mile instead of eighty-mile days, but unlike Eric and Emmanuelle I have this deep-seated urge to explore my physical limits and so I ride on, bullying the extra distance out of protesting muscles, cursing the hills that I enjoy so much when I'm fresh and fuming when the road surface deteriorates. On a recently laid stretch I consign a lorry driver to eternal damnation as his vehicle bombards me with dust and loose chippings and I blast an insubordinate gear cable on the bicycle. When fatigue causes me to fumble or drop or forget something I curse myself aloud.

Hot and thirsty after crossing Mangalore, and struggling with a sore throat, I order a Pepsi and two samosas from a roadside stall. The lisping vendor can make freshly squeezed pineapple juice, so I order a glass of that too. I have the usual difficulty in persuading my incredulous host that I have cycled all the way from England and not taken the plane to Bombay, and that the trip has so far taken over six months.

He asks me when I expect to return home.

'Next September.'

'What ith your profession?'

'Transport,' I reply with my customary vagueness.

'What ith your thalary?'

'About twenty thousand pounds a year.'

'In England what ith the average thalary?'

I hazard a guess. 'About twenty-two thousand.'

After making the conversion into rupees, he asks me if there are any poor people in England. Like so many I've met in the developing world, he has failed to equate higher salaries with the greater cost of living in Western Europe and assumes that we are all dripping with disposable income. When I try to convince him that there are plenty of poor people he looks disbelieving, particularly as I can't tell him 'what percentage'. Where do you draw the line between wealth and poverty – and isn't it all relative anyway?

'Are you married?' he asks.

'If I was married I wouldn't be free to cycle round the world.' The question continues to make me slightly defensive; amongst people who regard bachelordom beyond the early twenties as an aberration I feel that I have somehow to justify my singleness. 'I will find a beautiful woman and get married when I get back home.'

'Marriage ith thecurity but not freedom,' he pronounces solemnly.

Before leaving I shake his hand.

He likes that. 'I wish you all thuctheth on your journey!' he says with that inimitable Indian sideways waggle of the head, half way between a nod and a shake, which seems to signify perfect contentment with the general nature and order of the universe.

'Thank you!' I reply. 'I wish you every success in your business.'

*

Some of the climbs between Calicut and Trichur are both long and steep. The population of Kerala, boasting a literacy rate of 91 per cent against a national average of only 52 per cent, is India's best educated and the state has the subcontinent's lowest birth rate. For centuries Chinese, Arab, Jewish, Dutch and Portuguese traders fought over the rights to her booty of rubber, teak, cashews, tea, cardamoms and pepper until the British bully finally established a stranglehold in 1795. In 1957 Keralans voted in the world's first democratically elected communist party. Through a gap in the roadside foliage during one ascent I glimpse an undulating tropical green sea of palms stretching into the distance. Transfers on the back of one of the three-wheeled auto rickshaws proudly trumpet that it is a 4x4, and with gravity on my side I freewheel behind it, giggling.

Solitary travel has much to recommend it. You travel at your own pace and on your own budget, and you stop when and wherever you like. Life is so much simpler with only oneself to please, for fellow travellers will inevitably have different schedules and inclinations and contrasting budgets and levels of fitness. When on the move I'm too absorbed by the sights and sounds around me and too distracted by the sheer physical effort required to grind out eighty-mile days to feel any need for company; it is during breaks in the travelling that I tend to miss the fellowship of other human beings. Excellent company was provided in Goa by a delightfully eccentric English couple I'd met in Esfahan who were driving around the world in an elderly Citroen 2CV, but at Varkala, where reddish-brown cliffs tower above half a kilometre of sandy shoreline and the tourists are predominately English, Dutch, German, French and American, I reflect that it is odd that I can feel so much more alone on a crowded beach than when camping out in the middle of a desert. Although surrounded by potential company, some of it doubtless pleasant and interesting, I have no idea how to make a connection. Ironically, now that I find myself amongst people who respect my space and privacy, I'd be positively delighted if one of them were to approach and ask me *which country?* or *what profession?* but of course, just like me, they don't want to intrude – and without the travel-stained bicycle to provide my credentials I have become just another sun-seeking tourist.

It is a romantic setting and a love affair would be a terrific way to pass the time but attractive single women don't usually travel alone, and with good reason. The only such woman I've met so far was French. Having spent nine months finding her way from Montpellier to Esfahan via Egypt, Jordan, Syria and Turkey, she arrived at the Amir Kabir the evening before I left. I thought she was *formidable* and admired her hugely, but as I was already committed to leaving the next day there just wasn't enough time to do anything about it. An email I received from one of the Dutch cyclists who accompanied Eric and Emma through Eastern Europe graphically and rather charmingly highlighted the problems faced by women travelling solo:

Just before Shimla, there was this terrible guy on the road, making stupid signs with crossed fingers, wanted me to stop. I told him I don't speak Hindi and I don't understand you. He came after me and grapped me in my teets, I pushed him away, try to get away, but it was so steep. He came after me again and did it again. I start shouting, from far I saw somebody walking, then he left me alone. I was really shocked. The first hotel I saw I stayed, even for the price of 300rp! This was only 3km before Shimla.

Now there are three swiss cyclers behind me, they also should come to Shimla, but the swiss girl had pain in her legs, so they don't want to many mountains. Now I see them in Nahan, about two days cycling from here. With them I continu to Kathmandu.

Well this was my story, a bit different then yours, but that's because of the men. The men here have such stupid thoughts about western woman. They boder you all the time, say that you are sexy, even in this very wide and big cloths, want to make a picture and starring all the time. But I don't let them spoil my trip, tomorrow I jump on my bike, enyoing all the things I see on the road, because it is such a great experience.

As a male I am naturally far less vulnerable to sexual predators and the possibility of harassment is one that I've scarcely considered, but it can and does happen; I was propositioned a number of times by homosexual men when hitchhiking abroad as a student. Although they left me feeling acutely embarrassed and unaccountably filled with shame and self-loathing, these incidents were (with one exception) brief and harmless. Most would take place in the form of an advance – usually a speculative hand placed on one of my thighs – followed by a swift rejection (I'd take the hand off and return it firmly to its owner). If the driver persisted with his groping or unzipped his flies I'd ask him to stop the car so that I could get out.

The exception occurred when I found myself trapped inside a tent on a beach in Morocco by a very large fisherman filled with gin and lust. When I repeatedly pushed his hand away his mood turned ugly and his eyes flashed.

'*Te mato!*' (I'll kill you!) he hissed in bad Spanish.

The phrase 'caught between the devil and the deep blue sea' can rarely have been more appropriate. Nobody knew where I was. He could bump me off, tie my body to a lump of rock, row out to sea and chuck me overboard, and nobody would have been any the wiser. The equally unthinkable alternative would be to submit to an experience that I have little doubt would have left me psychologically scarred for life. Talking him out of it was my only hope and the tactic succeeded, thank goodness. It turned out that he wasn't bad, only drunk, and I think that my fears of being beaten-up or bumped-off were probably groundless but the danger had seemed real enough at the time. Like Eric and Emma's Dutch cycling friend, I didn't let the experience spoil my trip and I went on to make many more.

I am carrying two talismans, both of negligible size and weight: one is a tiny sock that my three-year-old niece left behind when my brother last paid me a visit, and the other – presented to me with great ceremony at a farewell dinner party I had hosted a week before I left home – is a standard matchbox. A bright-green piece of paper bearing the slogan *A.A.A.K. (Miniature)* has been taped over the front of it, and crammed inside are a needle and thread, a vintage three-penny bit, a folded stick of chewing gum, some sticky tape, an aspirin tablet, and two tightly folded sheets of A4 paper headed *ACME ANTI-ANAL ATTACK KIT (Miniature Version)*. An entertaining preamble detailing the traumatic exploits of an office junior dispatched by the company on a lone cycle ride across Asia in the interests of market research (too replete with explicit references to tumescent male members and tightly clenched buttocks to be reproduced here) is followed by an equally unprintable set of instructions concerning the use of the items in the box. *NB: No Live Matches Contained Within This Kit!* it concludes sternly. *We feel that anyone stupid enough to cycle halfway across the world alone and without apparent concern could not be trusted with live matches.*

Having come within a whisker of being sodomised in a Moroccan tent all those years ago, I decided to take the A.A.A.K. with me – just in case. And if at any stage of the journey I became lonely, I felt that I would only have to open the matchbox and inspect its obscene contents to hear again the drunken hilarity of my dinner guests as, struggling to keep a straight face, I read out the instructions on a distant English evening last May.

The Internet provides company of sorts and a visit to one of the cyber cafés surprisingly yields an email from Ralf:

Ho Ho Ho Duuuude!
I thought I was moving pretty fast from Quetta to Lahore – that was until I heard that you beat me there by 2 days – to watch a #@*%ing cricket game ?!!?! C'm oooooon !
Anyway: reached the border on Oct 31 – the Austrian Berserker was already waiting there – turned around on my heels and grabbed a oneway to Bangkok (us$ 350) 3 days later – I gotta tell you: after all these months in this dumpster called the Middle East, Thailand was the promised land! I took in life at a

pretty leisurely pace there – even for my standards, I'm afraid.
I'm in Sydney now for almost 4 weeks, spending most of them at Kings
Cross, probably the most fucked up area on the entire continent! Thanks for
your cards – I had the idea of checking out hotels in Lahore, looking for you,
as well – after 5 minutes I realized there were 200 around the train station
alone...
I'm sure I'm missing out on a lot of shit (literally) in India – but man, was
it ever time for the (cycling) trip to end! The first days in Lahore walking up
the stairs to my room took the living crap outta me (literally)! I'm not sure
what I'm gonna do next, but I'll stay in Australia at least 6 more weeks.
Hope everything is running smoothly – not only on the toilet – for you!
In that sense: so long   -rh-

The majority of the lodges and restaurants in Varkala are concentrated on the
north cliff, along with the Internet cafés, second-hand bookstalls, handicraft
shops, 'beauty parlours', establishments offering massage, meditation or yoga
classes, and travel agents advertising bicycle hire, elephant rides, fishing
expeditions, adventure sailing, houseboat trips and discount train and air tickets.
Nevertheless it is all pleasantly low-key, buildings of wood and thatch nestling
discreetly amongst the palm trees.

On Christmas Eve I wander along the cliff-top path with a dark void and
the pounding of the sea far below to my left and bustle and light and hard sell
on my right.

'Good evening sir!'

'Yes? Can I help you?'

'We have Special Menu for tonight and (voice lowered conspiratorially)
special drinks...'

Fresh shark (in some cases over three feet long), snapper and squid have
been laid out on tables outside restaurants. Seduced by its promise of a 'special
menu', drinks and live music, I eventually settle for the Sunset Restaurant and
order shark with chips and a side-salad. The neighbouring palm trees and the
poles supporting the awning on the veranda are festooned with strings of
coloured lights, paper streamers and balloons. A few fireworks are let off. No
live music just yet, but offerings from Bob Marley, Sade and Abba are issuing
from concealed speakers. The fish is served in great meaty chunks, lightly spiced
and with the consistency of fillet steak. It is quite delicious. Local licensing laws
are clearly being infringed, for my Kingfisher beer is brought to me in a teapot
'in case the police come'.

'May I compliment you on the excellence of your tea?' I say to the waiter,
ordering another Kingfisher.

Clearly enjoying the subterfuge as much as I am, he grins delightfully. 'You
are drinking *special* tea!'

The peace and goodwill to all men that I'm experiencing owes more to a belly full of shark and two Kingfishers than the time of year. Pouring more beer into my teacup, I contentedly watch the waiters attempting to reel in passing tourists, admiring a technique doubtless honed by years of diligent practice. Two elderly American women are wearing Santa-Claus hats and the three men and two women sitting at the adjacent table have brought a tiny, inflatable Christmas tree with them. One of the women, an exquisite brunette of mixed blood, is perfection in female form. She is speaking faultless English with scarcely a trace of an accent, and all of a sudden I feel self-conscious, acutely aware of my solitude. I don't know where to put my eyes any more and my contentment abruptly vanishes. No longer at ease, I drain my teacup, pay the bill and leave.

*

Shortly after cycling through Kerala's sleepy, multi-syllabic capital city Thiruvananthapuram (try saying that when you've had a few), I cross into Tamil Nadu, India's southernmost state. The sky is overcast but the atmosphere is heavy and clammy. Stores laden with watermelons, bananas, coconuts, pomegranates and pineapples, and cool bars displaying bottles of brightly coloured fizz are a constant temptation. Indians appear to love noise and in many of the villages loudspeakers mounted on trees blare out Hindi pop or devotional music at ear-splitting volumes. Colourful murals continue to advertise products and services as diverse as Tantex Vests and Briefs, cement and film developing.

Kanniyakumari perches upon the apex of the inverted triangle that is India. The temple is one of the most sacred in India and businesses selling rolls of film, souvenirs and handicrafts have sprung up to fleece pilgrims and holidaymakers alike. Apart from the two young women who glance at me speculatively as I march into a restaurant in clothes covered in dark, cloud-shaped patches of sweat bordered by white salt deposits, I appear to be the only foreigner in town. At 'Land's End', where the waters of the Arabian Sea, the Bay of Bengal and the Indian Ocean meet in sacred confluence, there is a tiny beach where a number of pilgrims are bathing fully clothed.

I have seen off one entire continent and made substantial inroads into another, and I've just crossed a whole subcontinent. Although the distances on my maps appear huge and the prospect of the effort still to be expended remains daunting, there are nearly nine thousand miles on the trip computer to reassure me that I am probably past the journey's halfway point. Those thousands of miles already covered constitute a steadily accumulating bank of evidence that I really do possess the physical and mental tenacity to make it all the way to

Vladivostok and the Sea of Japan.

I make my way back to the hotel in a fine drizzle (the first rain since that spectacular storm between Kerman and Bam) experiencing a rare peace of mind.

Chapter Twelve
'A Long Way from France'

'Water!' I say to myself, breakfasting on bananas and oranges in my 350-rupee penthouse suite and watching several drops form on a crack in the ceiling and fall to the concrete floor.

'Water!' confirms the lady on the reception desk, glancing outside at the rain as I hand back my key and collect the 550-rupee deposit.

It is too warm to don waterproofs so, unlike fellow members of the cycling caste who are gliding along most elegantly with one hand on the handlebars and the other grasping an umbrella, I resign myself to a soaking. On my left the southern extremities of the Western Ghats are thrusting their knobbly green fists into the soggy cloud, but before long the landscape flattens. There are fewer trees than on the coast and more open spaces, some cultivated and others left for pasture. It is weather for ducks and a day for the frogs; a boy is shepherding about a hundred female mallards along the road with a stick and a stentorian croaking issues from the roadside ditch.

My singlet and leggings rapidly become soaked but getting wet is a little like a visit to the dentists, the anticipation invariably being worse than the reality. Being English I'm used to it of course, and once you've reached that stage at which you can't become any wetter, there is even something strangely exhilarating about cycling in the rain. In the tropics my clothes very rapidly become saturated with sweat anyway, but for once I remain pleasantly cool; thirst no longer dominates every thought and the water in my bottles is refreshing and potable instead of hot and tasting of plastic. Sign reading is a little more awkward than usual because I have had to take off my glasses, and water has penetrated the insides of the multi-tone horn I bought in Goa, causing it to play the same tune over and over again. I can't be bothered to dig out my knife to prise open the battery cover so I wrench the useless contraption off the handlebars and toss it into the undergrowth where, after a final protesting bleep, it expires. It was far too puny to compete with the lorries and buses anyway.

The Iraqis have a saying *whoever is wet does not fear the rain* but the wind is a more intractable problem; God has switched on his celestial ceiling-fan and a spiteful nor-westerly is spinning the propellers on the wind farms. The distance has to be wrung from the road, mile by reluctant mile, like individual drops of juice from an exhausted lemon.

I eat rice and curry off a banana leaf to the sound of the rain drumming relentlessly on the corrugated-iron roof of a roadside café. In Kovipatti people are splashing barefoot through the huge puddles. It is still raining when I sally forth from the Ananda Lodge to explore, buy tomorrow's breakfast and get my head shaved. It is drizzling when I go back out for an evening meal and pouring by the time I return to the hotel. It looks like the rain will never stop, and my newly-shaven head is as brown, hairless and smooth as a peanut.

*

'Chance' encounters in Madurai's waterlogged streets are all with opportunists. People greet me with great enthusiasm, welcoming me to their country and asking me how I am and *which country?* before getting down to the real business of finding out if I'm looking for a rickshaw or hashish or if I need to change money. Or it turns out that they happen to work in a place that sells souvenirs to tourists or their uncle owns a tailor's shop ('just look, no buy!'). This machiavellian behaviour has the effect of promoting cynicism within me and raises barriers to more natural, genuine encounters in much the same way that the few persistent gropers I encountered when hitch-hiking around Europe all those years ago made me wary of perfectly innocent offers of hospitality from drivers.

On the way to a Masala Dhosa breakfast I purchase *The Hindu.* Under the headline *Cyclone Weakens* is the following explanation for the bad weather:

The deep depression over South Tamil Nadu further weakened into a depression and lay centred over South Kerala and its neighbourhood, close to Aleppey at 5.30 p.m. on Thursday. The storm damaged standing paddy and banana crops, fishing boats and houses in Tuticorin. The southern districts continued to experience widespread rainfall.

The city is a vast open-air bazaar in which you can buy anything from a compressor to a new suit. Drooling, I wander around the air-conditioned interior of a shop in which the shelves are stacked with Mars, Bounty, Metro, Twix, Cadbury's Dairy Milk, Nestlé Crunch, Toblerone and Kit-Kat bars, M&Ms, Ferrero Rocher, Quality Street, Cornflakes, Coco-Pops, Digestives, Hobnobs, peanut butter and other half-remembered delicacies you don't expect to find outside Europe, but it is all prohibitively expensive. There are also luxury soaps, shampoos and deodorants. I give a rupee to a beggar who cunningly plays on my conscience as I emerge with a couple of Metro bars.

A much larger beggar is patrolling the roads around the spectacular Shri Meenakshi Temple, acting as a collecting box. The elephant has brown, gentle, very human eyes and its skin hangs in thick folds so that from behind it looks as if it is wearing baggy trousers. When you place a coin in the end of its trunk it pats you gently on the head with it, like the Pope offering a benediction. Paddling barefoot around the flooded complex of the temple itself, I reflect that the Shri Meenakshi has nothing of the serene, understated beauty of the Golden Temple in Amritsar; it seems almost a little – dare I say it – *vulgar*. The massive fifty-metre-high gopurams, exuberantly covered from top to bottom with a riotous, multicoloured assembly of carvings and statuettes of gods and goddesses waving their many arms and exposing their bloated bellies, tower over the surrounding streets. Most of the 330 million deities that – by some estimates – comprise the Hindu pantheon appear to be represented.

*

Large, polluted and full of traffic lights, Coimbatore reminds me of Ahmadabad. I ask two policemen if I'm on the right road to Ooty.

They look blank.

'Ooty? Is this the right road to Ooty?' The full name of the place escapes me for the moment, but *everyone* knows it by its diminutive and even the road signs (where they exist) are usually marked 'Ooty' instead of the more formal 'Ootacamund' or 'Udhagamandalam'.

'Trichy?' queries one of them.

'No, Ooty! *Ooty!!*' Frustration is beginning to get the better of me now. 'OOTY!!!'

His mate decides it's time to help. 'Where are you going?' he asks.

I give up. *Never* ask an Indian policeman for directions.

Beyond Mettuppalaiyam the road begins to climb back into the mountains and the tropical sun unhelpfully breaks through the cloud just as I engage low gear. The hill stations were built so that India's British rulers could take refuge from the heat of the plains, which becomes intolerable around the months of April and May. The entire governments of Delhi and Calcutta would head every year for Shimla (which became known as India's summer capital) whilst the colonial administration of Madras retreated to Ooty. It isn't refuge from the heat that has drawn me to these mountain retreats, however, but rather the challenge of some sustained hill climbing (a little practice before the rigours of the Karakoram Highway would be no bad thing) and the lure of the scenery.

Kodaikanal, perched on precipitous slopes, is reputedly the most spectacular of all the southern hill stations but I never got to see much of it because of fog and low cloud. Involving a climb of 1,750 metres over the final thirty miles, the seventy-three-mile, single-day ride from Madurai had been a physical feat to rank alongside the ascent from Of to the Ovitdagi Gecidi and was a classic example of the journey being more memorable than the arrival.

GHAT ROAD STARTS HERE. YOU HAVE BEEN CAUTIONED declares a sign ominously.

SPEED IS A FIVE-LETTER WORD. SO IS THE DEATH points out another, a little unnecessarily for those of us hoo kan spel.

To the right is a towering hillside and gushing waterfalls and on the left an abyss and the sound of gurgling water. A riot of tropical greenery surrounds me on all sides, grass, flowering plants, shrubs, bushes and trees all competing for a share of the soil and the sun. Several monkeys sitting on the low wall at the roadside scrutinise me as I pass. During a halt at one of the roadside stalls to rest, drink mineral water, eat bananas and admire the view of a spectacular waterfall on the other side of the valley, I throw the banana skins to the monkeys and attempt to take photographs of them but the little wretches won't stay still.

Four-wheel-drive Tatas and Mahindras are careering along the narrow road and buses lurch round the bends, honking their horns furiously. A goat bleats piteously as a man carries it aboard a bus; I'd be doing exactly the same if forced to entrust my life to an Indian bus driver.

'Good morning! Welcome to Ooty!' bellows a head from a passing Tata. On a couple of occasions I have to dismount in order to hurl stones and invective at pursuing dogs, incensed at having my rhythm interrupted.

ELEVATION 1,250m. At 5 mph the occasional light breeze is heaven-sent. Progress is measured as much in terms of accumulated height as distance, and although I welcome the respite afforded by the occasional downhill stretch and the sight of the kilometre stones passing by more quickly, I find myself regretting the loss of altitude – it feels almost as if I'm cycling backwards. The roadside halts become more frequent as tiredness takes over. A stallholder gives me three satsumas free of charge and a girl and boy scamper down the hill from a waiting car to ask me my name and *which country?* As I cycle away I hear the sound of clapping: a young man is applauding me. I'm awkwardly situated to take a bow, but I grin my appreciation and he gives me the thumbs-up.

During another pause to relieve my aching back a Mahindra (a derivative of the Jeep) draws to a halt alongside. A middle-aged European face is staring quizzically at me from the passenger seat.

I decide to break the silence: 'Hello!'

'Well *hello*!' it replies in a broad Irish accent. 'Is that as hard as it looks?'

He works for 'a trading company' in Dubai and is on holiday visiting his Indian girlfriend's relatives and doing a little tourism at the same time. Initial incredulity changes to awe and then to frank admiration when I tell him that I've cycled all the way from England and that I intend to carry on pedalling until I finally run out of land at Vladivostok.

'What made you decide to set out on such a trip?' he asks.

Although *why?* must be the question most commonly posed by westerners, it is one rarely asked by people living outside Europe. I think that in Asia, and particularly in India (where thousands of pilgrimages are in progress all the time), the benefits of sacrifice and the idea of making a journey for its own sake are understood better than in the West. The greater the discomfort endured by the pilgrim, the greater his reward in the hereafter, and sometimes I wonder if people here assume that I'm just another pilgrim intent upon obtaining extra merit points for the next life.

Many westerners, on the other hand, cannot see beyond the hardship and sacrifices involved in such a journey. 'Rather you than me!' they say doubtfully, or 'He's never right!' or 'Why don't you fly, catch a bus, take the train?'

As a general rule, the more energy you invest in an enterprise the greater the dividend, and although there are easier ways of travelling, few can be as physically and mentally fulfilling. Every day on the road is a trial of strength and a test of determination, and even though there are occasions when I feel like throwing the bicycle onto a bus (or over the nearest cliff) and making for the nearest international airport, I've only failed the test once so far – when illness forced me to take that bus ride into Kerman. And I have discovered that the rewards of abstinence are manifold. How can you truly appreciate food if you've never known hunger? The exquisite beauty of a cold drink if you've never experienced real thirst? The lifting of the spirits induced by the warmth of the sun on your back if you don't know what it is to be cold and wet? The sheer pleasure of luxuriating in a hot bath if you've never been reduced to washing with a bucket of cold water?

It has become clear to me during the past few months that without periods of turbulence and deprivation intervals of greater calm and plenty would be worthless. Just as I have come to value each uphill slog for the interval of freewheeling joy it promises (without the hills there wouldn't *be* any freewheeling), I should learn to welcome adversity, for days of plenty can be identified only when they succeed periods of famine, blue skies enjoyed only when they follow grey.

'I split up with my girlfriend and then lost my job. There didn't seem to be an awful lot to stay for,' I reply, keeping it simple.

'Are you doing it for some kind of a cause?'

'No, just for the hell of it.'

'Well fair play to you! It takes real guts to do what you're doing – visiting all those places you've never been to before, facing all the dangers.'

Guts? I think despair had more to do with the decision than guts. Abandoning a high-flying career would have taken guts, but fleeing an unpalatable situation might be seen as cowardice. Cycling halfway round the world may not be most people's idea of an easy or logical response to a failed relationship and redundancy, but for me it might have been the simplest in the end.

'Have you had any problems?' he continues.

This has to be the next most common question asked by westerners after 'why?' He is visualising ambushes, robbery, kidnapping, sodomy, or some other unspecified villainy perpetrated by horrid, wild-eyed, bearded men wearing turbans – doubtless bearing an uncanny resemblance to Bernard Bresslaw playing *Bungdit Din* (opposite me as Charles Hawtrey's timid, bungling, victimised *Private Widdle*) in *Carry On Up The Khyber*.

Travellers are indeed rendered vulnerable by their ignorance of local customs, prices and laws, and in every society there are hyenas waiting for a chance to exploit signs of weakness or naïvety in others for their own profit. All things being equal, however, I don't think you are any more likely to encounter villainy out here than at home, and in people the world over the instinct is almost always to offer succour to a fellow human being in distress. That instinct was evident in the spontaneous kindness of the barman in Nordausques, the generosity of the manager of the filling station in Greece who shared his lunch with me when I was struggling to repair punctured tyres, the Iranians who offered me food, drink and refuge when I fell ill in the desert, the frequency with which I've had to turn down offers of a lift, the innate hospitality of people such as Khosrol, Zhosai and Sasan, and the countless kind souls throughout Europe and Asia who stopped their cars or otherwise approached me to volunteer advice whenever I appeared lost or uncertain of the route. Even the axe-woman of the Iskar Valley would have been far more likely to invite me home to experience some rural Bulgarian hospitality than to chop me up into little pieces.

When faced by the unknown, however, people tend to imagine the worst. Although I was no different from anyone else in this respect, the friend (an experienced traveller who really ought to have known better) who advised me to pack a pair of binoculars so that I'd be able to spot trouble on the road ahead seemed to be taking paranoia a little too far; whilst it is advisable to travel with prudence, it would be impossible to do so in the constant expectation of being robbed or attacked. The steady accumulation of miles and days has done wonders for my confidence and I've travelled far enough and for long enough in the past to have learnt that self-preservation is above all a matter of commonsense. Commonsense, for instance, dictates that I don't wander the streets of Lahore or Bombay alone late at night, but then I wouldn't dream of doing so in certain areas of London or Birmingham either. I've encountered plenty of wild-eyed, bearded men wearing turbans, but thus far they've offered me only courtesy, respect and rather disgusting tea. I find myself telling the Irishman that, aside from the odd stomach bug and a few punctures, I've had remarkably few problems so far.

'You know what?' he says. 'When you get back you'll find that people will be doing exactly the same things and talking the same old shit, and you'll have been halfway round the world!'

Indeed. And I should imagine that many of those people, absorbed by their careers and families, would say 'so what?' Nevertheless, his admiration is flattering and provides a welcome boost to morale.

Finally he extends his hand and wishes me luck.

'Perhaps I'll see you in Ooty!' I say.

He laughs. 'Yeah, perhaps you will! We'll celebrate with a beer!'

*

Sitting at a pavement café drinking coffee on a glorious morning above the clouds in Ooty (elevation 2,240 metres), it feels good to be alive. The boisterous competition to be found on the average Indian high street mirrors the unregulated variety and exuberance of the rainforest. Instead of soil and sunshine, businesses compete fiercely for life-sustaining rupees. Konica Sindhu Studio And Video Coverage, Hotel Hills Palace, Kishinchand Chellarams (India) Pvt Ltd (Self Selection One Of Its Kind In The Country All Your Requirements Under One Roof), Irani's Hotel, Radio Corner (Authorized Philips Dealer), Kashmir Gift Emporium (Imported Carpets And Handicrafts), Star Painters, Sagar Supermarket, Western Selection Megasale (Churridhars, Jeans, T-shirts, Handloom, Bedsheets), Shuraani Home Essentials and JC Air Travels For Air Ticketing are all jostling shoulders on the one small section of Commercial Road opposite as I refresh myself at the Kurinji Snack Bar (Pizza, Ice Cream, Milk Shakes, Fruit Juice).

*

During the long and precipitous descent from Ooty a patchwork-quilt asphalt surface makes my teeth rattle and the dappled confusion of light and shade projected onto the road by sunlight filtered through trees renders it particularly awkward to pick out the potholes and corrugations. Bad surfaces disturb me least when I'm cycling uphill because I'm going slowly anyway, but on downhill or level sections there is a sacrifice to be made: either I have to make a considerable reduction to my speed or risk damaging the bicycle. Usually I settle for an unsatisfactory compromise and find myself fretting about both the lack of progress made and the hammering taken by my trusty steed. The anticipated freewheeling descent from Ooty to the plains below never materialises and I feel cheated after the hard work I put into gaining so much height.

'Well, you can forget about making it to Mysore today!' I tell myself aloud.

The air becomes appreciably warmer as I lose height and my hands have begun to ache with the effort of pulling on the brake levers. When I stop to give them a rest I'm still above the clouds and the views are tremendous, as if from an aeroplane. Distant waterfalls are tracing silver threads on steep green mountainsides with terraced slopes. Some mountaintops are hidden by low cloud and other summits are poking up through the mists. After taking a picture I tuck into some savoury snacks left over from breakfast, admiring the fairytale landscape – there must be witches, dragons and castles down there.

Two young men on a motorbike whizz past, brake, and do a U-turn. A frisson of resentment, for solitude can be a difficult habit to break. I want to savour the silence and the magnificent view before me rather than be distracted by another interrogation, but to Indians the European On A Bicycle is a phenomenon that requires explanation and I still haven't quite got used to that yet. We sail through all the usual biographical details (Which country? Your good name, sir? What is your profession? Your monthly salary?). Although I had deliberately chosen a method of travel that would bring me into contact with local people, I hadn't realised quite how overwhelming their attention could be. Making a conscious effort to relax, I decide to turn the tables and ask them some of the same questions. They are on their way to Coimbatore. One sells vegetables and the other is in the fast-food business. In the end we get along rather well and they shake my hand before leaving me once more to the view and my thoughts.

If it ain't broke don't fix it (and if it is broke get somebody else to sort it out) is a maxim I apply to everything from household maintenance to dental repair, so when the chain finally snaps after 9,450 miles of sterling service on a steep hill outside Gudahur it is with little confidence and some apprehension that I contemplate carrying out my first major roadside repair. Urs assiduously replaced his chain every three thousand kilometres according to the manufacturers instructions but I have always suspected manufacturers of having a vested interest in making such recommendations – and besides, I loathe getting dirt under my fingernails (a predicament now made inevitable by a general reluctance to spend time cleaning the bicycle when there are so many more interesting things to do).

On the outskirts of the town three or four men are working on a car in what appears to be a small repair business, their tools scattered about them. I ask their permission to borrow some tools and everything happens exactly as I planned it. Indians are intensely curious. The car is abruptly abandoned and they crowd round the bicycle, eager to help. Using the new chain as a strap-wrench, I borrow one of their spanners to detach the worn sprocket (a job that would have been feasible but deucedly awkward on my own). Then they slap fresh grease on the freewheel, help me to replace the worn gear cluster, and hold the new chain steady for me while I carefully join the two ends with the chain-tool. The newly formed link is predictably a little stiff, but by wrenching and flexing it with hands blackened by grease, they eventually free it. Then they pour petrol into a hubcap so I can wash my filthy hands, and top up my container of oil. The hundred rupees I give them is probably well above the going rate, but as far as I'm concerned they've thoroughly earned it.

*

In the centre of Mysore a skinny, ill-favoured old tout tells me he knows 'a good hotel, a *very* good hotel'. He repeats this litany over and over again as if trying to convince himself of its truth as I push the bicycle through a labyrinth of narrow alleys playing host to dozens of small businesses and workshops. Indian cities are a multi-coloured, symphonic, percussive and olfactory assault on the senses. We pass bicycle, moped, scooter and motorbike repairers, electricians, panel-beaters, arc and gas welders, radiator repairers, a 'Mixy Doctor' specialising in the repair of washing machines and food mixers, and the usual purveyors of fast food and *chai* presiding over their tiny pavement stalls to the roaring of petrol stoves. People everywhere are hammering, banging, clinking, clunking, clanging and bashing, dismantling and assembling, welding and soldering. Improbably squeezed between these holes-in-the-wall is a tiny optician's, a tailor working at his sewing machine, a clinic or a sari centre. The spicy aroma of cooking food mingles with the less fragrant smells of burning rubbish, stale urine, cowpats and exhaust fumes. The Adarsh Lodge is by no means as salubrious as I've been led to believe but it is conveniently situated and reasonably priced, and I'm satisfied that the bicycle will be safe in the ground floor parking area.

Beyond outstanding sights such as Madurai's Shri Meenakshi Temple and Mysore's Palace I have a pretty relaxed attitude towards monuments and museums; I prefer the buzz of the bazaars and the bustle of the streets, and to sample the culinary curiosities on offer in restaurants and cafés. Having located a satisfactory base, the initial priority is to find my bearings and just to explore, soaking up the atmosphere of a town or city, examining stalls and goods for sale, and maybe having a coffee or a snack somewhere. Wandering around Mysore is a pleasure, for the city is elevated enough to prevent one from breaking out in torrents of sweat at the slightest movement. You can get almost anything repaired in India if you know where to look and a chap mends my watch for only ten rupees. At an Internet café I open my Inbox with the greedy anticipation of a child confronted by a pile of Christmas presents to read emails sent by those who are prepared to spend a little of their time thinking about me.

When performing their ritual ablutions Indians clean out their insides as well as their outsides and the next morning I wake up to what has become a familiar and deafening dawn chorus of coughing, hawking, spitting and blood-curdling retching sounds. On getting up I discover that there are no less than three giant cockroaches milling indecisively around the shattered corpse of a colleague I exterminated last night. It's a shame that I can't make them into soup and save some money on food. The blue paintwork of the walls around the head of the bed is splattered with what looks like blood – or could it be Chicken Tikka Masala? Has this room witnessed some terrible atrocity? Or merely an unfortunately-timed sneeze?

Absorbed by the view over Gandhi Square, I breakfast on toast and butter, omelette and a pot of coffee at a rooftop restaurant. From below comes the constant honking and beeping of traffic, the fainter tinkle of bicycle bells, the buzz of scooters, mopeds and auto rickshaws and the cries of street vendors. A middle-aged Dutch couple who spied me casually cycling across Bandipur National Park from the comparative security of their bus inform me that a notorious bandit who specialises in robbery and murder is thought to be in hiding there and that he recently kidnapped an Indian film star.

*

COLD BEARS SOLD HERE proclaims a sign on the road to Bangalore. Bright yellow advertisements regularly extol the benefits of Coromandel King Superior Grade 53 Cement.

In Bangalore itself several people on motorbikes and scooters slow down to ask *which country?* I suppose I should be flattered by their interest, but this really isn't a good time to ask; they are a distraction and keep getting in the way, and I get hopelessly lost in the heavy evening rush-hour traffic while trying to find Mahatma Gandhi Road. When at last I locate the Imperial Lodge I'm told that they're full.

Having just cycled over ninety miles from Mysore, this is positively the last thing I need to hear. I am sweaty, filthy, drained of energy and longing for a shower and a cold drink and the chance to put my feet up; instead I must continue the search for cheap accommodation in a sprawling metropolis of six million inhabitants and I have no idea where to start.

'My God! You're a long way from France!' observes a cool, sardonic voice. 'Did you get lost during the Tour?'

Too weary to formulate any riposte beyond a tired chuckle, I glance upwards to see a slight, wiry looking man addressing me from the hotel balcony. He is a puzzle: he looks Indian but his English is better than mine, and whilst thus far I've been unable to fathom the Indian sense of humour, this twit has just manufactured something clearly identifiable as a joke.

I ask him if he knows of any cheap accommodation in the area and he suggests that I follow his auto rickshaw back to the YMCA, where he has a room. Two hundred rupees a night is acceptable, so I dredge up some energy from somewhere and pedal behind the rickshaw in a hair-raising dash across the city centre, having to keep one eye on the whereabouts of the rickshaw and the other on the traffic. When I check in he insists on paying for my room. 'You're my guest,' he says firmly.

We take a rickshaw to a restaurant for dinner, where I learn that Shaun Rana (Indian name Shankarsinh Rana) is a descendant of Rajput princes but was born and raised in the south of India because his father's stepsister married the Maharaja of Mysore. This is his first time back in India since leaving for Britain in 1977 with his Indian wife at the age of twenty-four. A slender, improbably young forty-eight, he is divorced and lives in Harborne with an English girlfriend half his age and their two-year-old son. He is a freelance broadcaster and returned to Bangalore in November to commentate for one of the satellite television channels on the Legends Tennis Tournament, which featured the likes of Bjorn Borg and Pat Cash. He has commentated on Radio Four's *Test Match Special* with the legendary John Arlott, Henry 'Blowers' Blofeld and Brian 'Johnners' Johnston (who naturally christened him 'Raners') and is well acquainted with such luminaries as David Vine, Des Lynam, Gary Lineker and David Gower. Full of smooth charm, he numbers after-dinner speaking as one of his accomplishments and oozes the kind of self-confidence I can only dream about. He also happens to be a formidable chess player who won the Asian Open in 1975. 'I was obsessed with the f*****g game!' he admits in his impeccable English. 'People would talk to me and I wouldn't hear them because my head was full of chess positions. I nearly went loopy.'

*

There is no trace of the expected *chai* stalls, cows nosing in piles of rubbish or bullock carts in Brigade Road. As I tuck into an insipid pizza, washing it down with a delicious iced coffee in the Fifth Avenue shopping arcade to the sound of that inane western music composed specifically to slow pulses, dull sensibilities and loosen purse strings, I reflect that, for all the thousands of miles I've cycled, I might as well be in Slough High Street.

This is a sobering thought. Brigade Road in downtown Bangalore hosts a Wimpy, a Pizza Hut, a Kentucky Fried Chicken, a number of cyber cafés and several rather ostentatious looking clothes shops full of western brand names. Reasoning that an occasional visit to these places is necessary just to remind oneself why one never normally bothers with them, I follow the pizza with an ice cream from the Baskin Robbins parlour in nearby Residency Road.

Wandering back up Brigade Road, I feel the urge to spend a penny so I pop into Kentucky Fried Chicken and order two chicken pieces with fries and Pepsi. While I'm eating a party of expensively attired young men in grey suits and stunning women in saris come down from upstairs and make a poised exit. The place is doing brisk business and Raners later tells me that to be able to afford to eat this stuff is considered a status symbol. The visit is made thoroughly memorable not by the food but the thrilling discovery that the toilets have automatic hot-air hand-driers – when did I last come across one of those?

Bloated with overpriced junk, I ponder my next move. A delivery van is reversing cautiously up the street, its warning bleeper playing a complete rendition of *Fur Elise*. Fortunately the ubiquitous auto rickshaws and the dilapidated pale-blue and white buses periodically shatter the nightmare illusion of being back in Berkshire's finest, but even so Brigade Road is globalisation in progress, the shape of things to come. These days empires are built by big business instead of armies and the developing world is being colonised by the likes of Toyota, Sony, Nestlé, Volvo, McDonalds, Philip Morris, Nike, Coca-Cola, Levi Jeans and DHL (and I was staggered by the sight of a vast Tesco hypermarket outside Kecezmet in Hungary). In another ten to twenty years Indian cities will doubtless be full of arcades, malls and fast-food joints. When every town centre between Istanbul and Singapore looks like Brigade Road there will be much less incentive to travel, and I hope it doesn't happen in my lifetime.

At the Plaza Cinema they are showing *Bedazzled*, a Liz Hurley epic that was panned by the critics, but I opt to wait until tomorrow and see *Charlie's Angels* instead. I have little doubt that the film will be awful but it has at least been a box-office hit. The evening meal, a vegetable dopiaza in the YMCA's excellent restaurant, is infinitely cheaper and more filling than the expensive rubbish I ate earlier.

*

Booming Bangalore is India's I.T. capital and one of the fastest growing cities in Asia. Under the headline *For Good Home Join I.T. Club* an article in the next day's *Times of India* laments the formation of an 'I.T. divide':

If you are on the wrong side of the Information Technology (I.T.) divide in the country's Silicon Capital, you don't belong. Despite its name, the bricks and mortar class, for example, cannot afford a decent home here. Driven by the have-money-will-spend I.T. cult, house rents have shot through the roof. (...)

Says Feroze's Estate Agency managing director Feroze Abdulla, "Several significant announcements made by the new government saw businesses, specially of the I.T. kind, gatecrash into Bangalore. The fact is that rents have shot up in step with the higher salaries of the I.T. people. And that has seen the others getting left out." (...)

As for the I.T. man, his happens to be a world apart. Higher salaries and better perks have ensured that his lifestyle is dramatically different from that of the typical adjust madkoli Bangalorean.* And he couldn't care less so long as the Microsofts and the Oracles fight to pander to his caviar dreams, champagne in hand.

The Readers' Grievances section on Page Two contains letters protesting about the proliferation of stray dogs, potholes and power-cuts, problems common throughout India, and Page Three carries details of a proposed one-way traffic management scheme to cut rush-hour delays. As personal wealth is on the increase so is the number of cars, and the roads in many Indian cities are unable to cope with rising volumes of traffic.

*

'Come along, Smithers old bean!' says Raners one evening. 'I want you to meet some friends of mine.' He attributes his old-fashioned English and impeccable manners – he *always* holds doors open for ladies – to his maternal grandfather's friendship with the Earl of Burma.

We have to shout above the noise of the engine of the ancient, underpowered auto rickshaw taking us to the Badminton Club. Acrid fumes from the dense traffic sandpaper our throats, and Raners maintains between bouts of coughing that there are more potholes in Bangalore's streets than when he was last here twenty-three years ago.

---

*'Salpa adjust madkoli' is a saying popular in Bangalore that means 'make do with what you have.'

We are joined at the Badminton Club by Dilip, a chartered accountant crippled by polio who nonetheless makes light of his disability, his sister and her husband Madhav, who is one of the I.T. brigade. The latter can't be much older than thirty but a developing paunch is suggestive of a comfortable, silicon-enhanced lifestyle. Raners is the life and soul of the party, delivering jokes like an erratic fast bowler. Some are a good line and length, but others a little short-pitched or wide of the mark. As the number of whiskies mounts up a few beamers, wides and no-balls are delivered, the rest of us fending them off with varying degrees of difficulty.

On the morning of my last day in Bangalore I wake up at 7.30 to the sound of bat on ball outside on the YMCA's sports ground. A youth surrounded by a ring of small boys is batting the ball back to them for fielding practice in the warm early morning sunshine. Indian children from the age of five walk along rehearsing their batting and bowling actions, displaying a passion for the game that most Englishmen of my acquaintance consider boring. Yesterday afternoon we watched a cricket match between the YMCA's side and a local team; one of the bowlers was fearsomely fast and I asked Raners if we could find out if he had a grandfather or a great aunt somewhere with a British passport. English cricket's decline will only be arrested when more people take an interest in the game, which will only happen when the national team starts winning on a regular basis – which won't happen until more people take an interest in the game. Catch 22. Britain's most talented athletes and sportsmen can earn more money elsewhere – look at the salaries commanded by top footballers and tennis players.

After a bucket shower I climb the stairs to the second floor and knock on the door of Room 18. Raners is sprawled in his dressing-gown with a coffee and a Sunday paper, his celebrity status affording him the privilege of having them delivered to his room every day. The man who complains that the pollution in Bangalore is killing him is already drawing deeply and appreciatively on his second cigarette of the morning and the room is filled with smoke. Books (mostly Frederick Forsyth thrillers), magazines and papers are scattered about the room in homely disorder. The gaunt figure, the dressing gown, the untidiness, the English faintly reminiscent of a bygone era (he regularly uses words like 'splendid') and the dense smoke bring to mind Sherlock Holmes and the room in 221B Baker Street. *Ah, Watson my dear fellow!* he might have said. *So good of you to have come!*

'Smithers, old bean!' he says instead. 'Splendid! Ready for some breakfast?'

Chapter Thirteen
Maintaining Momentum

In Andhra Pradesh the landscape has become drier. A boulder-strewn plateau covered with long, dry grass and randomly dotted with trees makes me think of Africa as I race along undeterred by the signs *BETTER TO ARRIVE LATE ON EARTH THAN EARLY TO HEAVEN*. I'd strike out *HEAVEN* and replace it with *HELL*; if heaven is all it's cracked up to be I wouldn't mind arriving early, and by causing a damn good road accident I could always do others a favour by taking them with me. The squeal of brakes and deafening blast of a horn behind me is a lorry driver's signal that he wants to overtake, but he is prevented from doing so by an oncoming convoy. Maintaining my position on the road, I raise two fingers in his general direction. He can wait. Other signs wish travellers a pleasant journey on behalf of the (R&B) NH Division Anantapur.

Fascinated men pore over the Nelles map of Southern India at a dhaba and I show them how the trip computer works. Instead of the four-egg omelette I ordered I am served four of the standard Indian two-egg omelettes – plus a vegetable curry, two chapattis, a Pepsi and a mineral water. The waiter shakes my hand and wishes me 'good trip', and I cycle off bulging with egg and empathising with Paul Newman in *Cool Hand Luke*.

Built around a dusty crossroads upon which there is a bus depot and an auto-rickshaw stand, Gooty is about as far as you can get from Brigade Road and a reassuring return to what I've come to regard as normality. Cows, monkeys and stray dogs roam the streets. A man walks by holding a squawking hen upside-down by its feet. Pavement stalls offer bananas, oranges, grapes, pineapples, tomatoes and onions, the vendors sitting on the dusty verges with a pair of scales and their produce spread out before them on a groundsheet. I am certainly the only European in this small Indian town and I feel like a goldfish in a bowl.

I've been agreeably astonished by the lack of traffic on the undulating road linking India's fifth and sixth largest cities. Roadside homilies continue to provide a diversion as it follows India's bony spine northwards:

ROADS INDICATE THE CULTURE OF A NATION.

The *wealth* of a nation, I'd have thought; driving habits are more indicative of its culture. An overtaking tractor pulls in far too early and I narrowly escape getting mown down by its trailer.

WHILE DRIVING, DIP HEADLIGHTS FOR OPPOSITE VEHICLES.

Always assuming of course that your headlights are working.

Teams of oxen are lumbering between the shafts of carts half-concealed beneath untidy loads of hay. People have converged in the villages, some waiting for buses and others attempting to flag down lorries. I watch with my heart in my mouth as a mother pig leads her two little ones across a busy dual carriageway in Kurnool. They narrowly miss being run over by a couple of auto rickshaws but make it safely to the other side. Thus far I've seen plenty of dead dogs, cows and even a monkey at the roadside, but never any pigs. Presumably they have some road sense and might even make half decent bus drivers.

*

That quintessentially Indian sound of horns, bicycle bells and Hindi music reaches me faintly through shuttered windows as I gradually wake up to a new day. Hyderabad is noisy, congested, polluted and bewilderingly large. When I go for a wander up Mukarramjahi Road in search of some breakfast a predatory shoe-repair wallah pounces, having observed me approach with the soles flapping disgracefully at the toe-ends of my boots. Sitting cross-legged on a raised section of pavement with the tools of his trade spread out in front of him upon a piece of plastic sheeting, he is bald, unshaven and middle-aged, dressed in a faded blue denim shirt and black jeans. Laid out in neat rows are some nasty looking pointed metal implements, rusty scissors, a wedge-shaped blade with a wooden handle for cutting rubber, nail extractors, tins of polish and pots of glue, brushes and several small bottles containing mysterious coloured liquids.

I sit on the pavement while the traffic roars by only feet away, watching him apply his craft and ensuring that the cleats are given enough clearance to engage with the pedals. From time to time he turns and spits neatly onto the dust at the edge of the road and I find myself wishing that I too could spit like that. After repairing the boots he polishes them so that they look like new. This may be a mixed blessing, for it is rumoured that when assessing the susceptibility of foreign tourists to exploitation, Indians examine their footwear. If the shoes are new and shiny the wearer is clearly fresh off the plane and promising material for a sting.

On the way back to my hotel in Station Road I have to step round several inert figures covered from head to toe in blankets and stretched out on pavements and in doorways outside the public gardens. A beggar woman approaches me with her arm outstretched.

'Hiya Hiya Hiya!' she screeches.

Having deduced that this isn't a friendly greeting but more likely Hindi or Urdu for 'Gimme Gimme Gimme!', I ignore her, but she grabs my arm as I walk past. Although I regularly give small change to beggars, I make it a point of principle never to do so if I'm hassled or manhandled. The language I use on this occasion is regrettable but aggression has to be vigorously countered. The stench of urine rising from the hot pavements along Mahatma Gandhi Road is so overpowering that I elect to walk in the road.

*

I leave Hyderabad with none of the regret with which I left Mysore or Bangalore, a brisk hour's cycling taking me clear of the sprawling suburbs. At the end of the day I check into a lodge in a small town called Suriyapet. The streets are a maelstrom of pedestrians, bullock carts, cyclists and pedal rickshaws, and I realise why I feel at home here and didn't in Hyderabad; a bypass has taken traffic away from the town centre and the streets have been reclaimed by the people. Occasionally a bus struggles through at walking place ineffectually blasting its horn, but the throng is in control and won't be intimidated or dictated to. In Mysore there were oases of traffic-free side streets and in Bangalore relief was provided by parks, but in charmless Hyderabad the traffic drove noisy, polluting, alienating barriers through the city, and at certain times of the day it was all but impossible to cross the street from my hotel to the restaurant opposite.

The NH5 is the main road that follows India's east coast from Madras all the way up to West Bengal. I've lost count of the number of times the stampeding lorries have forced me off the road. A sign near Eluru warns traffic that it is approaching a *CONJUSTED AREA* where I chalk up a record number of near misses and even collide with a scooter that pulls out directly in front of me. Two cyclists decide to turn right while I'm overtaking them and a car pulls across me to avoid a pedal rickshaw. I really must get a bell, for unlike the Indian versions that clunk, creak, squeak and rattle, my bicycle gives no warning of its approach. Deafened by horns, poisoned by exhaust smoke and periodically blinded by dust, I wonder at times a trifle wistfully if I wouldn't have been better off travelling by train after all. The electrified Madras to Calcutta line runs alongside the road and high-speed passenger trains rush effortlessly past, flaunting their comfort and security.

Refreshment stops provide temporary relief from the madness. Near Tadepallgudem I drink two litres of mineral water and eat chicken curry and rice off a banana leaf to the strains of Hindi music drifting over from an adjacent dhaba. On the opposite side of the road a lorry is jacked up minus its rear wheels and brake drums. Figures in dhotis and lunghis are squatting around the exposed axle, and one of them is doggedly bashing it with a hammer. A hen and her five furry chicks (four yellow and one black) scratch around in the dust by my feet and half a dozen men are discussing the astonishing 'gear-cycle' propped up a few feet away. It never ceases to amaze me that in a country in which millions depend upon the bicycle as their personal transport, gears remain virtually unheard of; cyclists are obliged to dismount and push their machines up even moderate inclines and even the poor, straining pedal-rickshaw wallahs have no gears.

A tiny girl, about three years old and wearing nothing but a pair of knickers, is staring at me with huge, solemn, dark eyes. I'm clearly *different*, but she can't quite figure out why. A man playfully flicks some water at her. Puzzled by the source of the wetness she puts her hand to her head. I can't help grinning at her and a number of bystanders giggle. She smiles radiantly and cackles with laughter, delighted to be the centre of attention, but by the time I get up to wash my hands after finishing my meal the attention has shifted back to me. I turn to see a crow swoop down to my plate from its perch on the canopy and make off with a chicken bone.

For a while the road follows a small river where people are immersing their laundry in the water and others are laying it on rocks and scrubbing it. Brightly painted wooden boats are moored to the bank.

'Please give me five minutes of your time!' entreats a man on a small motorbike, his voice muffled by his helmet.

'I'm sorry, I can't stop!' I reply, continuing to pedal. A lorry, separated from its rear axle, has turned onto its side and another is upside-down in a ditch. Maybe they should equip Indian lorries with a bigger version of the sort of stabilisers that were fitted to my first bicycle. The trouble is they'd have to widen the roads to accommodate them.

A maroon Tata four-wheel drive pulls into the verge ahead and the driver sticks his head out of the window: 'Sir! Sir!'

I cruise past. Seconds later he overtakes again, this time cutting in dangerously and forcing me to slam on my brakes.

'Get out of my bloody way!' shouts Sir.

On the edge of a village a man in a loincloth is washing two baby water buffaloes in a large pond, with two bigger animals (Mummy and Daddy?) looking on. It would have made an enchanting photograph of rural Indian life but yet again I find myself unable to stop. To cycle a loop that encloses almost the whole of India in only five months demands a degree of single-mindedness, but the maintenance of progress at all costs is in danger of becoming obsessive.

For the whole of the next day I follow Andhra Pradesh's fertile east coast from Tanuku up to Annavaram. Palm trees, watermelons, sugarcane and bananas all grow in abundance and the paddies are a lush, emerald green. Convoys of bicycles are weighed down by great bunches of bananas hung from the handlebars and the rear carriers and other cyclists are struggling with wicker baskets laden with coconuts, watermelons and limes. Carriers have been ingeniously adapted to accommodate churns, urns, sacks and even mattresses. Naturally all of them are single-geared and have to be pushed up hills. I am shocked by the number of people to be seen squatting unselfconsciously by the side of the busy road in full view of the traffic. Some even squat in pairs, for defecating is clearly a social occasion, rather like sharing a pot of tea. When the road runs through a small village the verge on my left is a minefield of glistening brown deposits, a perfect breeding ground for disease.

In Anakappali I read in *The Hindu* that an earthquake has hit Gujarat and that up to 1,500 people are so far feared dead. Tremors were felt as far away as Madras.

*

Further north, India's eastern flank appears less fertile. The hills are rocky and the greens have turned to yellows and browns.

SPEED THRILLS BUT KILLS.

No, *bad driving* kills.

The road crosses a series of rivers that have been reduced, no doubt by upstream irrigation schemes, to little more than sorry trickles. One of the bridges spanning the Godvari delta measures all of 2.38 kilometres in length but beneath there is only a narrow channel of water surrounded by a vast area of silt.

Halfway between Srikakulam and Berhampur three lorry drivers, dressed in nothing more substantial than some rather grey Y-fronts, are cleaning their teeth and washing their clothes at a concrete water tank outside a dhaba. When I join them to wash my face and hands they grin companionably and offer me their soap.

'Jesus?' says one of them, the tone of his voice suggesting a question rather than an exclamation. Assuming that he is enquiring about my religion and not my name, I smile and nod assent.

'Cooling glasses!' observes another as I replace my sunglasses before leaving.

*

One of the poorest states in India, Orissa is optimistically referred to by the tourist board as 'The Emerald East', but isolated hills are bony and barren and the palm trees and paddies appear to have been left behind in Andhra Pradesh. In view of a warning received from the proprietor of a dhaba that the roads in Orissa are swarming with bandits and that Calcutta is a city overrun by thieves and brigands, a mobile conversation with a man riding a scooter with two young ladies squeezed lusciously behind him appears particularly ominous:

HIM: Which country?
ME: England.
HIM: And where are you going?
ME: Calcutta!
HIM: Are you religious?
ME: No, not really.
HIM: I'll pray for you anyway!

An email has brought news that Sandra and Elliott are staying at the Derby Hotel in Puri.

Sandra and Elliott ran a pub in Bexhill-on-Sea until their fragile relationship with the landlord finally and irretrievably broke down. They promptly purchased a tiny Citroen 2CV for the princely sum of a hundred pounds. Elliott resourcefully extended the rear of the car to allow them sufficient room to sleep comfortably inside it and Sandra contributed a multi-coloured, customised livery of blue, red, green and yellow overlapping spheres, stars and stripes. Then they sold the house and set off for New Zealand. During the crossing of Turkey a love-struck local, dazzled by the car's beauty, offered to swap it for a two-year-old Ford Transit van or £2,500 in cash.

Having met initially at the Amir Kabir hotel in Esfahan, we discovered during four idyllic days spent reading, sunbathing and swimming on Goa's immaculate beaches that our respective journeys had a good deal in common. Over meals of vegetable fried rice served with mineral water so cold that there were shards of ice floating in it, we discussed the unfathomable behaviour of Indians, the vileness of Indian driving and the perils of the NH8, checkpoints in Iran and Pakistan, bowel problems, bad hotels, the beauty of Indian women and the ugliness (according to Sandra) of the men, Loralai, Lahore, Jaisalmer and Pushkar, the relative merits of Nelles and Geocenter roadmaps, and the thorny issues of whether or not pork pie ought to be accompanied by HP Sauce and the advisability of including black pudding in breakfast fry-ups. Coincidentally we left England on the same day and it became a standing joke that a man on a bicycle first beat their car to Esfahan and then caught up with it in Goa.

And again in Puri, which boasts a magnificent temple and a turd-infested beach that immediately discourages any thoughts of sunbathing or swimming. The Derby Hotel turns out to be a pleasant, laid-back establishment with a central courtyard in which to congregate and eat interminable breakfasts and drink Thums-Up or Marinda fizz. Like my bicycle, *Deuchie* the rainbow-coloured Citroen has been tapped and prodded at every halt and Sandra and Elliott are full of stories of nights spent attempting to sleep in the car while curious locals poked and pushed and hammered at the bodywork, stood on the bumpers and bounced it up and down. In Mamallapuram they discovered two children using the sloping bonnet as a slide. 'It's amazing that they don't *feel* the fury emanating from inside!' says Elliott, who has painted *Horn Please* on the rear bumper.

Malcolm, a sixty-year-old Irish film producer with his long, white hair tied back in a ponytail, made two return overland journeys to India in a long-wheelbase Land Rover in 1962 and 1964 and has some enthralling tales to tell about independent travel at a time when there was no need for visas, borders were unmarked, Baghdad was a town of mud huts, and metalled roads were virtually non-existent beyond Europe. A fifty-two-year-old Canadian called Jan works as a hot-tub cleaner at a ski resort in Western Canada for eight months of the year and spends the rest of his time travelling.

Every morning at breakfast the five of us gather to compare and contrast our respective journeys. We discuss India's limited resources and unsustainable population growth, politics, the books we've read, the environment, the changing face of the world since 1962 when Malcolm made his first journey – and Germans.

One of the German travellers staying at the hotel has told me that he met a holy man at the Khumbh Mela in Allahabad (a religious festival that attracted thirty million souls) who had kept his right arm raised in the air for several years without altering its position. This incredible achievement must have been excruciatingly painful and tiring and struck me as magnificently futile, but then it suddenly occurred to me that many people might view my cycling odyssey in exactly the same light.

One sweltering afternoon while I'm servicing the bicycle with my customary reluctance and most of the others are either reading or taking a siesta, my German acquaintance regales me with tales of his visit to Western China in 1993. Between explosions of barely controlled hilarity he informs me that somewhere in the deserts of Xinjiang is the town the furthest from the sea in the world! Sandra's puzzled frown tells me that – like me – she's waiting for the punch line, but it never materialises. I think it was Oscar Wilde who said 'For Germans a sense of humour is no laughing matter' but I reflect that Ralf's comment 'It's not that Germans don't *have* a sense of humour, it's just that nobody else understands it' is probably closer to the truth.

An hour out of Puri the air whistles out of the front tyre. After ten minutes of blissful solitude, two people on a scooter stop to watch me at work and I reflect sourly that I could justifiably levy a charge for the entertainment I provide on these occasions. By the time I've packed away my tools and cleaned up, a crowd of no less than sixteen has gathered at the roadside. India appears to be filled with directionless people who spend their entire time searching for something to engage their attention.

Jan said that you never get bored with India; you just get tired of it sometimes.

I'm beginning to feel that he hit the nail on the head. The landscape beyond Cuttack, consisting mainly of fields of stubble, remains flat and dull, the sky overcast, the NH5 packed with lorries, and the wind – blowing from precisely the wrong direction – is literally becoming a pain in the back. Billboards advertise Coca-Cola, steel, menswear and even Bliss Lubricated Condoms 'For Those Exciting Moments'. Pedal rickshaws are half carrying and half dragging thirty-foot lengths of bamboo. An epidemic of punctures has resulted in a temporary loss of confidence in the bicycle and I find myself repeatedly glancing down to check the inflation of the troublesome front tyre.

A group of young men gathers round at a dhaba on the edge of Bhadrak.

'Which country?'

'England.'

'To India by plane?'

'No, by bicycle.'

This outrageous statement produces the usual exclamations and doubtful glances.

'Is the bicycle for sale?' asks their spokesman.

'Certainly not!'

Another man picks up my sunglasses. 'Goggles!' he announces to the assembly.

'How old are you?' pursues the spokesman.

'Forty.'

'And so handsome!' (That Indian waggle of the head.)

'Yeah.' I smile involuntarily. 'I know.'

'Are you married?'

'No.' My smile grows broader. 'Are you intending to propose?'

Fortunately they fail to understand this riposte and I tell them about that fictional fiancée I'll be marrying as soon as I return home.

Teams of perspiring men are digging a trench on the left of the road, taking days to do what one man with a JCB could accomplish in a few hours. A series of signs, red lettering on a yellow background, provide food for thought and keep me amused.

DESERVE BEFORE YOU DESIRE
Excellent advice!
PLEASURE IS THE INTERVAL BETWEEN TWO PAINS
How true!
FISH IS BETTER THAN SELFISH
Indubitably so! (Especially if you like eating fish as much as I do.)

*

An expressway takes cyclists across the River Hooghly illegally via the Vidyasagar Setu, an elegant suspension bridge that was completed in 1994 in order to relieve the congestion on the Howrah Bridge. Like the Punjab, Bengal was split in two by Partition and Calcutta was affected more than any other major Indian city. Although the bloodletting never attained the scale of that seen in the Punjab, the city experienced communal rioting in which thousands were massacred and there was widespread arson and looting. Gandhi's arrival a week before Independence Day and his threat to fast to death unless peace was restored eventually put an end to the rioting, and Muslims and Hindus celebrated Independence Day together with cries of *Jai Hind!* (Long Live India!).

Consulting a street map and using the Maidan and the racecourse as landmarks, I find my way onto Chowringee Road and thence to a guesthouse in Sudder Street, astonished at how easy it was; the traffic was considerably lighter than I expected and I wasn't once attacked by robbers or mauled by beggars.

Along with Istanbul, Esfahan, Quetta, Amritsar and Kanniyakumari, Calcutta is a landmark city, one of the names marked in heavy type on the cerebral map charting my progress. Sudder Street and the surrounding area is clearly something of a tourist ghetto, but locals are filling buckets and washing themselves at the standpipe on the pavement opposite the hotel.

'Hashish? Grass? Very good quality opium too!' murmurs a discreet voice.

I shake my head without breaking stride. Calcutta is the last city in India to use human-powered rickshaws and a couple of them are parked on the opposite side of the street, the pullers sitting on the foot rests. I step over and around sleeping dogs and inert human shapes huddled under blankets on my way to meet Sandra and Elliott for breakfast in the Blue Sky Café, where we sip coffee and crunch muesli fruit curd and buttered toast amongst French, German, American and Japanese backpackers.

The arrival in Calcutta of millions of economic migrants from the countryside and refugees fleeing East Bengal following Partition led to living conditions that became internationally notorious, but although men urinate with carefree abandon against walls and there are people living under canvas on one side of Strand Road South, Calcutta appears to be no more or less squalid to my eyes than any other large Indian city. It is full of fine old British buildings and it feels uncannily like London at times, particularly as auto rickshaws appear to have been banned from the city centre. People get around by cramming themselves into battle-scarred buses painted silver or Victoria plum with a custard stripe that bear slogans such as *India Is Great, God Is One* and *Hypothecated To The Punjab National Bank* (whatever that means), whilst the more affluent elect to travel in the fleets of black and yellow Ambassador taxis. Wide, teeming pavements are packed with stalls selling oranges, bananas, grapes, pomegranates, mangoes, tomatoes, and hot savoury snacks including samosas, parathas, bhel puri, and whole curries. Others display sandals, belts, wallets, socks, underwear, shirts, trousers, coat-hangers, watches and calculators.

There appears to be a movement to 'Indianise' Calcutta, which, until 1911, was the capital city of British India. Several street names have been changed and the city itself is sometimes spelt 'Kolkata', but it will take more than a few strokes of a pen to erase the memory of the Raj. They'll have to raze the city to the ground and start again from scratch if they really wish to forget, and even in the absence of architecture the British legacy would remain in India's parliamentary and judiciary systems, her military traditions, her railways, the games of cricket on the Maidan, the widespread everyday use of the English language, the carefully groomed and uniformed schoolchildren, and the fact that some people – some of the time – drive on the left.

Another British legacy is the Howrah Bridge, built in 1943 to replace the old pontoon bridge. Providing safe passage across the Hooghly for an estimated hundred thousand vehicles and innumerable pedestrians every day, this huge cantilevered construction of grey metal girders is reputed to be the busiest bridge in the world. Crossing with the hordes of pedestrians, many of them supporting huge bundles on their heads, I discover that people keep to the left on the wide walkways and overtake on the outside (or the inside if there's room), but sometimes they attempt to squeeze past even if there isn't. Exactly like the roads, albeit with slightly less carnage.

After visiting an Internet café, Sandra, Elliott and I wander down to the Maidan where a young man rushes up to us, greets us with enthusiasm and shakes Elliott and me by the hand. When he offers his hand to Sandra, however, she ignores him.

'She's my wife,' explains Elliott gently. 'She doesn't shake hands.'

'That trick has been tried too often before, mate!' adds Sandra frostily. She discloses that on the first few occasions she'd shaken hands with local men they had run back to their companions giggling, the handshake evidently being a ploy to make physical contact with a white woman. There is something very childish about some of the locals, which perhaps explains their capacity to charm and infuriate in equal measures.

Within seconds of sitting down on a bench by an artificial lake in front of the Victoria Memorial we are surrounded by staring youths.

'Yes? Can I help you?' asks Elliott dryly. Evidently he has come to share my resignation.

Sandra, who with her long, blond hair is undoubtedly the star attraction, hasn't. 'It's so *rude*!' she fumes.

Undeterred, they continue to gawp, wordlessly. Although I've become accustomed to local scrutiny, I find the constant invasion of one's space disconcerting. In the wide green expanses of the Maidan it's rather as if a group of people have just got onto an otherwise empty carriage on the last train home and, ignoring the rows of empty seats, sat down directly opposite.

On my last day in Calcutta I finally buy myself a bicycle bell. I have received several warnings about India's notorious Grand Trunk Road and I have a feeling that during the forthcoming weeks I may come to need it.

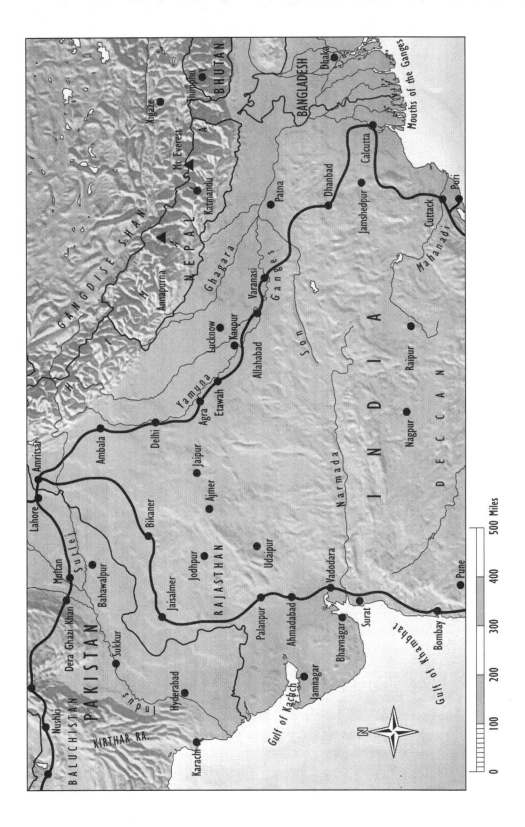

Chapter Fourteen
Grand Trunk Road Rage

Three hours after leaving Calcutta I lean the bicycle against a large tree a couple of yards back from the road to ensure a little privacy and sit down on the ground to eat some samosas. The execrable road surface has pulverised the savoury triangular pillows, separating them into unappetising shards of pastry and boluses of vegetables. I pick at them unenthusiastically, gradually becoming aware of an unpleasant smell and the presence of an unusual number of flies. Belatedly it dawns on me that I'm sitting in the middle of a public lavatory, archipelagos of human yuk in various stages of decomposition mingling gruesomely with the roadside weeds. Gingerly I pick myself up, praying that I haven't inadvertently sat in anything nasty, and transfer myself to a dhaba half a mile further up the road opposite a brick kiln, where I accompany an omelette with a couple of cooling Pepsis in the shade of a banyan tree.

I had been labouring under the misapprehension that the Grand Trunk Road was a British creation, but Kipling's 'river of life' is ancient, far older even than the Silk Road. It was used as long ago as 1,500 BC by Aryan invaders from Afghanistan and Central Asia, and over a thousand years later in 326 BC it was to serve as a conduit for the invading armies of Alexander the Great. Sher Shah Suri, the Afghan warlord who displaced the Mughals and declared himself emperor for six short years between 1539 and 1545, rebuilt it. He declared the road toll-free and lined it with mango, neem, peepul and banyan trees to shelter travellers from the sun, placing caravanserai at regular intervals to provide sources of rest and refreshment. The British contribution was merely to realign and improve sections, and to give it the name by which it is currently known.

Halfway through my second Pepsi two young men arrive on a motorbike and plonk themselves down at my table. No disarming 'Do you mind if we join you?' or equivalent phrase; to a European, Indians can appear to take an awful lot for granted. Like many, they are astonished that I have chosen to travel alone but, as they have themselves just so clearly demonstrated, one is rarely left alone for long in India – and the possibility that no-one was daft enough to accompany me evidently hasn't occurred to them. One of them is a PE teacher who informs me that two hundred years ago this small town on the banks of the Hooghly used to be a thriving port. It must have been made redundant when deforestation and overgrazing caused the river to silt up, eventually making it impossible for large, ocean-going vessels to reach Calcutta, let alone ports further upstream.

'Hallo, friend! Which country?' beams a tubby man on a bicycle as I cycle into Burdwan past panel beaters, spray shops, coachworks, dusty Ambassadors in various stages of dismantlement, tyre fitters, workshops and dealers in spares and parts.

'Where is lodge?' I counter.

He instructs me to follow him. The first hotel is full, but nothing daunted, he takes me to another. At reception he acts as a translator and helps me with my bags and to install the bicycle. When I offer him ten rupees for his trouble he bursts out laughing and waves it away.

'God bless!' he says as we shake hands.

*

Raners advised me to avoid India's poorest and most lawless state completely, but it is impossible to travel from Calcutta to Varanasi without crossing Bihar unless you are prepared to make a huge detour via Nagpur (for which I have neither the time nor the inclination). Bihar is India's bandit state and the same rules of thumb that saw me safely across Baluchistan – not to deviate from main roads, travel after dark or camp out – will have to be rigidly observed.

Eastern Bihar is a mining area. The road undulates between slagheaps and tall chimneys vomit smoke into the air to create a haze of pollution that defaces the azure sky. A lorry has overturned, spilling its load of coal onto the road. I pass several bicycles laden with bulging jute sacks of coal, the jockeys unable to pedal in the conventional manner because the heavy sacks are slung through the triangle formed by the frame and attached to it by ropes. Instead, leaning forward to grasp the handlebars, they perch on the rear carrier and coast down the hills, using a foot to propel them along as the road levels out. For flatter and uphill stretches they have no choice but to dismount and push. It is brutal, demeaning work that ought to be done by lorries, or at the very least by bullock carts. I can only guess at the dreadful Victorian conditions existing in the mines themselves; subterranean fires have been left to rage unchecked for decades, adding their poisonous fumes to an already blighted atmosphere because the technology required to extinguish them is unaffordable.

After a night in a lodge in Bagodar during which my sleep was interrupted by rustling and excited squeaks as mice investigated the contents of one of my bags, I awake to the sound of what I could swear is rain. This scarcely seems possible: the sky was clear all day yesterday and the evening dry, but when I open the door onto the veranda, water is cascading from the roof and it is raining steadily.

'Rainy season!' remarks the grinning proprietor.

Unable to share his apparent enthusiasm for the change in the weather, I ask him if this is normal for the time of year and if it is likely to last all day.

'Thank you very much!' he replies, seizing my hand. 'God bless you!'

An hour after setting off I begin the search for something to eat, but within seconds of my arrival at what appears to be a deserted dhaba people are converging from all directions. Abruptly I wheel the bicycle back onto the road and cycle away, ignoring protesting shouts. *Sorry chaps! The show's cancelled!*

I just can't face eating breakfast in front of an audience today.

The bumpy and cratered road surface beyond Dhanbad is preventing me from attaining any momentum or rhythm. At length I lean the bicycle against the parapet of a culvert that is conveniently shaded by an adjacent tree, and sit down in the roadside dust to rest and nibble at Indian sweets, propping my back up against a pannier while convoys of lorries thunder past, blaring their horns. Since leaving Calcutta I have been struggling with a stomach bug and, with my appetite affected, I have been drinking more than eating in the hope that sugary Indian tea and saccharine Thums-Up cola-flavoured fizz will provide the energy I require.

My second attempt at breakfast is more successful.

'Good morning!' smiles the proprietor of a dhaba as I prop the bicycle against a charpoy bed.

The place looks a little primitive, but one of my favourite plastic chairs is immediately brought out for me with great ceremony and a couple of minutes later the proprietor emerges with a glass of tea. 'Present from me to show my respect to you,' he says gravely, placing it before me. 'I will bring tea also with your order!'

I used to detest the blend of water, tea leaves, milk and sugar all boiled up together that the Indians erroneously call tea, but how can it taste anything but delicious when accompanied by such a gesture?

There are no lodges in either Dobhi or Sherghati and I don't fancy the prospect of a noisy and sleepless night on a charpoy bed at the roadside, so it will be a race against time to get to Aurangabad before the sun goes down. Duelling with India's deranged bus and lorry drivers is unpleasant enough during the day, but at night it would be a pretty certain way of committing suicide

('Tata Everyone!' probably being the most appropriate epitaph). Moreover the likelihood of highway robbery by armed bandits – whose tactics include staging roadblocks and mock accidents to stop traffic – increases significantly after dark. All I've had to eat all day is an omelette, but there is no time to stop for more food. By a tremendous stroke of luck the road surface has improved and for two hours I ride on an empty stomach, dancing on the pedals like Lance Armstrong and racing the sun. I arrive in Aurangabad at dusk with streaks and smudges of soot on my face, the 110 miles covered since dawn testimony to the powers of omelette, tea, sugary fizz and adrenaline.

One of the least pleasant aspects of cycling the Grand Trunk Road is the layer of dust and unburned diesel that builds up on skin and clothes. The insides of my nostrils have become filled with a sinister-looking black substance and black solids have lodged in the corners of my bloodshot eyes. The clean white polo shirt I put on two days ago has turned grey, and more than ever I regret the sentimental impulse that induced me to pack that particular shirt. To make matters worse, I am unable to wash properly because there is no shower and not even a bucket in the hotel's combined toilet and washroom. I manage to get the worst of the grime off my arms and hands and to shave in a reluctant dribble of cold water from the tap while I get bitten several times on both feet by the hordes of waiting mosquitoes, surely (with the possible exception of one or two human beings that spring to mind) the most repellent and unnecessary creatures on God's earth.

The streets outside the hotel are packed with barely distinguishable figures moving about in near pitch-darkness during another power cut. I slake a raging thirst with one ice-cold Pepsi after another at a dhaba to a distinctive throb of generators that reminds me of Baluchistan.

*

Varanasi's Old City is a bewildering maze of crowded alleyways that are too narrow for cars and auto rickshaws, but unfortunately not narrow enough to prevent yobs from riding their scooters and motorbikes at insane speeds, using their horns to clear a path through terrified pedestrians. They should be yanked off their machines and trampled to death in a pedestrians' revolt.

I sit down on the steps of Dasawamedh Ghat to watch a number of men dunk themselves in the filthy waters of the Ganges. Once upon a time the river would have been pure, an innocent young girl bubbling with energy and leaping laughingly down the mountainsides of the Himalayas, but by Varanasi she has become fat and sluggish and middle-aged, a bitter old whore defiled and corrupted by the abuse she has received at the hands of mankind. Innumerable sewers discharge untreated effluent into a conduit for water-borne diseases such as cholera and dysentery, and the corpses of infants, women who die in childbirth and those unfortunates who die from snakebite are consigned to the river un-cremated. I find the idea of bathing in a lumpy porridge of holy water, raw sewage and dead bodies both repulsive and counterproductive – not to mention downright dangerous. In a union every bit as incongruous, a group of western travellers is sharing a chillum with an orange-robed *sadhu*, one of India's peripatetic holy men. Salesmen approach at regular intervals, offering wooden flutes, boat trips, postcards, tea, caged birds and massage. Further downstream people are slapping wet clothes against rocks and I weave my way around and underneath washing lines sagging with the weight of drying sheets and garments.

'How are you, man?' asks a precocious ten-year old. Cow and buffalo dung has been collected and laid out in the sun to dry. Two men are waist-deep in the river, energetically scrubbing their shining black water buffaloes as one might wash a car.

When the ashes of the dead are consigned to India's holiest river the soul is released from the cycle of rebirth. At Manikarnika Ghat I watch from a balcony as firewood is carefully weighed on gigantic scales, pyres are constructed, and bodies enveloped in white shrouds are laid upon them to be consumed by the flames. The wood is priced per kilo and the corpses of those who were unable to afford their own pyres are weighted with stones and dumped in the river. A corpse's bearded face is gradually turning to charcoal and one of its feet, untouched by the flames, is sticking out at the other end of the pyre. Will it drop off when the leg burns through, to be seized by one of the mangy, scavenging curs (doubtless attracted by the smell of barbecuing meat) roaming hungrily amongst the groups of grieving relatives standing nearby? There is, as far as I can make out, little outward demonstration of grief; the process is conducted with far less ceremony than you'd find at a western funeral, Indians evidently being more reconciled to the idea of death than we are.

In the darkness just before dawn on 21 February, Shiva's birthday, I make my way down to the Meer Ghat through steep, winding alleyways accompanied by Martin van Doorne, a tall, lean and bespectacled Dutchman who cycled from Budapest to Istanbul with Eric and Emma. The bicycle parked in his room at the hotel is a splendidly eccentric mode of transport and I almost wish that I'd thought of travelling on a recumbent myself. He has informed me that you get only half the wind resistance that you would on a conventional bicycle and that it also has the advantage of allowing one to cycle straight underneath closed barriers at railway crossings. It has terrified horses on two continents and in Romania people assumed that he was disabled.

Having settled upon a fee of seventy rupees, we slide out onto the black waters of the Ganges just as the horizon to our left is beginning to turn grey.

Our grizzled boatman, wrapped in a blanket to keep warm, is well past his prime and the boat is large and heavy looking. Several other tourists have also made the effort to rise early on this important day in the Hindu calendar and their boats, smaller and faster than ours, race past. Little distance is going to be covered during the hour for which we have paid; I should have felt our oarsman's legs and examined his teeth before agreeing the price.

By sunrise the main bathing ghats are overflowing with people, many already performing their ritual ablutions on this auspicious day. A boat draws alongside us, the oarsman offering us lighted candles set in tiny watertight vessels made from some kind of leaf; placing a candle on the water is supposed to bring you luck. Martin will have no truck with this superstitious nonsense and I generally believe that you make your own luck, but for some reason I find myself parting with ten rupees and carefully placing my little vessel on the water.

'Look!' jeers the Recumbent Dutchman, pointing a contemptuous finger. 'Good luck?' The massive prow of the sellers' boat is bearing straight down on my tiny candle, but somehow, when all seems lost, the brave little vessel with its lighted beacon nimbly evades the huge black shape like a matador avoiding a charging bull.

'Survival against the odds!' I retort triumphantly. 'Most auspicious!'

*

Two hours after leaving Varanasi I'm cruising along nicely at a purposeful 14 mph on a road stained red with splashes of betel juice when a scooter with four youths squeezed onto it makes a highly inauspicious U-turn immediately in front of me and I hit it broadside on with sufficient force to throw me off the bicycle.

No apologies, offers of help, or any signs of concern at all from the w*****s on the scooter as I carefully untangle myself from the bicycle and pick myself up. Fortunately I'm not hurt and at first sight the bicycle appears to be none the worse for the experience. I embark upon a lengthy diatribe congratulating them for their anticipation, judgement and clarity of vision, just beginning to warm to my theme when, grinning idiotically, they zoom off at high speed, leaving me boiling with rage.

How can people be so irresponsible? Whereas in the West drivers accept without question that they are personally responsible for their own and other people's safety on the road, the Indians put their trust in the Gods and it is the casual fatalism of their driving that makes the road such a deadly place. Hundreds of roadside notices exhort those who can read to drive with care, but what's the point of being careful if road safety doesn't depend upon abstention from alcohol, observing speed limits and *mirror-signal-manoeuvre*, but the effigy of Ganesh dangling in the windscreen? It is almost inconceivable to me that anyone can execute a U-turn on a busy road *without looking* but that is the way Indians drive – which is precisely why there is so much use of the horn. To pre-empt further collisions I really must get into the habit of using the recently acquired bell more often.

Resuming my interrupted journey, I discover that the trip computer has been torn from its mountings and I find myself regretting that I hadn't been in a lorry instead of on a bicycle. I'd no more trust an Indian with a driving licence than I would a ten-year-old. Even the stray dogs have more road sense.

Later I pay what is clearly a 'special tourist price' for two Pepsis and a small pulao. It doesn't amount to much, but I hate being taken for a mug. Has the world price of Cola just increased by a third? There is little I can do to prevent such rip-offs short of checking the price of everything in advance, and that would be ridiculous. You have to trust people to some extent, but curiosity turns to cupidity as soon as a nation becomes bored with its tourists.

*

In Kora Jahanabad the bicycle begins to handle strangely and I realise that the rear tyre is soft. Wearily, I find an empty area of pavement and go through the familiar and detested routine of detaching all the panniers and turning the hateful contraption upside-down. *I really don't need this.*

By the time I've taken off the wheel the pavement is no longer empty. I have learnt to cope with spectators as long as they don't crowd me, but when the audience to a man presses closer to discover *exactly* how I attach the pump to the valve on the inner tube, I beseech them to allow me some room. When, having located and repaired the puncture I experience some difficulty in forcing the tyre back onto the rim, a slip of a twelve-year-old boy intervenes and replaces it with such dexterity that I suspect that he's been employed as a puncture wallah. In the meantime one of the assembled crowd has taken my diary out of an open pannier and is busily leafing through it. Another is tinkering with my stove and his friend is trying on my sunglasses.

I bite my tongue.

Halfway between Pukhrayon and Etawah the air vanishes from the rear tyre once more and I swerve to a halt. Something is clearly very wrong somewhere. Fortunately there is a ditch on the left that appears to offer some concealment from the madding crowds, but within five minutes I become aware that I'm no longer alone. Three cyclists are staring at me from the roadside.

'Oh for God's *sake!*' I yell. 'Find something else to do!'

Many western travellers gravitate to India on a quest for Inner Peace and to 'find themselves', but my own Inner Peace remains as elusive as ever and on the Grand Trunk Road I have found a part of myself that I don't like very much. I'd never dream of acting so rudely at home, but India and its masses can exert a strange effect upon one's equilibrium. Each day on this wretched road has become a drip, drip, drip accumulation of irritations and when I can take no more all that stored-up exasperation has to be released and I sound like Alf Garnett or Basil Fawlty – full of impotent fury. The language I use is horrible; India must have extracted more expletives per kilometre travelled than any other country, the majority directed at my fellow road-users.

The surface of the road out of Etawah is abominable. *Why can't these people do anything properly?* The mental aggression that is so crucial to the coercion of weary muscles is being diverted towards anything (or anyone) perceived to present the slightest hindrance to my immoderate agenda and I find myself echoing Ralf's lament (between farts) about a similar stretch of cratered asphalt in Baluchistan.

The landscape, not unlike a much larger version of East Anglia, remains a mosaic of flat green and yellow fields randomly scattered with trees. In the villages, walls of brick, stucco or mud support thatched roofs. Water buffalo are tethered to stakes and a whole fleet of them is having a luxurious wallow in a pond. Their excrement has been dried and neatly stacked into pyramids, ready to be used as fuel. The pedalling is hard work and I could swear that the road is imperceptibly rising (later I discover that this intuition is correct: India's vast northern plain is on a slight slope, dropping a very gradual two hundred metres eastwards from Delhi to the Bay of Bengal).

I continue to be pursued by the usual shouts of *oi* and *allo* and their myriad variations. Young men on bicycles apparently see the strange looking foreigner with the flashy 'Gear Cycle' as a chance to test their manhood and they overtake on their single-geared rattlers and squeakers, legs whirring in a blur of frenzied motion, but they can rarely sustain such speeds for long and I usually cruise past shortly afterwards.

When I eventually stop for food and drink it is more to lose two youths on bicycles who have been shadowing me with unusual persistence than because I'm particularly tired or thirsty. As I lean the bicycle against a tree they stop at the roadside to stare. It's like being under surveillance. One of them wheels in his bicycle just to make sure that he witnesses my order.

'Haven't you got anything else to do?' I growl, baring my teeth at him like a dog whose territory has been invaded.

Territory. *Space.* That's what this is all about. It occurs to me that after nearly four months in this country I should be handling these situations with more equanimity, but during the months in India my personal exclusion zone has been infringed as never before and my capacity for tolerance appears to be diminishing rather than increasing. Just below the civilised surface of each and every one of us exists a maelstrom of basic instincts and emotions, and the Grand Trunk Road has finally stripped away the thin veneer of sophistication, exposing the snarling beast that lies beneath. This is the reflex antagonism that can sometimes be witnessed between rival sets of supporters at a football match or amongst the inebriated at pub closing time on a Friday or a Saturday night, but I can claim neither mass-hysteria nor alcohol as an excuse for my behaviour. I have fallen prey to the atavistic, alcohol-free rage – increasingly seen on Britain's roads – that accompanies overcrowding. Instinct has taken over and I am acting the part of the male animal whose territory has been invaded, snarling and baring my teeth.

So much for Inner Peace. Moments of real pleasure have become few and far between and usually occur only after I've finished cycling for the day. Perhaps I've simply cycled too many miles in India – I would surely miss very little and save myself further aggravation if I were to jump aboard a bus or train to Delhi, but that option remains out of the question for the moment, for I haven't yet reached the end of my tether.

Nevertheless, my mood is becoming increasingly morose, relieved by occasional flashes of fury directed against the bicycle, the perforated road surfaces (does anyone else ever wonder why level crossings are called *level* when they so emphatically aren't?), the traffic, myself, but most often of all, *other people*. Crammed into Uttar Pradesh are 166 million of them, more than in any other state in India and numbering almost thrice as many as the entire population of the UK. The trauma of incarceration with two hundred fellow students in a university hall of residence twenty years ago induced me to seek solitary relief with a backpack on the roads of Europe every summer, but here in Uttar Pradesh the road offers no refuge from other people. Never have cyclists tailed me so frequently or so determinedly, and the crescendo of whistling and yelling that greets me as I pass through towns and villages is wearing me down. Bellowing at somebody because they are different may not have the provocative or racist implications that it would at home, but I have convinced myself that such conduct in anyone over the age of ten can only be interpreted as moronic, irrespective of their cultural origins. During pauses to rest and refresh myself I feel like a caged animal in a zoo.

Like a sponge, I can absorb only so much. I need to *escape*. Making my way towards Agra radiating primitive nastiness, I am aware that the hostility I feel is disproportionate and I'm becoming alarmed by the boorishness of my behaviour, but peace, privacy, anonymity and space are all vital to my sanity and India is slowly but surely driving me crazy.

The road into Agra is a bumpy, cobbled street choked with ox-carts, pedestrians, cyclists, pedal rickshaws, slow-moving tractors towing trailers loaded with bricks, timber or people, LML scooters, and honking buses and trucks. Auto rickshaws and tempos (a noisier, smellier big brother of the auto rickshaw) stop unexpectedly to pick up or decant passengers, and right turns, left turns and U-turns are all made without signalling. Pedestrians persistently step out without looking and cyclists periodically approach on the wrong side of the road. Frequently the traffic grinds to a halt in a sweltering haze of dust and pollution. A tractor drives gently into the back of me, and within minutes a scooter does the same. A bus drives with considerably more force into the back of a tractor and trailer. I recall being trapped in an unmoving crush of pedestrians in one of Varanasi's tiny streets with somebody relentlessly shoving me in the back. At length I felt obliged to turn round and point out that I wasn't able to move forward because there were people immediately in front of me who weren't moving forward either.

Madness. I can hardly wait for the vast, depopulated spaces of Xinjiang.

Revived by a cold shower, I watch the sun set over the Taj Mahal from the Shanti Lodge's rooftop while monkeys leap about on the neighbouring roofs. Built by the Mughal Emperor Shah Jahan to commemorate his beloved second wife Mumtaz (who died in childbirth in 1631), the Taj is flawless and almost hypnotically beautiful, the visual equivalent of a piece of Bach or Mozart. The Emperor (whose hair is said to have turned grey overnight after his wife's death) wouldn't have been someone I'd have chosen to work for, however, for a number of the twenty thousand craftsmen who worked on the building's construction later had their hands amputated to ensure that such perfection would never be repeated.

Krishna, the owner of the second-hand bookshop next to the hotel, is a portly and distinguished looking white-haired gentleman with an enviably low hairline, mutton-chop sideburns and a convex belly straining exuberantly at the buttons on his shirt. Treating me like a fellow human being rather than as if I've got three heads and have just landed from outer space, he tells me in excellent English that he is the eleventh descendant of the designer of the Taj Mahal and a master craftsman who works on repairing and maintaining the monument. Most of his time is now spent supervising the work currently in progress and teaching his craft to others. He runs the bookshop as a sideline and his card makes impressive reading:

VICE PRESIDENT: Agra Tourist Trade Sports & Welfare Association
MEMBER: Buddhist Publication Society - Kandy Sri Lanka
MEMBER: Servas International
EX-PRESIDENT: Agra Dist. Table Tennis Association
EX-PRESIDENT: Youth Congress Agra Div Unemployment Cell
FOUNDER: Vibhav Nagar Youth Sports Club

With his wife having departed to visit some relatives in Rajasthan, Krishna cooks dinner in a large house full of mosquitoes and I chip in with a bottle of Indian whisky. Mukesh, his nephew, practices palmistry and astrology and believes that everyone's destiny is mapped out for them.

I strongly disagree; although we have no control over the hand we are dealt, I believe that it is entirely up to us how we decide to play it. Consequently I see most events affecting my life as having been induced by some past action (or inaction) on my part. I'm eating at this table thanks to an unconventional response to redundancy and because I decided this morning to cancel a planned trip to Fatehpur Sikri and to return *Animal Farm* to Krishna's bookshop, and *not* because my path through life has been predetermined. I have come to believe even that I colluded fully in the loss of my job, for had I given the same dedication and intensity to my work as I had to my cycling and writing I'd surely have made myself indispensable. Just as a four-year-old relationship had died a few weeks earlier because it was no longer sustained by passion, my employment ended – at least in part – because I had never developed any passion for deskwork. I'd actually admitted as much to my boss, who may well have concluded when eventually forced by a difficult economic climate to 'downsize' that I'd be less upset by redundancy than the others.

Every individual's unique personal story is forged by billions of decisions, even the most apparently insignificant of which has the power radically to alter the course of a life. What I do (or decide not to do) with my own life is entirely up to me, not Destiny or the Gods; I am the author, director and starring actor in a unique production. Although others, of course, have parts to play in it just as I may have a part to play in theirs, it is mine to fashion and to shape, mine to give a happy ending, and mine alone to screw up. If people see themselves merely as puppets in the hands of a master puppeteer (God?), acting out parts already written for them, how can they take personal responsibility for their actions? This seems to me to be the perfect alibi for a life of failure and wickedness, for how can they either claim credit or accept blame for anything they do? How indeed can there be any morality? Morality exists only if there is a selection to be made between good and evil; if human behaviour is predetermined then there can surely be no such choice.

Krishna shuttles between kitchen and dining room with various concoctions, plays devil's advocate, laughs a lot and pours more whisky. He asks me if I'd like a fried egg.

'I have a funny feeling that Destiny has decreed that I'm going to have at least one fried egg tonight!' I reply with a sideways glance at Mukesh.

Krishna laughs uproariously, shakes my hand, and disappears into the kitchen once more.

It is late by the time I take an auto rickshaw back to the hotel. There is an empty bottle of whisky in Krishna's dining room and I'll have to get up in little more than six hours time to cycle ninety miles to Palwal with a hangover because I have arranged to rendezvous the day after tomorrow with a Dutch cyclist in Delhi.

I don't half make things difficult for myself.

Chapter Fifteen
Closing the Loop

We ask our rickshaw wallah, who has been waiting for us outside the Chinese Embassy, to take us to the cricket. A President's XI are playing the all-conquering touring Australians and Klompjes* has agreed to be instructed in this most noble of sports. On the way to the ground the rickshaw wallah points out the residence of the Indian prime minister.

'Can we pop in for a cup of tea?' asks Klompjes.

'Oh no, no, no! No, no, *no*! Not possible!' giggles our faithful wallah, a trifle uneasily.

Unlike the impressive Qadaffi Stadium in Lahore, the Ferozshah Kotla Ground in New Delhi is small and fairly decrepit and the atmosphere is more like that of an English county game than the seething cauldron of sound and fury in Lahore. The match has been arranged principally to give the Australian tourists practice before the forthcoming test series.

Explaining the rules of cricket to a foreigner is far from an easy matter. Eventually, however, Klompjes begins to understand that there is a *bowler* who *bowls* six *deliveries* which is an *over*, after which he takes a rest and another bowler bowls an over from the other end. The *batsman* must prevent the ball from hitting the *stumps* and he must at the same time try to score *runs* without being *caught, bowled, trapped lbw, run-out* or *stumped*. Each side has eleven players. When ten batsmen are *out* then the *innings* is at an end and it is the other side's turn to *bat*. Each side plays two innings each. To score runs each batsman must hurtle between the *wickets* (which are also called the *stumps*) and make it to his *crease* before the *fielder* returns the ball and the bowler or *wicket keeper* has a chance to remove the *bails*. If the shot is well timed and placed so the ball makes it straight to the *boundary* without being intercepted then the batsman scores four runs. If it does so without first touching the

*Klompjes is Dutch for 'Little Clogs'. (The Dutch 'J' is pronounced the same as the English 'Y')

ground then he adds six runs to the score. I do my best to explain the difference between fast, swing and spin bowling, and that the bowler must always keep the batsman guessing by varying the pace, length and direction of each delivery, and something of the tactics involved, but I avoid terms such as *long-hops* and *yorkers* and the complicated matter of field placings because she's looking confused enough already. As the President's XI attempts to build a telling reply to the Australians' formidable first innings total of 451 and batsmen cut, pull, hook, drive, glance, sweep and scamper between the wickets, score the odd boundary and are out, however, I think she begins to cotton on, and even to enjoy it.

The Indian crowd is of course made up of true enthusiasts. I ask my friendly neighbour, who insisted on buying us both a cup of tea, how many more runs the President's XI would have to accumulate to avoid the *follow-on*, another tactical ploy I attempt to explain to Klompjes.

He consults briefly with a friend. 'Forty.'

A voice of immense authority addresses us from the row behind. 'The Australians won't enforce the follow-on. Slater, Langer and Hayden all need extra batting practice.'

During the luncheon interval Klompjes teaches me how to swear in Dutch. A thoroughly instructive day for both of us then, but I think learning the rules of cricket is easier.

*

Klompjes is a tall, slender thirty-seven, comes from Haarlem, and is appalled at how seldom I clean my bicycle. After being employed for several years as a nurse she worked for the Dutch Post Office for a while, and then, after taking voluntary redundancy, for a travel agency. She left Holland with Martin van Doorne in May, and between Budapest and Istanbul they teamed up with Eric and Emma. The Dutch couple later found that they weren't suited as travelling companions and split up in Bam. Klompjes cycled on to Kathmandu with some Swiss cyclists and eventually arrived in Delhi following a six-week break from cycling to tour India by bus and train. Two months ago she emailed to ask if I'd allow her to accompany me on the Karakoram Highway, and I'd cautiously replied that I'd have no objection to a little company – always assuming of course that we got on OK in Delhi. Like her emails, she is pleasant, chatty and has a ready sense of fun, and I've reassured her that the more filthy and abject the appearance of my bicycle, the less likely it is to be stolen. Fears that she might turn out to be a nightmarish, female version of Milo have already been dispelled but it remains to be seen how physically fit she is, particularly following a long break from cycling. The Karakoram Highway is sure to be one of the most gruelling sections of the whole journey and I'm not prepared to compromise on my schedule; with the deserts of the Tarim Basin like a furnace in summer I need to be at the Chinese border by the time it opens on 1 May.

Neither of us are overly enamoured of Delhi. The air of the city is so foul that I can taste it in my mouth and I have to suppress a constant inclination to spit, but I have succumbed to a mild but persistent stomach bug that has left me feeling weak and lethargic and I don't yet feel ready to take to the road.

The main bazaar in Pahar Ganj is a narrow and crowded thoroughfare in which pedestrians mingle with cows. Scooters, bicycles, auto and pedal rickshaws force a passage in the usual reckless way, sounding horns and bells. Tradesmen, café owners, auto-rickshaw wallahs and beggars pester you from all sides, and with several of the cows apparently sharing my current affliction it is advisable to tread carefully. The Ajay Guest House opposite our hotel has a German Bakery that boasts a selection of mouth-watering western delicacies such as apple crumble, apfelstrudel, chocolate and lemon cake, cheesecake, croissants and bagels. The offerings from the clothes shop are even more intriguing:

T-SHIRTS & NIKKER	*Rs70*
TROGER	*Rs150*
FULL PAINT	*Rs200*
JACKET	*Rs150*
HALF SCORT	*Rs150*
FULL SCORT	*Rs160*

The following article catches my eye in *The Hindustan Times*:

40 CHARRED IN BUS MISHAP

In one of the worst road mishaps in Kerala, at least 40 people were burnt alive on Sunday when a private bus carrying them caught fire after colliding with a car in Malappuram district of the state, the police said. Only five managed to escape with serious injuries and were admitted to the Kodhikode Medical College Hospital. Among those in critical condition were the four passengers of the car. The mishap occurred when the bus tried to overtake a State Transport Corporation bus at high speed and collided with a car coming from the opposite direction at Pookiparambu. The vehicle capsized and its diesel tank immediately burst into flames, giving no chance to the passengers to escape.

Since when has culpable homicide been known as a mishap? I reflect that the brevity of the article is probably all too indicative of the frequency with which this sort of incident occurs in India. At home the accident and its repercussions would have been front-page news for several days, and countless editorials and column inches would have been devoted to sober discussions of road safety, driver fatigue and even bus design.

Drawing upon her experience as a nurse, Klompjes has placed me on a strict diet of dry toast and mashed potato and eating has become so dull that I felt compelled to spend an astronomical 250 rupees on a tiny jar of Marmite. Insensitively, she demolishes a large plate of delicious looking cannelloni while I nibble at an offensively bland mountain of mashed potato.

'Don't ruin it!' she warns me as I show signs of wavering. Although her English is excellent, occasional misunderstandings do occur. When discussing the films that we'd seen, I asked her if she'd heard of Michael Caine.

'*What* did you say? Something about *your cocaine*?' She was much taken with the performances of 'Huge' Grant and 'Yoolia' Roberts in the film *Notting Hill*.

*

At 7 a.m. on Sunday 25 March we finally cycle out of Delhi a full three weeks after we arrived. The jumble of small, rectangular shops, businesses and homes and the wide, rubbish-strewn verges of the suburbs gradually give way to the flat, prairie-like landscape which has become so familiar over the last few weeks, and the congested and bumpy roads of the city have been replaced by a smooth, horizontal dual carriageway. Klompjes confirms my belief that it is very like cycling in Holland (all we need is a few windmills and rather more wind and rain) but when we pass a dozen people apparently asleep on the grass of the central reservation and groups blithely defecating on a tract of waste ground outside a village, we are firmly back in India again.

Recovery from the stomach bug took longer than expected, and then we were obliged to wait a further week for a consignment of new inner tubes and rim tapes to arrive from the UK because a fresh outbreak of mystifying rim-side punctures had curtailed two previous attempts at departure. Despite having fitted new tyres, tubes and rim tapes, I am on tenterhooks, expecting at any minute to hear the dreaded hiss of escaping air that will signal yet another puncture. I have become mildly concerned by the sound of something rubbing against one of the tyres, but after a few minutes it ceases.

'My noise has stopped!' I roar.

'Do you want to get off and blow it?' shrieks Klompjes. She has set a cracking pace on her flashy Koga Myata tourer, but after a short break to refresh ourselves on icy Pepsi at a small, flyblown dhaba, she pedals as if her brakes are stuck on and we're battling a force nine. Anxious to put the foul air of Delhi behind us, she started too fast, and after spending over two months without cycling her legs appear to be experiencing some sort of delayed shock.

'Come on, Gran!' I chide her callously as our speed drops to an inglorious 10 mph.

She maintains that she is suffering from *verzuring* and *pap in de benen*, but she has no idea how to translate these sinister sounding afflictions into English. It isn't cramp or stiffness, nor are her legs particularly sore; there is just no strength left in them. For the rest of the day I have to bottle my frustration at having to cycle at less than two thirds of my natural pace, and doubtless she feels guilty at holding me up.

*

Although they are still outnumbered by bicycles, scooters and small motorbikes, the percentage of private cars appears to be significantly higher in the state of Hariyana than anywhere else in India. Most are modern Japanese and Korean imports, and on the outskirts of the towns the dual carriageway is lined with immaculate showrooms displaying gleaming Marutis, Hyundais, Toyotas and Tatas. After stopping to check the map at Ambala Cantonment I replace it in the bar bag and routinely check that my wallet is still zipped into the pocket in my raincoat.

No reassuring bulge and the pocket is unzipped. With a feeling of numb disbelief, the mind's protection mechanism during moments of overwhelming disaster, I turn to Klompjes. 'No wallet!'

'*What?*'

'My wallet isn't here!'

The awful realisation is dawning that I'm going to have to cycle twelve miles back on what will almost certainly be a wasted journey to the dhaba where we last stopped for food and drink to see if I left it there. Only then do I notice the precious black plastic bag* resting on top of the holdall slung across the rear carrier. I have just ridden for nearly an hour with my wallet exposed to the forces of wind and gravity (not to mention the danger of theft) and against all probability it is still there.

A force of unimaginable power and complexity keeps the planets spinning in their orbits; it is master of the seasons and of the tides and it governs the rising and setting of the sun. Those who believe that it is possible to harness this force by entering into a dialogue with it call it God. I set out on this journey

*The policy of disguising my valuables by making them look like rubbish paid handsome dividends when I left my camera behind on a park bench in Greece and was able to return, palpitating, to reclaim it fully twenty minutes later.

in the belief that its ultimate success or failure would depend almost exclusively upon factors such as determination, physical fitness and thorough preparation and planning, but when I told Dave Larsen about the episode in Nordausques he had been in no doubt that God (in the unlikely shape of a French barman) had entered my life – and to Mukesh the encounter would have been a rendezvous with Destiny.

By perching on top of the holdall instead of falling onto the road my wallet has broken all the natural rules of cause and effect, and when an event defies logical explanation the temptation is to attribute it to supernatural powers. I have been rescued twice already on the very brink of disaster, first by the unlikely intervention of a French barman and then by the honesty of two impoverished Turkish peasants, but who or what has stepped in this time? Destiny? Allah? Ganesh, the elephant-headed Hindu God of good fortune? My Lucky Stars? Has the same entity been responsible for ensuring my survival on the killing grounds of India's roads? Occasionally I am seduced, despite myself, by the dangerous belief that this foolhardy venture is somehow *meant* to succeed. Somewhere in the overpopulated Hindu Pantheon there must be a God who looks after fools.

*

I cycle fast into Amritsar, frequently glancing behind to see if Klompjes is keeping up, weaving in and out of the traffic and unerringly finding the path of least resistance. There are tricks you can use to ensure that you keep moving; like a pilot fish attaching itself to a shark, I try to cycle alongside or in the wake of a truck or bus at major intersections or roundabouts because these bullies of the road intimidate other traffic into giving them priority. The adrenaline and the cut and thrust evoke memories of driving articulated lorries on anarchic racetracks such as the Paris *Peripherique*, the Milan *Tangenziale* and Moscow's abominable ring roads. The cardinal rule is exactly the same now as it was then: *always* act swiftly and decisively. Be aggressive, and don't give ground unless you absolutely have to. Hesitate and you are lost, engulfed by the tide.

After sluicing off the sweat and dust in a hot shower we sit down at a table in the sun-drenched courtyard of the Castle Shiraz Hotel and order lunch. I have just closed the ends of a gigantic loop and the second phase of my mission, the *Tour de India*, is complete. With Klompjes' highlighter I trace my route through Pakistan and around India on the Geocenter map of the Indian Subcontinent. Looking at that long, fluorescent, yellow line and feeling enormously proud of myself, I wonder how many pints of sweat were expended during those thousands of sweltering miles. It is what my brother-in-law would have called *A Perfect Moment*.

Later in the afternoon a boy is dispatched from the hotel to get us a couple of Kingfisher beers and we purchase cream cakes from the nearby bakery in Queen's Road to celebrate our respective achievements (Klompjes having just passed the twelve-thousand-kilometre landmark). We spend the evening in our room, drinking beer and munching walnut cake (a bizarre juxtaposition of tastes) and watching Spielberg's *Empire of the Sun* while lighting flashes, thunder rumbles and the rain pours down outside.

*

On Queen's Road there are the faint but unmistakable marks of a zebra crossing. I can't imagine anything more superfluous; the idea of Indian drivers stopping voluntarily to allow pedestrians to cross a street is ludicrous. It must be the only one in the country and I can only surmise that it is a relic left over from the days of the Raj, when there would have been less traffic and more enforcement. When we step out experimentally a four-wheel-drive Tata Sumo packed with Sikhs immediately blasts its horn at us, causing us to make a rapid retreat.

'This is a pedestrian crossing, you bunch of t*****s!' I bellow at the passing car. Incandescent, I turn to Klompjes. 'In England they would have been had by the police for that.'

Yes, but this is India, you fool.

Although I have passed every physical test that India has thrown at me, she has presented me with the greatest mental challenge yet and I have failed to meet it. *Layers of habit learned and developed over a lifetime cannot easily be peeled away within a few weeks.* Remaining too stubbornly European in my attitudes, I have been unable to adapt. Well, it's too late to do anything about that now. The knowledge that others (including those veteran travellers in India, Sandra and Elliott) have buckled under similar stresses and strains, is some consolation. Maybe I'll do it better next time.

Klompjes, who has had much less exposure to the teeming hordes of the subcontinent, maintains that I should answer people when they shout *Allo* 'otherwise they think you're just another arrogant tourist'.

'If people in England say "hello" to you, do you ignore them?' she asks.

'No, of course I don't. But have you never wondered why Indians never shout like that to *each other*? They shout at *us* only because we're different, and I resent being singled out because of the colour of my skin. It would be like me shouting *Namaste!* to every Indian I see at home – stupid and offensive.'

'But I think that sometimes they just welcome you to their country.' She is being far too reasonable.

'If I feel that the greeting is genuine I return it. But 99 per cent of the time I think that they are just trying to provoke a reaction from me, or worse, attempting to attract plaudits from their peers by showing off. I like to be left to do my tourism in peace, so the last thing I'm going to do is encourage such behaviour by taking any notice of it.'

'Maybe it's time you went home!'

Although I resent being criticised by someone who is relatively new to India, I have a nasty feeling that she may have a point. On my first visit to Amritsar back in November I was as excited to have finally reached India as I am now exultant to be leaving it. Everything then was fresh and new and I revelled in the unfamiliar noises, smells and colours, but having spent nearly five months travelling around this vast country, my senses have become immunised through repeated exposure to the same stimuli and previous sources of fascination have become normality. The brilliant colours of the Sikhs' turbans and the women's saris have faded and the stench of urine evaporating from the pavements in Queen's Road no longer appals me. I have become inured to the pollution, scarcely register the noise, am no longer intimidated by the traffic madness, and I even find the tea drinkable.

In many respects India is the most welcoming of all the Asian countries for a cyclist. Although the distances are immense and cycling on some of the busier main roads is an uncomfortable and dangerous experience, hills, heat and headwinds have all been manageable, and food, drink and accommodation have been plentiful and cheap. Notwithstanding the occasional upset stomach I never fell prey to any of the really nasty bugs and, with the possible exception of Bihar (and that was rather through its reputation than anything I sensed in the atmosphere myself), I never felt threatened; the only hostility I had to deal with was my own. The quality you need above all others in India, however, is patience. After months of struggle mine finally ran out on the Grand Trunk Road somewhere west of Varanasi.

You never get bored of India; you just get tired of it sometimes.

Jan was so right. I grew tired of the crowds. Perhaps the people were just a little *too* friendly.

Time to go home? No, not yet. But although I'd love one day to return, it really is high time I left India.

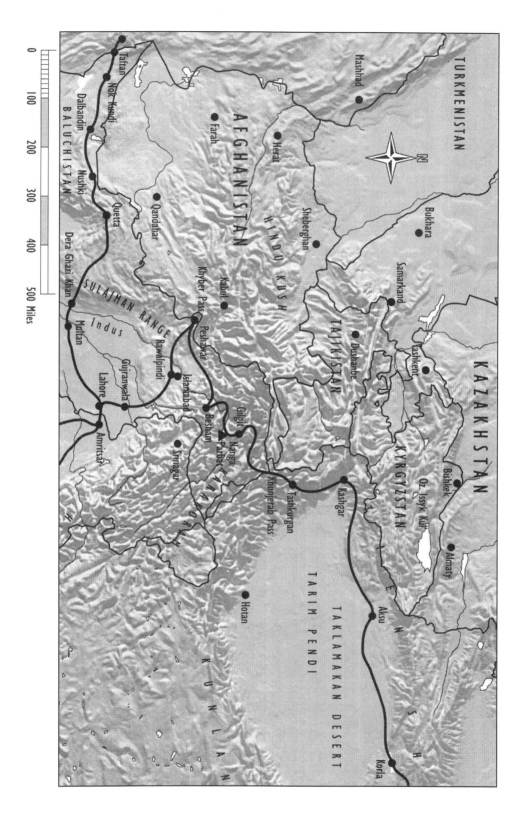

Part Three: Beyond India

Slaving night and day for one whom nothing pleases, enduring rain and wind, ill fed and short of sleep!

Leporello in Act One Scene 1 of Mozart's opera 'Don Giovanni'. (Translated from the Italian)

Chapter Sixteen
Pakistan Revisited

Beyond Amritsar's western suburbs traffic is scarce and the Grand Trunk Road, effectively a cul-de-sac, has become eerily quiet. The bullying lorries and long-distance buses have disappeared and the road, bisecting an endless vista of flat, cultivated farmland and bordered by eucalyptus trees, has become the preserve of ox carts, bicycles and the occasional tractor. Able to proceed in peace and relative safety instead of amongst braying horns and the hot, stinking breath of rampaging Tatas and Ashok Leylands, I am enjoying the cycling once more, almost for the first time since Calcutta.

Although it is firmly against my principles to cycle any road twice, retracing my tyre marks from Amritsar back to Lahore has been unavoidable because there is only a single crossing point on the 1,800-mile border dividing India and Pakistan. The Indian side at Attari Road is almost deserted and the officials are pleasant and interested in us. We are shepherded through immigration and customs with minimal fuss.

'See you again!' they say.

'We hope so!' I reply.

Teams of sweating coolies are jogging across no man's land supporting on their shoulders heavy looking, irregularly-shaped oblong objects wrapped in white muslin that remind me incongruously of the bodies on the funeral pyres in Varanasi. Two container lorries are parked on the Pakistani side of the border and the goods are being transferred to other lorries waiting on the Indian side, cross-border traffic between the two countries (with the exception of the occasional tourist bus or car or deranged cyclist from a third country) being prohibited.

A single people and a single country have been divided into two by a hastily and ill-conceived border. I find the comparison with the post-war division of Germany irresistible, but the cold war in the subcontinent has outlasted its European counterpart and shows no sign of ending. Neatly dividing India along religious fault lines proved to be impossible: not only were the heaviest concentrations of Muslims inconveniently situated on opposite sides of the country, but pockets of Muslims also existed in predominantly Hindu areas and vice-versa, and other regions contained an evenly mixed population. Was the partition in 1947 of the Punjab and Bengal worth the slaughter of up to a million Muslims, Hindus and Sikhs and the creation of seventeen million refugees? Since India's Muslims (although still a minority) today outnumber Pakistan's and don't appear to be noticeably worse off than their counterparts across the border, it can hardly be argued that all those people died and millions more lives were irretrievably ruined so that successive generations might enjoy a peaceful and prosperous future.

Their sacrifice was in vain and thousands more continue to perish needlessly in that futile, debilitating squabble over Kashmir. Although Kashmir's Muslim majority would logically have made it part of West Pakistan, the state was governed prior to independence by a Hindu maharaja. When in October 1948 a Pathan army invaded with the intention of annexing the state for Pakistan, the maharaja promptly decided to join India and the Indians poured troops in from the east. The first war between the two countries was ended by the intervention of the United Nations and a line of demarcation was drawn between the two sides known as the Line of Actual Control. Neither country has ever accepted it as the official border and other wars followed in 1965 and 1971. Sporadic outbreaks of fighting have kept the two countries at loggerheads and on the brink of a fourth full-scale confrontation that could involve the deployment of nuclear weapons.

So precisely whose interest was served by Partition? Did Mohammed Ali Jinnah truly want what was best for the subcontinent's Muslims? Or was he driven more by personal ambition? Like Communism, Partition was one of history's great mistakes and it is fascinating to speculate what might have been had the division never taken place. Instead of two impoverished countries teetering on the brink of the world's first nuclear conflict, a Greater India – possessing roughly a quarter of the world's population and with so much more money available to invest in education, the economy and the infrastructure – might have become an Asian superpower with an economy to rival those of China, Japan or even the USA.

Without the interference of politicians cynically seeking to manipulate ethnic and religious divides people usually find a way to coexist peacefully enough with their neighbours; individual prosperity and security is far more important to the vast, silent majority of Pakistanis and Indians than the destiny of Kashmir. All too frequently, however, religions and politics are hijacked by a bigoted minority with open mouths and closed minds. In 1989 Eastern Europe's silent majority took matters into its own hands with spectacular results. It is probably too much to hope that the borders separating India from Pakistan and

Bangladesh might one day vanish like the Iron Curtain, but sometime in the future the subcontinent's own silent millions may likewise impose their will, sense will prevail at last, and India and Pakistan will be able to settle their hostilities on a cricket field instead of with bullets and bombs.

An Iranian tourist bus is parked on the Pakistani side of the border and the customs hall is packed with passengers and mountains of baggage. My heart sinks and I find myself wondering how I'd explain the contents of the tiny matchbox lying like an unexploded bomb inside the bar-bag to an inquisitive customs official. It looks as if we're in for a long wait, but we are ushered into a smaller room where the details of our passports are written down by a rotund, bearded individual who says nothing but smiles at us from time to time, radiating benevolence.

Aspirin: as yet not widely available in Asia, and still quite effective against minor ailments. Can also be held tightly between buttocks to deter anal entry.

What would he make of the A.A.A.K.'s list of instructions? Fortunately however, a search of our baggage isn't considered necessary and the mask of affability remains intact. One of the fetchers and carriers recognises Klompjes from her previous visit and is most anxious that we should stay for a cup of tea. When we leave he shakes my hand and says 'God bless you, sir!' with impressive sincerity.

During the short ride to Lahore the fertile fields of Pakistan's half of the Punjab, witness to unspeakable horrors fifty-three years ago, stretch flatly and greenly into the distance just as they did on the Indian side, emphasising the artificiality of the border. The sun shines innocently through the same trees, dappling a road surface stained by splashes of animal dung. Oxen are grazing or lying down tethered to stakes. Although people on this side of the border converse in the same Punjabi language, the brilliant colours of the Sikhs' turbans and the women's saris have been replaced by the pastel shades of the ubiquitous shalwar qamiz.

In a huge, almost empty cinema in Lahore we watch *Tomorrow Never Dies.* When the Pakistani flag appears on the screen before the start of the film everyone stands up and the national anthem is played. During the film a man makes periodic tours with a flashlight, presumably to check that nobody is using the concealing darkness to indulge in anything improper, for what we in the West would regard as a little harmless snogging is strictly forbidden in the Islamic Republic of Pakistan.

*

Powerfully reminded of squabbling cats, I shower and get dressed to the atonal wailing of the muezzin. Klompjes wakes up to rustling and crunching sounds as I get started on a packet of Bombay Mix.

'I thought there was some sort of animal in the room!' she exclaims.

'There is!'

After breakfast we stroll along Church Road to The Mall. Prior to independence approximately half of Lahore's population of 1.2 million comprised Hindus and Sikhs, but the ethnic cleansing unleashed by Partition reduced their number to less than a thousand. The women seem to have disappeared along with them.

'What beautiful buildings!' Klompjes has paused to admire the Cathedral Church of the Resurrection and the impressive red-brick buildings of the law courts.

'Built by the British, of course!'

'You are becoming very narcissistic!'

'Narcissistic? I don't think so. Jingoistic, perhaps.'

'Both are bad. Anyway, I'm sure the British didn't lift a single brick. They designed the buildings and just watched while the Pakistanis built them.'

Crossing the busy road is a little like stealing a quick single in a game of cricket. Having judged the distance separating us from the safety of the opposite pavement and the speed and distance of the nearest onrushing vehicle, I make my decision in an instant.

'Yes, yes, yes!' I shout.

'No, no, no!' shrieks Klompjes, trying to pull me back by my shirt.

Indecision by either batsman usually results in one of them being run out. Without the chance of a second innings we are fortunate to cross with our respective scores of forty and thirty-seven 'not out' remaining intact.

*

The proprietor of an isolated restaurant on the Gujranwala bypass has offered us a free room for the night. How could we resist? The food is excellent and the people overwhelmingly friendly. The smell of baking chapattis from the kitchen immediately below our room wafts deliciously upwards. A rooster crows repeatedly and from the nearby dual carriageway comes the faint hum of traffic. I am about a third of the way through *The Grand Trunk Road from the Front Seat* by Brian Paul Bach, puzzling how the American author can have written a substantial eulogy of over four hundred pages about the road that has so far provided some of the dullest cycling of the entire journey. I must have missed something.

Klompjes glances up from *The City of Joy.* 'What's a "test-tube baby?"'

'I'm not really sure. Something to do with artificial insemination, I think.'

'But a tube is something you have inside your tyre!'

'Yes, but a *test*-tube is a small cylindrical glass container used in a laboratory.'

'Ah yes! I know it.'

Beyond Gujranwala the Grand Trunk Road continues much as before, the wide four-lane highway discreetly bypassing larger towns and cities such as Wazirabad and Gujrat but making no such concession to smaller communities, a barrier of concrete and asphalt imperiously dividing them into east and west, traffic unencumbered by courtesies such as traffic lights, pedestrian crossings or roundabouts.

Inauspiciously conceived from the politics of fear and hatred the country may have been, but Pakistan's people are a thoroughly decent lot. The milkman pedals into a dhaba with two large metal churns attached to either side of the rear wheel of his bicycle and presents us each with a free glass of milk. When I get up to visit the toilet after finishing my parathas and scrambled egg someone switches on the light for me. A little later at a teahouse-cum-café a man rushes over with a couple of chairs, places them in one of the few shady spots, and invites us to sit down. People crowd round us while we drink our Pepsis. One man works at a commercial centre in Milan and another in Copenhagen as a bus driver. Both are on holiday visiting friends and relatives before having to return to Europe. They are friendly and articulate. Several elderly men with wizened, bearded faces and wearing either a skullcap or a turban above the inevitable baggy shalwar qamiz are squeezed into the small, windowless brick cell of a teahouse, gossiping and drinking endless cups of tea. Rice is being boiled outside in a great cauldron over an open fire and we are invited to stay and eat, but sadly we have to decline because we are already full from breakfast. Just as we are preparing to leave a young man arrives with a large entourage and entreats us to stay and drink tea. 'You are my guests and I am your host. It is my duty to offer it to you,' he declares.

Evidently foreign visitors are still rare enough in Pakistan to be appreciated. Yesterday two lorry drivers, astonished that we weren't exhausted after cycling the thirty miles from Lahore, insisted on paying for our drinks. During the initial crossing of Pakistan I was probably too overwhelmed by fatigue and ill health to notice them, but it is these charming little acts of kindness that have made travelling in the country such a pleasure the second time round.

The landscape is becoming steadily more dehydrated as we move north, leaving the moist, fertile plains behind us. Gentle shades of green have turned to more dramatic combinations of greys, browns, yellows and reds in a thirsty landscape that reminds me of Iran, an illusion reinforced by the silky-smooth surface of the road. The dual carriageway begins to roll and dip as it skirts the eastern extremity of the Salt Range, and after bypassing Jhelum the highway channels through barren hills, spans gorges and wends its way around and over craggy mountains. I attack the first hills I've encountered since Bihar with a surge of joy, revelling in the change from the monotonous flatness of the past few weeks. The air is hot and dry and the ground has become parched and stony, supporting only the hardiest thorn trees and bushes. Mountains, half concealed by the haze, rise in the distance and, closer at hand, deep gorges and dried up riverbeds carve their way through sepia cliffs that loom up from a dusty, boulder-strewn plateau. Dominated by the domes and minarets of the mosques and peremptorily bisected by the road, villages and small towns are a huddle of flat-roofed brick and stuccoed shops, businesses and homes baking in the sun. Colourful billboards advertise *Red & White* cigarettes, *Gold Leaf* tobacco and *Liptons Ice Tea*, and some low hills on the left remind Klompjes of the dunes on the Dutch coast near her native Haarlem.

The few cars on the road are almost exclusively Japanese. Local public transport is provided by the same Suzuki and Toyota minibuses that tore around the streets of Lahore blaring their horns and by vintage Ford Transits imported from Britain (some of them with the British number plates still attached). Long-distance Hino buses hurtle past, belching thick, oily smoke from their exhausts and buffeting us with hot air. The most eye-catching vehicles are unquestionably the lorries, elephantine beasts of burden resplendent in burnished chrome and startling combinations of colours, displaying slogans in Urdu and English and covered in clusters of lights and reflectors. The imagination, technique and extraordinary attention to detail devoted to their gaudy and exuberant customised paint jobs have succeeded in transforming them from familiar, unglamorous machines into spectacular mobile works of art.

With the roar and rush of the warm air filling our ears and drowning out the faint buzz of the freewheels, we swoop at break-neck speed down a long, long hill to the city laid out before us on the plain below, where the proprietor of the Rawalpindi Popular Inn welcomes us with a warm smile and a firm handshake.

*

The bus to Islamabad grinds along in low gear in the heavy traffic on Murree Road, stopping frequently and soliciting for extra passengers by sounding its horn, which makes a strange, tremulous noise a little like the whinnying of a horse. At each stop the conductor shouts out the name of the destination, reluctant to leave until the aisle is crammed with standing passengers. Through a window I watch a green and white PIA jet climb steeply into the cloudless sky, its passengers scooped up from one world and only hours later deposited in an entirely different one with little or no sense of what lies in between.

Considering the months of effort it has taken me to get this far it is all the more remarkable that England is only about ten hours away by air.

'Not very far!' agrees Klompjes. 'Aeroplanes make the whole world not very far.'

Half an hour later we are strolling along hot, empty, litter-free, even pavements, and past expensive modern properties protected by high walls, gates and intercoms. Only ten miles separate Rawalpindi from Islamabad but, just like the passengers on the plane, we have been catapulted into another world. The trees and bushes are heavy with red and white blossom, and carefully tended borders are filled with multicoloured flowers.

Klompjes remarks that we might be in Holland.

Or Milton Keynes with sunshine. Or Florida. Pakistan it certainly isn't.

The man in the office of ACB Pvt Ltd at Hill View Plaza in the Blue Area welcomes us warmly, offers us a complementary bottle of Cola each and fetches my package of bicycle parts. Then he presents us with free pens, points us to the bus stop, and we return to Pakistan in a segregated Suzuki minibus. Klompjes and the other women have to squeeze in the front with the driver, and so tightly are the men packed together in the back that I can scarcely get my hand into my pocket to give the conductor the fare.

*

Unlike Islamabad's, Rawalpindi's pavements are crowded and uneven, islands of concrete giving way to compacted dirt and gaping holes.

'You don't get bladders when you wear your new shoes?' asks Klompjes – whose English contains some endearing little idiosyncrasies – solicitously.

I reply that the new cycling boots I collected in Islamabad have given me a small blister on the right heel. The heat is intense and energy sapping, and I reflect uneasily that if Northern Pakistan is this hot in early April, how am I going to deal with the temperatures in the Tarim Basin and Inner Mongolia in May and June, and in Manchuria in July?

These concerns are abruptly banished by a stream of angry sounding Dutch. One of the local Lotharios has just squeezed Klompjes' thigh as he walked past in the opposite direction. With some men mistaking the greater freedoms and independence enjoyed by western women for promiscuity (a misconception bound to be strengthened by the porn sites on the Internet), these can be awkward and even dangerous countries for female travellers. I stifle an urge to chase after the miscreant, grab him by the testicles, grope his buttocks and then ask him how *he* enjoys being sexually assaulted by a total stranger, but a few moments later I find myself pondering the degree of ignorance and sexual frustration that would drive an individual to such lengths and wondering if I shouldn't feel pity rather than anger.

Travelling in a Muslim country with a woman has been a revelation to me. Not only are the sexes segregated on public transport but also in many restaurants and cafés, where we are quarantined in so-called Family Areas.

'There are some lovely people in this country but some really stupid rules,' observes Klompjes darkly as we sip cooling Pepsis behind the tinted glass of a Family Area inside a café in Rawalpindi's Saddar Bazaar. 'Being a woman makes you feel that there's something *wrong* with you.'

We collect her new smock (a long, loose garment designed to conceal the provocative protrusions of breasts, thighs and buttocks in ultra-conservative regions such as Indus Kohistan and Baltistan) from a tailor. She ordered it in Dutch orange and she remarks that she feels considerably more conspicuous in it than she did in her grey T-shirt.

'Pakistani women wear bright colours too,' I remind her.

But they don't ride bicycles. She risks being the target of considerable curiosity (and possibly even derision) in the remote, tribal areas further north.

*

We leave the Rawalpindi Popular Inn early on Wednesday 11 April with stomachs uncomfortably swollen by an enormous breakfast of yoghurt, chopped banana and honey. Apart from a couple of dogs copulating (the male with enthusiasm, the female with apparent resignation) on a small area of waste ground opposite, the streets are pleasantly deserted. Beyond the city limits, cows, donkeys and goats are nibbling at the sparse vegetation on a dry and dusty landscape. The low cliffs and ubiquitous brick kilns recall areas of Baluchistan.

Beyond Attock several vehicles slow down as they pass, bearded faces under turbans and skullcaps subjecting us to their scrutiny. We have just crossed the Indus and entered the land of the Pathans, a fiercely independent and warlike tribal group whose homeland extends from Pakistan's romantically named Northwest Frontier Province into Baluchistan and Afghanistan. They enjoy a legendary reputation for savagery and I can only hope that attitudes towards the British have changed, for soldiers of the Raj were reputed to keep the last bullet for themselves rather than risk suffering an appalling death at the hands of their captors – or even worse, their women.

Pungent wafts of marijuana drift towards us as we refresh ourselves at a dhaba near Jahangira.

'Do you think it will be possible to get some in Peshawar?' asks Klompjes.

'I should think so, but I'm not going to.' I declined the joints proffered by passing lorry drivers in Baluchistan on the basis that cycling on those precipitous and broken roads was quite demanding enough without the handicap of being stoned by the locally grown weed as well as by the locally grown children.

'Why not?'

'Because I'd never buy the stuff from someone I don't know, and especially not in a country in which I know nothing about the rules.'

'I might buy some if I could get it from a person I could trust. Another tourist, maybe.'

'Smoking gives me a sore throat but I might be persuaded to *eat* a bit. We could mix it into our banana, yoghurt and honey breakfasts.'

'And then go cycling! I think that will be nice!'

At a dhaba twenty miles from Peshawar I tuck into a meal of chapattis, dal, brown beans, mutton and a cucumber and tomato salad with a breezy confidence that would have been unimaginable back in October. A villainous looking man with the obligatory beard and a lazy eye sits down on the neighbouring charpoy and attempts to converse with us.

'It is very beautiful,' he sighs, gazing lustfully at my bicycle.

With its small diameter twenty-six-inch wheels and big, chunky tyres I have always thought of it as a pragmatic rather than a graceful machine; Klompjes' Koga Myata, although less strongly built, is much more elegant.

One of the two young men acting as translators presents me with a ring, after which they shake my hand and excuse themselves. They are off to say their prayers at the local mosque.

'I wonder why he gives you a ring?' says Klompjes. 'Martin was given one by a man in Iran.'

I shrug. 'Perhaps he wants to marry me.' It is small and light enough to take with me as another keepsake to go with Olive's sock and the obscene *Acme Anti-Anal Assault Kit*. I'm never sure whether I'm expected to accept or decline such gifts, for I have nothing material to give in return.

Six miles from Peshawar vehicles have braked to an unexpected halt in front of us. Like water, traffic in Asian countries finds the path of least resistance; if the lane ahead is blocked, enterprising motorists will attempt to find a way around the obstruction by driving along the verge, into the adjacent fields, along the central reservation, and against the traffic flow on the opposite carriageway. The result, of course, is utter, unimaginable chaos. Two lanes of stationary traffic have multiplied to become four. Throngs of pedestrians are milling around the unmoving vehicles, reminding me a little of the Tottenham High Road immediately after a football match. Several vehicles are displaying black and white horizontally striped flags and people are piled into and on top of them, and others are clinging to the roofs and the sides of buses. The springs of a dangerously swaying pick-up that has to be carrying at least thirty people bottom out with a crunch as it attempts to execute a U-turn across the central reservation and I think that it must surely topple onto its side, but miraculously it remains upright. The western infidels are obliged to dismount and self-consciously push their bicycles through the mayhem for fully two miles before the traffic at last begins to move.

*

Peshawar's Old City is a gigantic open-air bazaar full of wonderful smells of barbecuing kebabs, frying liver, tea and spices. Here, as in Quetta, I can sense the proximity of Afghanistan, for the city's population has been swollen in recent years by the arrival of millions of Afghan refugees and many of the women are hidden behind burqas. A return ride to the legendary Khyber Pass and the opportunity to peek across the border into another land (that obsession manifesting itself again) would indeed be achievable within a single day but, insisting that our security cannot be guaranteed, the authorities at the PA Khyber Agency have refused to issue us with the necessary permits. Accordingly a long and volatile relationship with the Grand Trunk Road finally came to an end upon our arrival at Peshawar's Hadyat Hotel, 1,562 miles (2,499 kilometres) from Calcutta.

According to *The Statesman*, the chaos we encountered on the western approach to the city was the end of the three-day International Deoband Conference at Taru Jabba. Unenlightened, I read on:

The participants chanted pro-Taliban slogans and condemned the US and other anti-Islamic powers for their attitude towards the Taliban. More than 10 lakh (1,000,000) people participated in the concluding session and prayed for the unity of Umma.

There wasn't a single woman to be seen amongst all that compressed humanity and Klompjes admits that she felt thoroughly discomfited by the experience. 'All those men staring! I felt like the little boy in *Empire of the Sun* when he lost his mother. If I'd lost you I think I would have really panicked.' Despite the specifically anti-western nature of the gathering I wasn't aware of any hostility as we struggled through the crowds, but I can't say I enjoyed myself very much either.

The auto-repair bazaar is an intriguing labyrinth of narrow alleyways crammed with small repair businesses stocking what I judge to be mostly recycled car and lorry parts, everything from nuts and bolts to entire engines. I need to replace a screw that dropped out from one of my cleats but it's infernally difficult to find the right type; they are all too short, too long, or have the wrong thread. After rummaging through several boxes I eventually get what I want from a rapacious ten-year-old presiding over a car-radio business.

Chapter Seventeen
Klompjes, Rosie and the Karakoram Highway

After crossing the 2,134-metre Shangla pass in torrential rain and running the gauntlet of hordes of stone-throwing brats who grabbed at the bicycles as we bumped through remote, sodden mountain villages on unpaved, slimy and potholed roads, we join the Karakoram Highway at Besham. At the hotel I discover that one of the little *bastards* has stolen my pot of Marmite; the zip on the holdall slung across the rear carrier has been broken for some time, making it easy for small hands to infiltrate it.

The following morning an elderly gentleman with a bushy white beard tells us in halting English that he saw us yesterday from his seat on the bus. 'When it rains you must go in hotel!' he admonishes us.

If only there had been a hotel to go to. We politely decline his invitation to take tea with him and cycle warily out of Besham on an unpaved section of mud and puddles, an unpromising introduction to an engineering feat that has been described as the eighth wonder of the world. For twenty years fifteen thousand Pakistani soldiers and between nine thousand and twenty thousand Chinese labourers fought against landslides, rockfalls, floods and vicious summer and winter conditions to carve a route through some of the most vertical and inhospitable terrain on the planet. On the Pakistani side alone there are close upon a hundred bridges, the hapless road criss-crossing the river time and again in an effort to find an easier passage. Accidents claimed roughly one life for every mile of roadway laid and maintenance remains a Herculean, never-ending task in an area of intense seismic activity. In 1974 an earthquake at Pattan killed more than seven thousand people and forty miles of road were buried under tons of rubble, but despite nature's best efforts the frail and scarred eight-hundred-mile asphalt thread that connects Rawalpindi to Kashgar remains a monument to human determination and engineering ingenuity.

The saturated sky resembles the canvas of a poorly constructed tent, sagging beneath the weight of rainwater; if it weren't for the nearby mountains propping it up it would surely fall in on top of us. Signs warn traffic that the area is prone to landslides as the road, clinging to a narrow ledge that has been chiselled out of the mountain wall that rises on our left, begins to climb away from the Indus. A fine drizzle has started to fall and longhaired mountain goats cower into the cliff walls as we pass. A terrified calf gallops away from us, searching in vain for an avenue of escape. On the right is a dizzying drop to the muddy-brown waters of the river, and on the opposite bank terraces have been improbably carved between perpendicular outcrops jutting from rocky green mountainsides that rise steeply to peaks concealed by low cloud. The road's name is misleading: I had been expecting at the very least a wide, modern, well-maintained thoroughfare, if not a dual carriageway, but the route remains narrow and its surface unpredictable, and it carries little traffic.

We are pursued into Dasu by a posse of small hooligans uttering shrill cries and cackles of malevolent laughter. I'd rather be chased by a pack of Rottweilers. Our hotel room is cramped and noisy and the bathroom window won't close; voyeurs in the busy street outside will be able watch us shivering naked in the draught under our cold-water bucket showers.

'Cycling Queen, can't you see, sweet seventeen – thirty-seven I meeeeean!' howls Klompjes (apparently unperturbed by the horror of our surroundings) to a tune vaguely reminiscent of an Abba hit.

Gangs of diminutive monsters pester us relentlessly during a two-mile walk to the District Forestry Office. Our noisy retinue diminishes as we leave the village behind but a giggling teenage half-wit accompanies us until I take a swipe at him with the guidebook. I blame the parents.

We are saved from the ordeal of walking back by the driver of a minibus who tells us that he is a teacher.

Poor sod.

He drives at a snails pace, stopping frequently to greet acquaintances or pick someone up.

'Do you like Pakistan?' he asks us.

We nod enthusiastically. 'Very beautiful!'

'Pakistan people?'

'Of course!' we reply. *Well, some of them.*

'Pakistan music?'

'You bet!' we lie.

A mistake: he eagerly inserts a cassette into the player and the confined space is filled with the excruciating atonal wailing and screeching that passes for music in Pakistan.

With the little darlings still clutching their teddies under their Winnie the Pooh duvet covers, it is left to the barking and snarling local dogs to give us a rousing send-off early the next morning, but when I slow down and give them the evil eye they lose interest – dogs are so much easier to deal with than children. Not once during our brief and unpleasant sojourn in Dasu did we catch sight of a woman.

I have become depressed by the surly attitude of some of the locals and the prospect of more skirmishes with aggressive juveniles. As we cycle through a village a youth threatens to hit Klompjes with a stick, and a little further on a young man is standing at the roadside holding up a very large, freshly caught fish as if to offer it to us. When I signal a polite 'no thanks' he makes as if to hit me over the head with it. It is the first time in my life I've ever been threatened by a dead fish. The reception isn't always hostile, however; lorry drivers toot their horns and return our answering waves; an old man offers me his hand but I can't stop; two children clattering down the hill in the opposite direction on a home-made go-cart wave at us; and when we stop at the roadside to re-hydrate and regain our breath, a smirking donkey confronts us with an erection.

'Do you think he fancies me or you?' I ask Klompjes.

'My God!' she gasps. 'It must be forty centimetres long!'

'Didn't you know about donkeys then?'

'No.'

'In England we have an expression "hung like a donkey" to describe people with very large penises. That animal is making me feel very inadequate.'

'Why?'

'Because mine is a lot smaller.'

'It doesn't matter!'

'So they say, but most men would like their willies to be bigger.'

'I'd like my teets to be bigger.'

'I think you've got nice tits. Bigger ones would only get in the way.'

'It is possible, but they'd make me feel more womanly.'

Shatial consists of a filling station and a few unenticing shops and eateries built alongside the road. Everybody stops whatever they're doing to stare at us, and twenty spectators follow us into an empty restaurant and take their places on the surrounding charpoy beds. Dal and chapatti is the only dish on the menu and there is no cutlery so we are obliged to eat using our fingers. A man who speaks some English tries a little evangelism: *Only with Allah's help can we hope to succeed and there is no God but Allah.* When he urges me to repeat the sermon I refuse; I'm damned if I'm going to allow myself to be converted to Islam, even to shut him up.

The rest house is a bungalow at the bottom of a steep track. Only after I've paid the two hundred rupees for a room do we discover that there's neither electricity nor water. There are no other tenants and we are forced by the scrum of yelling children outside to spend the rest of the day under a state of virtual siege.

*

The terrain becomes harsher and more forbidding as we forsake the greener slopes of Indus Kohistan and the North West Frontier Province for the exposed granite of the Northern Areas. Jagged cliffs and rocks embedded in vertical walls of dried mud rise to either side of a broad valley that can only be described as desert, its floor covered in sand, pebbles and boulders as large as lorries. The few leathery shrubs hardy enough to eke out an existence are almost as devoid of colour as the scenery. On our left are the eastern extremities of the Hindu Kush, and on our right the western ramparts of the Himalayas, whilst ahead of us rise the mighty Karakoram and Pamir ranges, a confluence of mountain chains thrust upwards by a collision between India and Asia that commenced fifty million years ago. Mountains are the geological solution to the 'unstoppable-force–immoveable-object' conundrum: India's momentum continues to propel her northwards at a rate of five centimetres per year, the impact manifesting itself in regular earthquakes and tremors and causing the mountains to rise by a rate of roughly two millimetres annually. Somewhere on our right is the colossal 8,125-metre massif of Nanga Parbat (Kashmiri for 'Naked Mountain'), demurely hiding its white face behind a veil of cloud. Unimaginable underground forces are causing the planet's eighth-highest mountain to grow at the prodigious rate of seven millimetres per year. Amongst this ferment of geological activity the Karakoram Highway is as vulnerable as an ant-run on a construction site, its surface scarred in several places by landslides and the tracks of the heavy machinery used to clear the rubble. Alongside the frail and twisting ribbon of asphalt runs the river, tranquilly wending its way between smooth banks of grey-pink silt deposits.

Summer heat turns this craggy, boulder-strewn valley into a furnace and winter temperatures plummet to several degrees below zero, but the cool and cloudy April weather is ideal for cycling. Although drifting clouds have run themselves aground upon the mountaintops and the highest peaks remain frustratingly hidden behind obdurate banks of cumulus, I revel in the sensation of sunshine and wind on my face, rejoicing in the bends and undulations of the empty road and the constantly changing vistas. After cycling past banks of piled-up boulders, we perch on a conveniently placed wall to refresh ourselves from our water bottles, gazing at the empty, pulverised terrain of the valley for a while in companionable silence. I wish I'd brought aluminium water bottles with me because they keep the water cool for longer and don't transfer their taste to it, but Klompjes prefers plastic ones.

'I like better to squeeze than suck,' she explains.

We grin obscenely at each other. Tiny, isolated islands of green in the immense monochrome backdrop denote the presence of people, who seem more kindly disposed to us in this sparsely populated area than the inhabitants of Indus Kohistan, whose suspicious glares, unpredictable reactions and unruly offspring made the crossing of villages and towns an experience to be dreaded.

We spend a relaxed afternoon sitting on the veranda of the rest house in Talechi, reading and drinking tea in the sunshine.

The view of the Grand Trunk Road, whether through wide-screen vistas from the front seat of a private car, or a few glances from the middle of a crammed coach, constitutes one vast mural, a continuous "mise en scene" of style, substance and survival which is not only unique, but superbly creative at the same time.

A gentle breeze ripples the grassy meadows and stirs the branches of the nearby trees; the sweltering, overpopulated plains of Uttar Pradesh are a world away. I tell Klompjes about some friends who rode an Enfield Bullet called *Dum-Dum* around India and Nepal and who wrote in an admirably succinct email that the Grand Trunk Road was 'shit'.

'Why did they call their motorbike Dum-Dum?' she asks.

'They named it after a type of bullet manufactured in India called the "dum-dum" bullet, and for the excellent reason that the engine went *Dum-Dum-Dum-Dum-Dum-Dum.*'

'Oh. What do you call your bicycle?'

'It hasn't got a name – except when I get angry with it. Then it gets called all sorts of names.' Although it is true that I scold it whenever it performs any of its duties less than satisfactorily, I tend to regard my bicycle more as a tool than as a person. The relationship is rather that of a master to a servant than a friendship, partnership or love affair. If I were to give it a name it might be Leporello – or perhaps Jeeves, since I probably identify slightly more with Wodehouse's effete, foppish Bertie Wooster than the philandering Don Giovanni of Mozart's opera. Besides, I haven't yet learnt how to swear in Italian.

'Mine is called Rosie,' says Klompjes.

'Why?'

'In Holland a bicycle is sometimes called a *stalen ros*, which means "steel horse". *Ros* is Dutch slang for "horse". I call her *Rosie* because I want the name to sound feminine.'

'Good idea!' I reply, turning back to my book.

Not all of the exhibit is brilliant, of course, but even at its bleakest, one is never very far away from some redeeming detail or innuendo. Subcontinental culture may not reinvent itself at every epoch, as Western culture tries to, but the imagination of aesthetics here is ever at work, varying themes, spinning out experimentation on subconscious levels, and producing an art based on life, rather than mere "ars gratia artis".

With his posterior insulated from the road's abominable surface by leaf springs and an upholstered seat, Mr Bach rode on the same buses that deafened me with their horns, poisoned me with their exhaust, covered me in soot and regularly forced me into the ditch. It is hardly surprising therefore that his memories of the Grand Trunk Road are considerably more sentimental than both mine and those of Jerry and Su (who on their motorbike would have been subjected to much the same experience as I was). I found the scenery of the Gangetic Plain insufferably dull. Life on the road is cheap; thousands meet their death every year on Kipling's 'River of Life' and the majority of those who eke out an existence alongside it are trapped in poverty and dehumanised by long, tedious and brutal hours spent in the fields, factories, sweatshops and mines that it serves. There is nothing noble or romantic or attractive about such penury. If I were to dedicate an entire book to the subject, *The Grand Trunk Road Is Shit* would make an admirable title.

When we walk our bicycles out to the road in the cool air of the following morning, the sky to the west is at last clear and Nanga Parbat is exposed in all its glory, the morning sunshine reflected off the dazzling snows of the summit. It is a thrilling sight; marvels such as the Masjed-e Emam, the Golden Temple and even the Taj Mahal all pale into insignificance next to this awesome killer mountain, so much older, vaster, more magnificent and infinitely more permanent than any of mankind's puny endeavours.

*

Lower average speeds beyond Gilgit are indicative that the cycling is becoming harder work in the thinner air. Klompjes stops to photograph a roadside memorial to the workers who died during the construction of the Karakoram Highway. 'I think it's important,' she says. 'Just think, they died so people like us could make this journey.'

So I do give the matter some thought. No names or numbers are mentioned. Many workers (particularly the Chinese contingent) would have died far from home.

The Hunza Valley emerges as a startling clamour of colour against a sepia background. Apricots, plums, apples, melons, maize and wheat are grown in irrigated fields. Karimabad, clambering up a mountainside on a steep staircase of terraces, is overshadowed on all sides by vertical cliffs whose icebound summits, including that of the 7,790-metre giant Rakaposhi, are swallowed up by cloud. On the veranda of the Hilltop Hotel I plough on with *The Grand Trunk Road from the Front Seat* to the sounds of village children at play, the bleating of goats, the cawing of crows, the occasional faint *beep* from the road, the clatter of a metal pail as a woman washes her clothes, the sighing of the wind in the poplars, and a snuffle from Klompjes' congested nose as she writes up her diary.

We breakfast the following day on cornflakes, milk and chopped banana in our room. There is usually little conversation to illuminate these early repasts, both of us still in the process of waking up and mentally preparing ourselves for the rigours of the day ahead. I am still uneasily pondering the allegorical implications of a dream in which I was sitting a written exam and all the other entrants were scribbling busily while I was still reading through the questions.

'Ugh! I'm not eating that!' One of the bananas is a mushy dark brown.

'Chris! It's only bruised at the top! Eat it up! You're acting like a spoilt child!'

'Leave it out, Klompjes – I'm a sick man!'

'Yes, I know. And men always behave badly when they are sick, like little children!'

When I stop to take off my overcoat halfway up the long, steep climb out of Ganesh, my legs turn to jelly, a mist develops in front of my eyes and I am overcome by giddiness. Abruptly, I sit down.

'Are you all right?' asks Klompjes.

'No. I feel sick.'

'That is because you eat too much before you cycle. Your stomach can't manage.'

I suspect that the colossal expenditure of energy in the thinner air at heights of over seven thousand feet combined with the heavy cold that has afflicted me for the past two or three days are more valid reasons for the sudden attack of dizziness.

'I think it's because you made me eat that disgusting banana.'

Her concern evaporates immediately. 'Don't be so silly!'

*

Terraced plantations separated by dry-stone walls tumble down to the river in Passu, a tiny village situated between the encroaching tongues of the Passu and Batura glaciers. Partially concealed by swirling banks of mist, there is something faintly sinister in the slender, tapering summits of the surrounding mountains; they resemble the conical hats worn by a coven of witches or an assembly of the Klu-Klux-Klan. The village people are very friendly; some of the men have abandoned the omnipresent shalwar qamiz in favour of conventional jackets and trousers and the women are no longer afraid to expose their faces or even to speak to us. An old lady informs us that her yaks' milk is much better than sheep's milk and that tomorrow's weather will be fine.

I hope she's right.

Beyond Passu the upstart road, pockmarked and broken in several places following landslides, chisels its way through a narrow gorge of towering shale and limestone. The Karakorams (a word meaning 'black, crumbling rock') are aptly named; beset by falling rocks and scree, the asphalt occasionally disappears entirely and the Karakoram Highway mingles seamlessly with the surrounding rubble. Sheer cliff faces loom over us, plunging the valley into shadow and blotting out much of the sky, and steep fans of scree appear ready to engulf us at a moment's notice. Signs warn of further rockfalls and several stretches of the road are narrow enough to be classified as single-track. The waters of the Hunza River have become shallow and turbulent, racing over the stony riverbed as if eager to escape the desolation. The occasional lone lorry, usually a hardy Bedford, bounces and sways past us, creaking on overloaded springs, the steady drone of its engine audible from afar in the silent, treeless valley.

Although there is constant sunshine and plenty of blue sky, the clouds have continued to accumulate around the peaks. Great galleons of cumulus, rudderless and drifting on thermal currents, have run aground and are tearing themselves to pieces on the rocks. Occasionally a portion of wreckage will drift away to show us what we have been missing and the shining spire of a vast natural cathedral is dramatically exposed, delivering a summons far more powerful than any church, temple or mosque to give thanks to who or whatever is responsible for the wonders of creation.

Near Khyber groups of workmen are walking along the road carrying shovels. Most of them raise their hands in friendly acknowledgement of us, and in the village itself even the women (who are unveiled) smile and call out to us, greetings that possess all the sincerity I found lacking in some other areas of the subcontinent. At altitudes in excess of 2,500 metres the cycling has become a severe, lung-heaving slog, and I'm so breathless that I can only raise my hand and return their smiles, rendered speechless by altitude and exertion. For the past eleven months the heat has been such that I have invariably sought shade in which to rest, but the climate has changed. Somewhere north of Peshawar ceiling fans ceased to be de rigueur in hotel rooms and when at length we stop – panting and with our tongues hanging out – for a much-needed break and to eat our bars of chocolate, it is only after we have found a patch of roadside warmed by sunshine.

'My Dad says mountains get in the way of the view,' gasps Klompjes, who didn't see her first 'mountains' (Dover's famous white cliffs) until she was twenty-one. She is thinking of applying for a job as a tour guide with one of the large Dutch touring companies when she returns home.

'Do you enjoy working with people?' I ask her.

'I think I'm good with people. Don't you?'

'I can't say I've noticed especially.'

'I'm good with *you*!' She smiles suddenly and with overbearing sweetness, as if to prove the point.

'No you aren't! You called me a dummy yesterday when I left my bag behind at reception.'

'Well you were! It's good I check that people don't leave things behind, and I call you a dummy so you don't forget next time!'

'That's all very well, but if I'd been in your tour group I'd have complained to your manager and you'd have been sacked!' I still haven't formulated any long-term plans and the thought depresses me. A return to a routine involving a telephone, a computer screen and the confines of four walls holds little appeal.

'Maybe you'll get married and have children.'

'Possibly. Who knows?'

'I don't think I will ever get married. I never find the right man,' she says sadly.

'Perhaps you're trying too hard to find perfection.'

'It's not that. Every time I really like someone they don't like me. And if someone falls in love with me, I don't like them!'

Chapter Eighteen
Over the Top

'Hey, peanut-head!' Klompjes addresses me irreverently. 'I've been on the road for exactly one year today. Aren't you going to congratulate me?'

The first of May has just dawned over Sost and at nine o'clock the border will be opening for the first time in six months.

'I thought you left home on the eighth.'

'The eighth of *June* is my birthday, you dummy.'

'Ah... I see. Congratulations then! But the fifth* is a very special day too, you know.'

'Yes. It's *Bevrijdingsdag.*'

'I beg your pardon?'

'Liberation Day.'

'No, far more significant than that! It will be exactly a year since I left London.'

During the two-and-a-half-day crossing of the bleak, high-altitude no man's land between Pakistan and China there will be neither food nor water, nor accommodation. As we leave the Mountain Refuge Inn on bicycles laden with extra provender and drinking water, it strikes me – not for the first time – that the more weight we carry the more energy we'll use up, and the more we'll therefore need to eat and drink. A substantial crowd of local tradesmen and foreign travellers has already gathered in the compound where customs and immigration formalities are carried out, but as the only two cyclists present we are given priority over those travelling to Tashkurgan by bus and everything goes swimmingly until we reach the checkpoint at Dih, where I discover that the bar-end gear shifter I replaced in Rawalpindi has worked itself loose. When I tighten it, the blasted thing jams.

The timing of this setback is exquisite. When the shifter jammed for the first time on the Grand Trunk Road to leave me with only half of my gears I

*We got a little mixed-up here. I was referring to the 5th June; the liberation of Holland is celebrated on the 5th May.

191

had coped adequately in the lowlands of the Gangetic Plain and the Punjab until I was able to fit a new one in Rawalpindi. The Karakoram and Pamir mountain ranges, however, are a different matter entirely; unless I can somehow resolve the problem I will have to continue the ascent to the 4,700-metre Khunjerab Pass using only the three gears on the chain-set.

I unhook the panniers, turn the bicycle upside down and take the shifter apart. Then I put it back together and replace the cable, swearing continuously while Klompjes busies herself making Marmite sandwiches. When you have just been let down by something upon which you have invested a considerable sum of money and upon which you depend entirely, filthy language isn't only entirely justified but necessary. By the time I've finished I can get only two out of the eight gears available on the rear-wheel gear cluster and I'm in no mood for Marmite sandwiches, appetite usually being the first thing to go in a crisis – along with my patience; machines, particularly expensive ones, ought to do what they're damn-well told. 'It's almost as if someone is *testing* me,' I rave bitterly. *'Back on the Grand Trunk Road he had it too easy, so let's f**k up his gears again and see how he gets on in the mountains!'*

Since it is highly unlikely that Chinese visa regulations will allow me sufficient time to wait for replacement shifters to be sent over from the UK, I can only pray that the road to Beijing will be flat and windless. Some hope. China dwarfs even India and the prospect of cycling all the way across the world's third-largest country from the Khunjerab Pass to the Black Dragon River is daunting enough even with a full range of gears at my disposal. I imagine that cycling in the western half of China might be a little like crossing Iran but without the immaculate road surfaces: searing heat, dust, headwinds, and a harsh backdrop of desert and mountains.

Comparing reality with the pictures conjured up by one's imagination is one of the enduring fascinations of travel. The crossing of China by bicycle won't be easy and it may prove to be impossible, but how do you know that anything is impossible unless you attempt it? This journey has taught me just how wonderfully *possible* everything is; all of my principal fears prior to leaving home have thus far been unjustified and pretty well everything I've tried has come off. If I'm looking for omens, what better than my floating candle's miraculous escape from the boat in Varanasi?

The air becomes distinctly colder and thinner as we progress up a sterile, desolate valley of ash-coloured rubble. Perpendicular rock faces emerge from treacherously unstable banks of scree, the veins of snow and ice on their upper reaches merging with the pale sky. Deprived of the appropriate gear ratios, my power isn't being utilised to its best effect but we are faced by gradients that are long rather than steep, and crucially, the wind has remained behind us. Despite a few awkward moments, the dearth of gears at my disposal is never critical and I decide that I'm going to cycle into China even if I have to walk the final, steepest ten miles to the pass. When the road – the only evidence that anyone has been here before us – and the river converge, squeezed together by vertical walls plunging from dizzying heights to the valley floor, I take the opportunity to refill our bottles with icy river water, at last finding a use for the expensive (and heavy) water filter I've lugged over so many thousands of miles.

By the time we reach the abandoned checkpoint at Koksil we have gained a breathtaking 1,500 metres in height since leaving Sost and are in a state of near-collapse. The rooms are bare and cheerless and the floors covered in rubbish, but the walls and roof will provide an effective barrier to the wind and any rain or snow that might fall during the night. We put on extra layers of clothing with which to combat the bitter cold and lay out our mats and sleeping bags. Klompjes tidies up the rubbish while I experiment with the tension of the gear cable, and after a while I find that I can coax as many as fifteen gear ratios out of the full complement of twenty-four. Although the situation remains far from ideal, I know now that I'll manage somehow. Feeling that an immense burden has been lifted from me, I apologise for my vile language earlier on.

'Don't be so silly!' says Klompjes, whose own language can be quite colourful.

We cook ourselves a tasty dinner of pasta with garlic, onions, tomatoes, tuna and green chillies, eating it straight from the saucepans in the light of the candles that she had the foresight to bring.

*

Rather as if one were sitting comfortably at home in front of a roaring log fire with a glass of port instead of in a freezing concrete cell contemplating the ascent to a 4,700-metre pass, Klompjes, who for once is first up in the morning, cheerfully reports that it is snowing.

After the painfully cold, finger-numbing experience of washing up and filtering more water from the river, we set off up the final ten miles of hairpin bends that separate us from the pass. Blizzards have been known to occur as late as June and the weather is unlikely to improve as we gain height.

Following forty minutes of steep climbing we stop to rest, the rarefied air making our lungs gasp and heave. An eerie silence has enveloped the watching mountains, all but the closest slopes of which have been concealed entirely by snow-laden cloud. It is still snowing steadily, but thus far the road has remained clear and with neither of us suffering from cold or any preliminary signs of altitude sickness, I'm optimistic that we'll make it to the top within a couple of hours.

Further up, however, whole stretches of asphalt have been covered and we are forced to dismount and push. Icicles have formed on the visor of my helmet, I have registered that my boots aren't waterproof and the snowflakes are continuing to fall. Klompjes suggests turning back, but we haven't enough supplies of food to spend another night at Koksil and a return to Sost is out of the question because our Pakistani visas have expired. Under the circumstances there is little alternative but to press on. I'm still confident that we'll make it to the pass even if we have to push the bicycles all the way, so when the only vehicle we've seen all morning, an ancient blue jeep pick-up, wheezes towards us with a couple of yaks in the back, we reject the offer of a ride.

Compacted snow and ice are nevertheless becoming wedged between Rosie's tyres and mudguards, and before long it is impossible for Klompjes even to push her bicycle. We stumble round a bend to find the jeep disgorging its cargo and, loath though I am to admit failure so close to the pass, the chance of another lift might be a very long time in coming and I am beginning to sense that discretion might on this particular occasion be the better part of valour. The driver offers to take us to the pass for fifteen US dollars and Kompjes counters with an offer of five. We compromise on ten dollars and, weighed down by a sense of failure, I heave the bicycles aboard in the painful knowledge that hardest part was all but over.

The jeep whines gamely up the mountainside in low gear, the driver peering through a spider's web of cracked glass and managing somehow to navigate in the absence of wipers. The snow is becoming ever deeper, burying the land beneath a thick white quilt, obscuring contours and making it difficult at times to pick out the course of the road. The heights above and the yawning chasms below are invisible and sensed rather than seen as we lurch round the switchbacks. Although the decision to accept the lift was unquestionably the right one (it would have been impossible to manhandle the bicycles through this), the conquest of the Khunjerab Pass was to have been a highlight of the journey and defeat within a paltry five miles of victory is the bitterest of pills to swallow. I am gloomily convinced that the indestructible Alois would have slung his bicycle over his shoulders and cheerfully yomped to the top, whistling *The Hills are Alive* and *Climb Every Mountain*.

We are deposited on the pass near a flashy scarlet four-wheel-drive pick-up with tinted windows from which a Chinese man is taking several pictures, including two or three snaps of a beleaguered Klompjes as she staggers through the blizzard towards China, dragging a recalcitrant Rosie through the snow. She has reported that her rear brakes have iced up and are no longer working, and it has become apparent to both of us that losing height in these conditions is scarcely going to be any easier than gaining it, so when the pick-up draws alongside us and we are offered a lift we have little difficulty in accepting it.

Because there is room inside the extended cabin only for one extra passenger, I volunteer to join the bicycles in the exposed cargo area behind. Assuming the foetal position to keep out of the icy blast of the wind, I try to make myself as small as possible. A group of shaggy, double-humped Bactrian camels is briefly discernible galloping along the road in front of the car amongst the swirling snowflakes. Within five minutes I am shivering uncontrollably and by the time we reach the Chinese checkpoint at Pirali an interminable ten minutes later I am frozen to the marrow. Fortunately, however, one of the passengers (a policeman who must have hitched a ride to the pass) disembarks, leaving a space for me on the back seat.

A long descent at last leaves the impenetrable, snow-laden clouds behind and we find ourselves unexpectedly crossing a spacious, grassy plateau. The shining domes of the Pamirs have replaced the saw-toothed ridges and tapering steeples of the Karakorams, and the monochrome, shadowy corridors on the Pakistani side have given way to light and colour and space, luminous, airy vistas of green, beige, white and blue. The pasture supports yaks, donkeys, sheep and the longhaired Bactrian camels that became a familiar sight when I was driving in Kazakhstan. Some rather wild looking Tajik or Kirghiz herdsmen can occasionally be seen patrolling the steppe on horseback.

Jubilation at having entered China is tempered by regret at the unsatisfactory manner of our arrival and for a while I wrestle with my conscience. There is no question that cycling has once again become possible, but I can't stop shivering and I'm far from convinced that I'm in any fit state to get on a bicycle. I need a hot bath, hot food and drink, and plenty of rest. Less puritanical, Klompjes appears to be content to relax and watch the landscape speeding by. Best perhaps to swallow my pride and accept the lift as far as Tashkurgan, where I'll be able to rest up for a day or two in a hotel if necessary.

At the Ice Mountain Hotel in Tashkurgan there is no hot water and nowhere to hang our clothes, I can't understand a thing anyone says, the toilet smells, and Klompjes – a great one for shutting the stable door – takes me to task for having failed to negotiate a lower price for the room (the Dutch reputation for parsimony is well founded). Using chopsticks in the gloomy restaurant next door is such a painfully slow process that we rather shamefacedly ask for spoons, and the 'noodles with meat' might more equitably have been described on the menu as 'noodles with gristle'.

After dinner we take an exploratory stroll down the single asphalt street. The buildings, shabby rectangular boxes, are uncompromising in their ugliness and powerfully reminiscent of Stalinist eyesores in rural Russia. Reports of police brutality in Tibet and the regular and arbitrary imprisonment and execution of political opponents throughout the People's Republic of China have engendered much the same sense of unease that afflicted me upon entering Iran – even though my experiences in that country taught me that however repulsive the regime, the people it abuses and intimidates are no less welcoming than anywhere else.

Four young Tajik women have dressed for a party, their high heels, figure-hugging clothes and lipstick coming as a shock after the austerity of Pakistan. An older woman gargles noisily and a great globule of phlegm crash-lands on the pavement with a resounding splat; that was even more shocking. I feel dismally cold and quite unable to function in this alien land. Even the food has failed to thaw out my frozen inner core and I am still shivering violently when I get into bed.

*

During the eighteenth and nineteenth centuries Russia and China annexed vast chunks of Turkestan, an immense area of Central Asia inhabited by Kazakhs, Uzbeks, Turkmens, Tajiks, Kirgyz and Uighurs. These Turkic Muslim peoples all regained their freedom following the disintegration of the Soviet Union in 1991 – with the sole exception of their Uighur cousins who remained trapped inside Communist China.

Cut off from the North, West and South by some of the mightiest mountain ranges in the world and from the East by one of the planet's greatest deserts, Xinjiang, a Chinese word meaning 'New Territories', is China's Wild West and one of the most inaccessible places on earth. The largest and most westerly province of the Peoples' Republic of China has also been known by the names of Sinkiang, Ughuristan, Ughuria, Tartary, Chinese Turkestan and Chinese Central Asia, reflecting a chequered history and perhaps something of an identity crisis. Despite occupying an area roughly equivalent in size to Western Europe, its mountains, deserts and steppe are home to a mere eighteen million people, Uighurs and Han Chinese mingling with smaller numbers of nomadic Tajiks, Kazakhs, Kirghiz and Uzbeks.

The Uighurs, who form the largest ethnic group in Xinjiang, significantly prefer to call their motherland East Turkestan, indicating a greater affinity with the Turkic Muslim lands that extend for thousands of miles westwards across Central Asia as far as the Caspian Sea than with their Marxist rulers over two thousand miles away to the east. Coal, gas, oil and a wealth of minerals exist in the region, however, and Communist China hasn't been prepared to countenance any movement towards an independent Uighur state. A policy of Han Chinese infiltration has been implemented to render impracticable any ideas of independence and at the same time bolster Beijing's tenuous legitimacy to exploit Xinjiang's mineral wealth. Waves of Han Chinese settlers have been lured across the Gobi Desert by the promise of jobs and high wages, reducing the Uighur percentage of Xinjiang's population from ninety per cent in 1949 to below fifty per cent at the turn of the millennium.

With the Han Chinese today numbering almost half of Xinjiang's total population, the disenfranchised Uighurs have become a minority in their own land, suffering a similar (albeit considerably less public) fate to that endured by the Tibetans. While Han Chinese settlers grow fat on the immense wealth that lies beneath the shifting sands of the Taklamakan Desert, most of Xinjiang's original tenants scrape out an existence as herdsmen and farmers. Their language (a derivative of Turkish), culture and religion are under siege; Chinese officials have closed down mosques and traditional Islamic schools, and devotional literature has been confiscated during regular crackdowns on 'illegal' religious activities. The overwhelming majority of books published in Xinjiang are in Mandarin and the few Uighurs able to afford higher education are unable to profit from it because classes are conducted in Chinese. Unable to speak Chinese and therefore unable to learn, they fall well short of the minimum qualifications required for the better jobs and face the prospect of becoming as marginalised in their own land as the Australian Aboriginals and the American Indians.

In practice there is precious little autonomy in the Xinjiang Uighur Autonomous Region. Separatist demonstrations in Kashgar and Urumqi were brutally suppressed in 1993 and thirty Muslim nationalists accused of 'openly agitating against government officials' were executed in January 1997 following riots in Yining. The Chinese don't mess around when 'the unity of the motherland' is placed in jeopardy. Incongruously, even the sun rises and sets to Beijing Time, several time zones east.

Although the shivers finally departed sometime during the night, Tashkurgan is sufficiently elevated at 3,200 metres to be decidedly chilly in early May and we escape the grim confines of the Ice Mountain Hotel wearing overcoats and gloves. The empty road bisects a broad, gleaming swathe of pasture crossed by sparkling brooks. High, drifting clouds in the vast, azure sky speckle the glowing beige slopes of mountain ranges with darker areas of shadow, like doubt invading a restless mind. Distant plumes of smoke indicate the presence of factories and settlements on the plain. Occasional roadside buildings are an uneasy blend of Muslim and Marxist, small traditional constructions made of baked mud juxtaposed with rectangular white-tiled monstrosities that remind me of public urinals. Two women wave at us.

'What ugly dresses!' remarks Klompjes.

'I didn't notice their dresses, only their smiles.'

'I notice everything!'

When two large dogs ambush us, barking and snarling, she wisely slows down. I ride straight at one of her pursuers and it runs off, but when it comes round in a circle for a second attack I throw down the bicycle. That dogs can sense fear is well documented, but they can also sense fury and most are cowards.

No handy rocks or stones available, so I vent my anger by turning the air blue and flinging handfuls of roadside grit at them, and by the time a woman emerges from a nearby mud-brick hovel to investigate the commotion they are in full retreat. I hurl a parting stone in their direction (*found one at last!*), glare at the woman, retrieve my bicycle from the roadside dust, and pedal off reflecting that the poverty of these remote farming communities, the savagery of the dogs, the Turkic physiognomy of the people and the empty grandeur of the landscape are all powerfully reminiscent of the Eastern Anatolian Plateau.

As the road begins to climb once more, gradually but inexorably towards the four-thousand-metre Subash Plateau, the terrain reverts from pasture to rocks and rubble. Telegraph poles march into the distance alongside a broad, stony, and for the most part dry, riverbed. To either side bald foothills, the colour of milky tea, rise to meet serried ranks of white cones. Every bend in the road and brow of a hill fuels the illusion that we might at last be approaching the pass but these are precursors only of further tests of our heaving lungs and aching legs. During regular breaks from the slog we refresh ourselves with water and Marmite sandwiches. Riven by glaciers, trailing plumes of cloud and looking like a gigantic iced bun, the dome of the 7,546-metre giant Muztagh Ata (Turkic for 'Father of Ice Mountains') towers above the rubble-strewn slopes on our right.

When we finally make the pass we are met by a stupendous view. Ahead of us a pewter sky is reclining upon a chain of snow-capped mountains dominated by the 7,719-metre Mount Kongur. The road can intermittently be seen zigzagging its way down the mountainside and, tiny and distant, tracing a path through the pasture in the wide valley far below.

*

Following a sub-zero night in a yurt* on the shore of Lake Karakul we set off under a cloudless sky fortified only by the last of our cornflakes mixed with a watery milk-powder solution which constituted a cold, soggy, depressing mush – even with ancient Iranian raisins added to perk it up a bit. After a couple of hours of exhilarating, gravity-assisted cycling on an empty road that winds its way down a valley, Klompjes (rather cheekily in my opinion) stops outside an isolated mud building to beg a cup of tea.

To my considerable surprise we are invited in. The single large room (which, like the traditional yurt dwellings, combines living area, bedroom and kitchen) is crowded with at least a dozen people of all ages, eating, drinking and chatting. I take my seat on the floor next to a baby goat placed in a cardboard box, its

*Traditional circular tent-like dwelling made from canvas or animal skins stretched over a wooden frame. Still used by the nomadic peoples of Central Asia.

head sticking inquisitively out from the jacket that has been wrapped around it. We are given large bowls containing pieces of bread floating in salty tea. The laughter and banter are incomprehensible, but as we examine our surroundings someone's eyes might meet ours and there is always an accompanying smile.

The sensation of space upon the broad plateaus and in the high, wide valleys of the Pamirs is intoxicating. The progress of the road has been more serene than in Pakistan, where it was constantly walled in and obstructed, forced by the vertical terrain to twist and loop and backtrack. When we enter the Ghez Canyon, however, mountain walls once again rise sheer and close and snowmelt races over a stony riverbed. The air has become much warmer and I estimate that during the preceding two hours of rapid downhill cycling we must have lost well over a thousand metres in altitude. For the past few weeks height has sometimes been a more relevant gauge of our progress than distance, and for the umpteenth time I regret not having thought to include an altimeter in my equipment.

Upal, only thirty miles from Kashgar and the first settlement of any size since Tashkurgan, marks the point at which the foothills of the Pamirs finally sink into the sands of the Taklamakan. The Turks migrated westwards from these areas of Central Asia from the sixth century, and although some of the villagers possess the high cheekbones that denote Mongolian descent, others wouldn't look out of place in Istanbul. Their dress is oddly old-fashioned to my eyes, many of the men wearing trousers and long-sleeved shirts or shabby suits with flat caps, making me think of a 1930s football crowd somewhere in the north of England – Accrington Stanley versus Bradford Park Avenue, perhaps. The Muslim faith practised in this region is plainly a gentler, more moderate version than the Iranian and Pakistani variety, for the women aren't afraid to take pride in their appearance or to greet a stranger. They wear skirts of varying lengths and every conceivable colour and pattern, some made of thin, almost transparent chiffon or nylon, and they are even permitted to ride bicycles. After a meal of *lamian*, the local staple of noodles with finely diced beef or lamb and spicy vegetables, a cheerful lady shows us to a Spartan five-bed dormitory next to the mosque. There is nowhere to wash and the toilet is the well-used patch of waste ground round the back, but for only ten yuan per bed, what can you expect?

Shops, cafés and businesses are compelled by the anomaly of Beijing Time to open at the crack of dawn and people are up early. Beyond the village limits a gale is picking up sand from the desert and flinging it across the road, stinging our faces and causing us to close our eyes. Is this the reception we can expect from the Taklamakan? We are forced by the bars of sand that have settled upon the asphalt to dismount and push. It is a fearsome demonstration of one of the hazards we can anticipate during the forthcoming weeks, but within minutes the desert turns from sand to shingle and the road obligingly changes direction so that the wind is at our backs.

At a café in a village I ask for a Cola. Coke, Pepsi or the locally produced Future-Cola will do, but they look blank. Coca-Cola must be the most widely known brand in the world and they certainly have it in China, so why don't they understand? Evidently I'm not pronouncing it in the right way. In India I had the same problem ordering *curd*, the word Indians fondly imagine is English for yoghurt; time after time I failed to make myself understood, whichever way I pronounced this unassuming but bloody-minded little monosyllable. After several weeks in China and much frustration I was to discover that *Cola* is in fact pronounced *colour* but with the stress placed on the second syllable instead of the first, but in the absence of this information we are obliged to settle for green tea, pouring it from a kettle into small bowls. At other tables people are devouring dumplings with their tea, and knots of inquisitive locals have gathered to examine the bicycles. Convoys of donkeys and horses are trotting past in the direction of Kashgar drawing single-axle wooden carts heavily laden with tree-trunks. The local taxis are two-axle carts, sometimes with a little canopy overhead, also drawn by donkeys or horses. The drivers nudge their animals along by regularly thwacking them across the back or the rump with a stick.

The road becomes flanked by poplars as we approach Kashgar, irrigation channels providing the necessary moisture to sustain crops and pasture. Several of the timber-laden carts we saw earlier are queuing outside the Xinjiang Factory for Musical Instruments. On the city's outskirts the road broadens to accommodate six lanes of traffic, undivided by any central reservation; it is like cycling down an airstrip. Large buildings to either side are guarded by green-uniformed soldiers or policemen, and a group of Han Chinese policemen is jogging briskly along the opposite pavement. Fitness is clearly prized by the Chinese, and rightly so. I've never been able to take pot-bellied policemen seriously – how are they going to chase and apprehend miscreants if they are overweight and unfit?

*

In Kashgar, for two millennia an important trading post on the Silk Road, ancient Uighur traditions collide head-on with the disciplines imposed by Communist China. Modern Kashgar is order and symmetry: wide, level boulevards and pavements, spacious squares, and intersections controlled by traffic lights. Multi-storey concrete office blocks and department stores identified by Chinese characters line tiled, patterned pavements regularly furnished with public telephones and even litterbins. Everything is broad, smooth and straight, and just in case anyone should forget that they are in the People's Republic of China, a gigantic statue of Chairman Mao towers over People's Park.

Uighurs, Uzbeks, Kazakhs, Kirghiz and Tajiks may mingle with Han Chinese on these ample pavements but their culture, language and religion are worlds apart, and only two blocks away life revolves once again around the mosque and the bazaar. Broad boulevards have reverted to narrow and winding lanes, pavements are uneven or non-existent, and the buildings, moulded out of mud instead of concrete, are modest in size and pleasantly asymmetrical. The twenty-first-century public telephones and litterbins have disappeared and games of pool are being played on pavement tables. Farriers, cartwrights, tailors, cobblers, hatters and carpenters ply their ancient trades to meet the demands exacted by a way of life that has changed little for centuries. Taxis and lurid pink minibuses have been replaced by donkey carts, and bicycles outnumber cars. A mild pong of animal dung mingles with the smell of charcoal smoke from barbecuing kebabs and the odour of savoury sheep's head and gonad of goat being boiled at stalls. One senses that the Han Chinese presence is every bit as dislocating here as Beijing Time.

The region's mercantile history is alive and well and thriving at the world-famous Sunday Market, the most overt celebration of traditional Kashgar. After a ride across town on a donkey cart we join the throngs of people converging on the livestock market to browse, barter and bargain. How could these people ever have embraced Marxist Communism? The quest for the best deal is evidently deeply ingrained in the Kashgari soul. Hundreds of sheep with protruding, fatty buttocks that look comically human, cows, horses and donkeys have been assembled to await buyers. Bearded ancients presiding over huge steaming woks placed over wood fires on the periphery of the enclosure appear to be doing a brisk trade, for the nearby tables and benches are packed with diners.

The bustling main bazaar is one of the biggest and most famous in Asia, but although its sheer size and the variety of goods available are indeed impressive, I've already wandered around so many Asian bazaars in recent months that it has little impact. More interesting is the ethnic diversity of the predominantly Central Asian faces in the jostling crowds and the variety and colour of dress on display, particularly coming so soon after the drab hegemony of the Pakistani Shalwar Qamiz. Every imaginable size and shape of hat is worn, from flat caps and skullcaps to trilbies, elaborately decorated pillboxes, and tall, fur-lined affairs. Most (but not all) of the women are wearing headscarves.

We toast our arrival at the end of the Karakoram Highway with bottles of excellent Chinese beer (our first since Amritsar) at a table outside one of the plethora of small restaurants in the Old City. It takes time to adapt to a new country's culture, language, people, currency, food and (in this particular instance) its eating utensils, but as the waiters bring us a feast of fried naan with meat, shish kebab, cucumber in sauce, and noodle soup ordered from a number of traders cooking at tiny mobile street stalls, I feel for the first time that I've really arrived – if not in China then at least in East Turkestan. I'm even beginning to get the hang of eating with chopsticks.

Chapter Nineteen
Sand and Noodles

A six-lane concrete freeway abruptly metamorphoses to corrugated two-lane asphalt as we leave Kashgar. Buses and taxis have given way to tractors and donkey carts, and tiled city pavements have been superseded by columns of poplars and mud-brick walls. Fields of maize and wheat eventually peter out into scrub, and after rising steadily towards a chain of low, biscuit-coloured mountains, the road descends, we gather speed and the landscape empties. On our left rise the barren foothills of the Tien Shan, and on the right the desert, a boundless, flat expanse of pebbles, shingle and grey sand, stretches southwards to merge into haze and a milky sky.

At Kashagar the Silk Road (never actually a single road but several organised caravan routes whose paths were determined principally by natural obstacles) forks in order to circumvent the waterless sand and shingle wastes of a desert the size of France and one of the most inhospitable in the world. Although my natural inclination was to follow the more remote, southerly branch that leads to Lanzhou via Hotan, Golmud and Xining, uncertainty about the number of visa extensions I'll be allowed by the Chinese has forced me for once to opt for the flatter, quicker looking alternative. Reputedly the better road, the northern arm follows the new railway link between Kashgar and Urumqi along the northern periphery of the Taklamakan to Korla and Turpan before eventually making its way to Lanzhou via a corner of the Gobi Desert and the Hexi Corridor.

Eight hundred miles of sand, gravel and rocky waste will have to be crossed before we reach the sweltering oasis city of Turpan. *Taklamakan* is an Uighur word meaning 'you go in but you don't come out' and the desert is a place of sinister repute. Local legend has it that these desolate wastes are inhabited by evil spirits which call out to travellers, luring them off the marked routes to their deaths just as the Sirens of Greek mythology lured sailors onto the rocks. Resist their calls and the demons would unleash the *Kara Buran* or 'Black Hurricane', a blinding, stinging, disorientating fog of airborne sand and shingle.

Temperatures in the Tarim Basin vary from an unbearable fifty degrees Celsius in the summer months to an equally hellish minus forty during the winter.

Ramshackle groups of transport cafés, tyre changers and automotive repair shops, the modern caravanserai, appear every so often to provide itinerants with a temporary refuge from the emptiness. We receive noodles, spicy diced meat and vegetables, bagels, bowls of green tea and much benign incomprehension from the Uighur oasis dwellers. The language barrier is all but insurmountable and it is indicative of the area's isolation that even words of global renown such as 'WC', 'Toilet', 'Hotel' and 'Kilometres' mean nothing to them. Nevertheless, they appear delighted to accommodate us. Uighur women are eager to know our ages and if we are married and have babies, but the men, as in every other country, are more interested in our equipment. They speculatively prod my Karrimat, judicially squeeze tyres and experimentally pull at the gear-shifters, and naturally they want to know where we've come from and where we're going. Whenever we can get someone to understand that we've cycled in from Pakistan and are on our way to Turpan there is much head-shaking and friendly admiration, and my map of China is repeatedly unfolded and spread across tables. At one teahouse a man grabs my foot to examine my boot. Then he seizes my wrist so that he can look at my watch. An old lady chuckles happily whenever our eyes meet. During draughty nights spent under the road in culverts (an unpleasant new experience for Klompjes), gusts of wind blow sand into our hair, nostrils, ears and our sleeping bags.

*

'I spy with my little eye something beginning with "R".'

For three days there has been precious little to spy apart from parched desert and barren mountains. The empty road has followed the railway into hot, monochrome monotony, plotting a course between the foothills of the Tien Shan to the north and flat desert the colour of ash merging with the hazy horizon to the south. From time to time great piles of rubble, the local equivalent of diversion signs, have blocked the route and forced traffic to detour into the dust and stones. Relief has been provided only by the occasional oasis, where poplars line both sides of the road and mud walls and irrigation channels subdivide the surrounding greenery into orchards, pasture and crops. These days wealth comes from under the ground and the modern caravans plying this section of the Silk Route are light-blue Chinese-manufactured lorries, usually weighed down not with ivory, silk or spices but rather less glamorous loads of coal. We have never been in serious danger of going hungry or thirsty because grim little huddles of transport cafés, tyre repairers, workshops, teahouses and filling stations have continued to appear at intervals of approximately thirty miles.

'Road!' replies Klompjes, with minimal inspiration.

'Correct!'

'I spy with my little eye and it starts with a "B".'

'Bicycle.'

'No.'

'Bar-bag.'

'No.'

'Bottom.'

'No.'

'Boy.'

'No.'

'Bastard.'

'Yes! …No, just kidding!'

'I give up.'

'Bidon.'

'Cheat! That's not an English word.'

'What do you call it then?'

'A water bottle.'

A sore throat is preventing me from raising my voice, and because Klompjes can't hear me I have to repeat everything I say – which only makes matters worse. The strain on my larynx forces us to abandon the game and we pedal on into the desolation in silence. At a transport café surrounded only by stony emptiness, Klompjes, who likes her creature comforts, rather optimistically asks if there is a hotel in the vicinity. I'm tempted to tell her not to be so ridiculous, but we are shown to a Spartan dormitory at the back of the building. There is no shower or even a basin in which to wash and the toilet is a small patch of well-used desert, but I had been expecting to sleep out during the entire crossing of the Taklamakan.

The next day my throat feels as if it is made of sandpaper. I cycle with a streaming nose and my eyes down, concentrating on wringing every last available drop of energy from reluctant limbs and, like *Gollum* (the repulsive character in *The Lord of the Rings*), hating the sun. I feel alarmingly weak, a predicament that is in no way helped by a disastrous loss of appetite, for I have developed a violent loathing of noodles. Since every single meal since Kashgar has so far consisted of noodles with the predictable meat and vegetable accompaniment, this is akin to travelling around India unable to eat curries. Even if alternative food is on the menu we have no idea what it is or how to order it. Whereas Klompjes dispatches her food with relish, I tackle each mountain of noodles as if it is Everest, taking an age to chew before being able to swallow the nauseating tangle of slimy worms. The more I eat, the less impression I appear to be making on the bowl in front of me, and usually I leave over half of the dish uneaten.

I spend mealtimes and rest stops wondering grimly how on earth I'm going to summon sufficient strength to cycle another twenty or thirty miles to the next pit stop. I feel tetchy and morose, and above all, bone-weary. Back on the road the soreness of my throat precludes conversation and each interminable mile is covered in silence. I have lost all interest in the surroundings and I have even run out of things to think about.

The snow-capped peaks of the Tien Shan, the Mountains of Heaven, are appropriately ethereal, resembling icebergs adrift upon a sea of haze as an unexpected stretch of brand-new motorway sweeps us past the oasis town of Aksu.

'This is the end!' says Klompjes encouragingly as we rejoin the original road at a T-junction.

This is the end, my only friend, the end.

The Doors dirge reverberates around the echoing cavern that has opened up between my ears. The last time I felt as bad as this was on that stretch between Dera Ghazi Khan and Lahore, when the symptoms (streaming nose, sore throat, loss of appetite and exhaustion) had been identical. I ought to be tucked up in bed but there is no time to be ill in China.

Just as we are beginning to think about searching for somewhere to spend the night we are treated to our first taste of the *Kara Buran*. A strong, gusting wind has risen and a dense brown fog of flying sand is barring the way ahead. A filling station mercifully appears in the nick of time and we cower inside with half a dozen other people similarly caught out in the storm.

'Ask that woman if we can stay here for the night,' I urge Klompjes listlessly. The wind is stomping around in a fury outside, hissing and flinging sand and debris into the air.

'*You* ask. You have dose beeg, brown eyes.'

'But you can act the poor, helpless female.'

Neither my cow-eyes nor Klompjes' thespian skills make any impression at all on the stony heart of the Han Chinese cashier, so after waiting half an hour for the storm to blow itself out we cycle a further four miles to the next town, where there's a real hotel with a real shower and a real toilet. I haven't seen Klompjes looking so happy for ages, but barely able to find enough strength to hold myself upright, I am far too exhausted to care. 'Undress me!' I croak pathetically, proffering a steaming foot encased in a sweaty Nike sock. My limbs feel like lead and the desire just to lie down fully clothed and un-showered and go to sleep is overwhelming.

'No! You refused to put my shoes on for me so I'm not undressing you.'

'Tell me, Klompjes, did you leave the Dutch Health Service of your own accord or were you sacked?'

'I left. I got fed up with dealing with sick people.'

'So I see! And then you decided to join the PTT, an organisation more suited to your temperament.'

'Yes. We had to go on a course to teach us how to treat people. It was hell!'

'I should imagine it was! But how on earth did you pass?'

With considerable difficulty we manage to order an evening meal with rice instead of noodles to accompany the inevitable portions of diced, spicy vegetables. I find eating easier, but by God I feel tired.

I apologise for being such poor company for the last few days.

'Well, you're sick,' replies the Cycling Queen with an unexpected flash of sympathy.

*

At noon the next day we sit down to drink water on the parapet of a culvert, dangling our legs over the edge. The sheer emptiness of the landscape is the most dramatic and eloquent of statements and usually I rejoice in harsh, lonely places, but I'm still not feeling myself and I don't have the energy to find it fascinating. The infection has taken its inevitable route down from throat to lungs and all I can look forward to is the end of the day's cycling.

'What a wonderful view!' I remark. I don't think I've ever seen anything quite so sterile.

'It is very boring.'

'I don't think it's boring per se – there's just too much of it. On the Grand Trunk Road everything was green and there were plenty of trees but we got bored with that as well. Variety is essential. I'd even get bored with mountains eventually.'

'*What?* You mean you wouldn't get your camera out every time you see a snowy top?'

'No. That's why I travel – because it brings change. I cease to take my surroundings for granted. You'd get bored with anything given sufficient exposure to it. Some things more quickly than others, admittedly...'

'You mean you even get bored with me?'

'Well... um... no, because you always have the ability to surprise me!' I reply, improvising hastily.

Our accommodation at the hotel in Xinhe is almost as surprising as Klompjes. There is a palatial en suite bathroom with complementary towels, soap, sachets of shampoo, and combs and toothbrushes wrapped in sterilised envelopes. Cycling across a desert is a dirty business and the shower is wonderful.

I am beginning to appreciate things again. I must be getting better.

In the restaurant Richard Clayderman, the ubiquitous blond French pianist, is banging out something bland and soothing on a giant colour TV connected to an amplifier and speakers, and there is even a menu with an English translation.

*

A detour round the north of Korla on the seventh day since our departure from Kashgar lifts the road into the moonscape of the Tien Shan, and as well as a good deal of climbing we have to contend with a strong, gusting headwind. We relieve our feelings by swearing. Although my appetite is back to something like normal and most of my strength has returned, violent paroxysms of coughing and retching have been generating further outbursts of profanity. Unceremoniously I discharge the contents of each loaded nostril onto the road, an operation which requires skill and timing if the wind isn't to blow long, slimy entrails of what Klompjes calls *snotje* back into me. I can hear the phlegm gurgling inside my labouring lungs but worries about my health have largely been displaced by concern about the bicycle, for one of the saddle stays has sheared off. There is nothing I can do about it and the remaining stay will henceforth be subject to double the stress on the rough roads. If it should break then I'll be left without a saddle as well as half my gears – and that would make life really interesting.

We pause for some sorely needed respite at a roadside café situated halfway up a mountainside overlooking Korla. When the increase in maritime trade from the sixteenth century onwards brought about the decline of the Silk Road many of the oasis towns in the Tarim Basin fell into oblivion and were buried by the shifting sands of the Taklamakan, but the discovery in 1989 of oil beneath the desert is bringing the area back out of its isolation. A former Silk Road oasis town has become a city of three hundred thousand inhabitants, a forest of bleached, high-rise concrete split by a grid of broad, straight boulevards having sprung up to service the booming oil industry. Xinjiang's very own version of Houston or Dallas is evidently still growing, for the skyline is regularly punctured by tall cranes presiding over concrete skeletons in varying stages of construction. The harsh conditions that prevail in the Tarim Basin nevertheless ensure that the extraction of oil from an area estimated by the Chinese to contain more reserves than Kuwait is carried out only at considerable expense.

*

Most of the following day is spent struggling up interminable hills against a gusting wind in a mountainous landscape. I have developed a theory that the recent worsening of my backache is due to the sagging to the left of the saddle caused by the absence of the fractured stay, an unhealthy state of affairs that twists my pelvis and effectively makes one leg longer than the other.

Behind me, shielded from the worst of the wind, Klompjes complains that I'm going too slowly.

'You're welcome to go in front if you want to,' I shout back.

She declines the invitation.

So I'm going too slowly, am I? Turbocharged by pique, I dredge up some extra energy I didn't know I possessed and, throwing my weight forward and stomping viciously on the pedals, I bore a path onwards into the wind. When at length I risk a quick glance over my shoulder, I find to my considerable satisfaction that she has dropped far behind. With no end of the hill in sight I stop at the side of the road to wait for her and recover my breath.

At length she comes to a breathless halt alongside me. 'What are you doing? I don't like it that you don't wait for me! You were going much too fast!'

Carefully, I study the composition of her features. Stony-faced and glowering. She *isn't* joking then; in fact she's furious. Women can be the most extraordinary creatures.

'I think you've had enough for today,' I reply, having counted slowly to ten and eschewed a number of blistering retorts. 'Let's sleep out here.'

Maybe it is as well that our time together is drawing to a close. With the uneven, boulder-strewn terrain providing ample concealment, we slide into our sleeping bags.

'Chris! Look at me!' pleads Klompjes. *'Chrisja! Look at me!'*

'You'll have to sleep on the other side if you want me to face you.'

She thinks I'm still angry with her but I'm not. Honestly. I just sleep better on my right side.

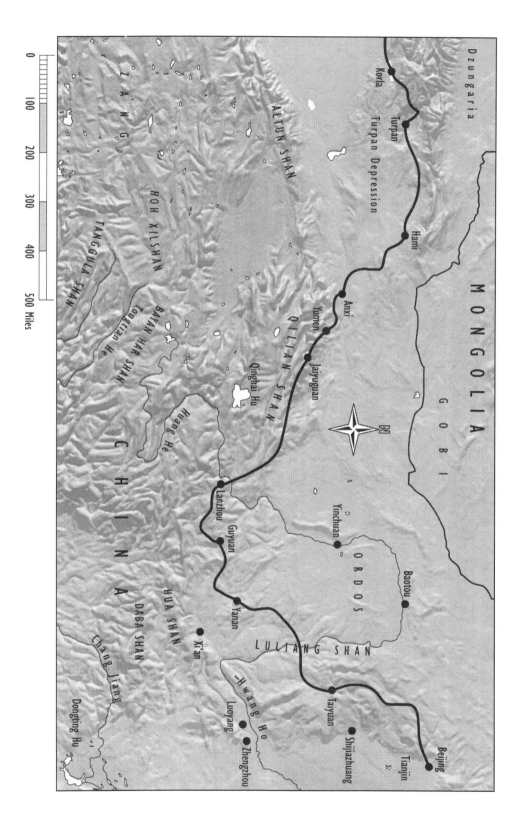

Chapter Twenty
The Lungs of the Gobi

At 154 metres below sea level and at the centre of the second-lowest depression in the world after the Dead Sea, Turpan is the plug at the bottom of the Tarim Basin and uncomfortably hot even in mid-May. The road east follows a narrow valley of unexpectedly lush vineyards squeezed between converging mountain ranges before ascending steeply and levelling out on a barren, dusty plateau. A constant headwind has caused that tiresome ache in my lower back to flare up again and is keeping my speed down to single figures.

'You have a good spirit,' the Public Security Bureau (police) officer at the visa section in Turpan had said after I'd turned down his well meant advice to take the bus at least as far as Hami. Clearly enjoying the chance to practise his English, he had warned against heat, lack of food and water, and language problems (all of which hazards I'd successfully overcome during the ten-day ride from Kashgar) but he had never mentioned the wind. There's nothing quite like a headwind to break your spirit. Klompjes called them *Kutwinds*.*

Just before I left home a thoughtful friend lent me *The Long Walk* by Slavomir Rawicz, a heroic and sometimes appalling account of the author's escape in 1941 from a prison camp in Siberia and subsequent flight on foot to India. Whether my friend had intended the book to warn or to inspire I'm not entirely sure; only four out of the original party of eight fugitives made it to freedom in India, two of them succumbing to the ravages of thirst, starvation and exhaustion somewhere here in the Gobi, where they were obliged to hunt and eat snakes to survive.

Gobi is a Mongolian word meaning 'waterless place'. The planet's northernmost and second-largest desert after the Sahara covers half a million square miles of Northern China and Mongolia, much of it averaging less than three inches of rainfall a year.

---

*This is *not* the conventional Dutch word for 'headwinds'.

We were heading into the desert (wrote Rawicz), *the extent and character of which we did not know. Had we been fully forewarned of its formidable terrors, we might have made more prudent preparations. The word Gobi was just a word to us. We hardly discussed it. (...) We were striding into the burning wastes of the Gobi waterless and with little food. None of us then knew the hell we were to meet.*

A little, but not a great deal better informed, I select a Coke and a mineral water from the fridge outside a village restaurant, where I'm given the inevitable bowl of noodles to eat.

'Where you from?' asks a Han Chinese girl of about fourteen.

'England.' I'm highly impressed by her unexpected fluency. 'Do you learn English at school?'

'Yes, very much!' she replies bashfully, not quite understanding the question.

A group of onlookers inevitably forms and clusters inquisitively around the loaded bicycle. A man picks it up experimentally and immediately drops it with an exclamation. Too heavy for him.

Too heavy for me.

The owner of the restaurant is lounging in an armchair, sagely surveying the quiet, sun-drenched road and the lines of white-tiled, single-storey buildings. Occasionally he fires a question at me and, not understanding a word, I reply with the help of sign language that I'm from *Yingguo* (England) and on my way to Beijing, but he seems happy enough with this explanation. Chickens scratch about in the dust by our feet while his wife snoozes contentedly on a nearby bed. An elderly gentleman sits down at my table and shows me his collection of coins. I think he wants to sell them to me, but I have no idea of their worth so how can I possibly make him an offer? Instead I examine them dutifully and nod appreciatively as I hand each one back.

Reinvigorated, I cycle on into the wind, straining at the pedals and missing Klompjes. She attached her Dutch key ring with its dangling pair of miniature wooden clogs (*klompjes*) to the zip on my bar-bag as a keepsake and the clacking noise they make, particularly when I stand on the pedals and the bicycle leans from side to side, are a constant reminder of her.

During a relaxing two days in Turpan we'd toasted the end of her cycling trip with bottles of chilled Chinese beer, traded emails with absent friends and dined under flashing neon signs at pavement cafés. Soothing female Chinese voices emanated from hidden loudspeakers in pedestrian arcades overhung with grapevine trellises, which were not only attractive but also provided welcome shade from the fierce sunshine in China's hottest city, a major producer of wine and raisins. After replacing the chain and cassette for what I hoped would be the last time, I returned to our room on the eve of my departure to find Klompjes weeping silently. Ten unforgettable weeks together were about to come to an end. The Dutch Cycling Queen had been splendid, robust company and, humbled and considerably moved by her tears, I held her close. If love had any foundation in logic I'd surely be in love with her.

In the afternoon the wind eases and I manage to pick up some speed. Miniature dust cyclones are dancing across the powdery surface of the desert and a haze all but conceals the rugged brown mountain ranges to either side. Distant rows of poplars denote the presence of an oasis, and chimneys spouting flame and phalanxes of 'nodding donkeys' periodically bear witness to the reserves of oil and gas that lie beneath the sands. The friendly woman at a café in a small oasis town offers to cook me a meal but as I'm not particularly hungry and the wind has dropped, I resolve to carry on for a few more miles and eat out in the desert instead.

As I lay out my Karrimat and sleeping bag an hour later in a culvert beneath the road, weighting them with rocks to prevent them from being blown away, I reflect that the decision to press on wasn't one of my better ones. The sudden return of the wind reduced my speed to a paltry 5 mph for the final half hour of the day and a gale is now howling through the narrow culvert, covering the pages of my diary with sand and preventing me from writing. Had I accepted the woman's offer of food instead of deciding to squeeze some extra mileage out of the day, I could have eaten and written in comfort and probably found a cheap bed in a dormitory. It is impossible to eat without getting sand in my food and I'm concerned by my proximity to a tollbooth. Am I being paranoid in imagining that the police within had binoculars trained upon me as I manhandled the unwieldy bicycle down from the road into the culvert? I can only hope that the possibility that anyone might be daft enough to sleep in one of these places wouldn't have entered their heads, for what I'm doing is almost certainly against the law. When I spit to get some sand out of my mouth the wind carries the gobbet fully fifteen feet before it hits the concrete floor. Can't eat for sand, can't sleep for the wind. Unusually for one accustomed to solitude, I experience a stab of loneliness.

When I wake up at dawn there is sand everywhere. It is in my ears, nostrils and hair, inside the panniers (where it has found its way into the food) and it has stuck to the oil on the brand new chain I put on in Turpan, creating a corrosive grinding-paste certain to induce premature wear. The first job of the day is to change the inner tube in the rear tyre because the valve is faulty and can no longer be relied upon. Next I rummage in the toolbox for the superglue because the blasted trip computer has broken free from its mountings again. Then I eat one of my bananas for breakfast. The skin has split on the other and the sand has infiltrated it, so I throw it away, along with some bread I bought in Turpan that is stale and as hard as a brick.

After an hour of cycling in comparative calm, all hell breaks loose. A howling northerly buffets me from my left, my speed halves, and it is all I can do to stay on the bicycle and avoid being blown off the road. A further half hour of mighty effort yields minimal progress so I opt to shelter in another culvert in the hope that the gale will blow itself out. Deciding that I might as well wait in comfort, I wriggle into my sleeping bag. Listening to the storm outside, I ponder two questions: first, how long will the wind last, and second, how widespread is it? Is it a local phenomenon, an obstacle I can ride my way out of, or is it affecting the whole of Xinjiang, an immense dustbowl as big as Iran? During lulls I wonder whether to make a break for it, but they prove only to be temporary and I spend the time alternately snoozing and reading the copy of *The Lord of the Rings* I bought in Calcutta. I'd already read the book at least half a dozen times, but tales (fictional ones included) of heroic endurance, great suffering and perilous quests have become especially compelling now that I am engaged on my very own quest, and death-defying accounts like *The Long Walk* and Joe Simpson's *Touching The Void* have the advantage moreover of making my own difficulties appear encouragingly trivial by comparison. Reclining inside a culvert in the middle of Chinese Turkestan, I am absorbed by the ghastly fictitious predicament of, well, not a human exactly, but a hobbit.

But nothing of this evil which they had stirred up against them did poor Sam know, except that a fear was growing on him, a menace which he could not see; and such a weight did it become that it was a burden to him to run, and his feet seemed leaden.

Xinjiang shares several topographical features with Tolkein's evil land of Mordor, each being a desert enclosed on three sides (north, west and south) by mountain ranges. I might almost be cycling across the Plateau of Gorgoroth, but unlike Sam's, my mission (although not without risk) is entirely self-imposed and the fate of Middle Earth doesn't depend upon its successful outcome. And unlike Slavomir Rawicz and his friends I am no desperate fugitive from tyranny – dying of hunger or thirst in the Gobi isn't a serious prospect because I can end this ordeal any time I like. I won't pay the ultimate price if I don't in the end make it to Vladivostok and I'll get over the disappointment; I have only my pride to lose by hitching a lift or jumping onto a bus.

I leave the culvert just after midday during a lull which seems to be slightly longer than most, but twenty minutes later the schizophrenic wind picks up again and I have to dismount and walk, for I can no longer control the direction of the bicycle during the unpredictable gusts and on a number of occasions I've almost been blown off the road. Mercifully, I'm not being shot-blasted and blinded by sand; the desert's surface, resembling an immense gravel pit, consists principally of pebbles, but even so it isn't hard to imagine that the evil genies of Uighur folklore are becoming annoyed by my impudence.

For the next four hours I alternate between riding and walking, stopping at the roadside from time to time in order to rest and eat dry bread and drink water from my bottles. Although riding doubles my speed it is much harder work, and passing lorries suck me towards them in the most alarming fashion before spitting me out again. Like the bottom of those bowls of noodles when I was feeling unwell in the Taklamakan, the horizon never seems to get any closer.

Thank God I'm not sick now.

I had expected headwinds, but never in my worst nightmares did I imagine that they'd reduce me to walking. Spurring me on as I lurch and stumble along as best I can is the thought that the next curve or brow of a hill (not that there are very many of these) might reveal a roadside teahouse or truckstop where I can sit out the storm with food and drink, but on each occasion I have to swallow my disappointment. Apart from a distant range of low, rugged hills on the left there is nothing but empty desert, stretching away in every direction as far as the eye can see. The road has been gradually gaining height for what seems like an age, but when it reaches a sort of low pass and begins a gentle descent through more barren mountains I get back on the bicycle and find that I'm able to increase my speed a little. At length I come to a few isolated, single-storey buildings on the side of the road where I'm able to get food and drink. An effervescent Han Chinese girl who speaks a smattering of English shows me to a small, unpretentious room with a bed in it.

The next day commences with a long descent between the mountains but I am unable to take advantage of gravity in my usual way because unpredictable gusts of intimidating power are threatening to knock me flat. The road eventually levels out and, turning broadside on to the wind, begins its long, slow climb towards another mountain range. Reduced to 5 mph by a hellish crosswind, I plough on, head down, legs pounding the pedals, and consumed by bitter hatred. The wind is by no means the only obstacle I've encountered since leaving home nearly a year ago, but my duels with it have never failed to take on a personal dimension. It is a powerful and fickle adversary, a callous, sly, ruthless and cynical bully, and yet one prey to occasional moods of abstracted largess during which I assume either that it has forgotten about me or that it has other fish to fry (or other cyclists to stew). It reminds me of a manager I once had the misfortune to work with.

A particularly brutal gust blows me off the road and I topple over onto a shallow embankment with my head pointing down and my feet pointing up and the bicycle lying on top of me. The fourth fall of the journey. It's as if I've just been swatted, like a fly, by a giant, invisible hand.

Undamaged, but raging at my antagonist, I pick myself up. 'You haven't finished me yet!'

Shouting is a release of pent-up fury, which having accumulated steadily during the past half hour, can no longer be contained. With nobody around to hear me I turn the turbulent air blue with my defiance, but my cries are faint and helpless, like the wailing of an abandoned child in a vast, empty cathedral.

Am I going mad?

I'll know for sure when I hear the voices calling me from the desert.

The wind is merely amused. The ascent is painfully slow and further gusts threaten to toss the bicycle into the desert and deposit me once more onto my backside. It is having a little fun at my expense, mocking me, making me aware of my frailty like a small boy torturing an insect. At length, feeling as impotent as a mosquito caught in the turbulence of a giant ceiling fan, I decide to halve my speed and walk, if that's the right word – the clubbing power of each gust is such that I stagger and lurch like a drunk. The climb shows no sign of coming to an end and there are no longer even any bends or brows of hills to instil hope. My destiny is apparently to follow a narrow black ribbon across this infinite, waterless, dun-coloured moonscape until the end of time, a punishment that might have been rejected by the Gods as being too harsh even for Sisyphus.

As I stumble along I consider my options. Slavomir Rawicz and Joe Simpson had stared death in the face and defied it to do its worst, but their brand of heroism isn't for me and I hope never to find myself forced to make that kind of journey. Whereas their adventures were fuelled by terror, mine is sustained only by considerable pride and a natural stubbornness, and although these qualities have served me admirably thus far, starvation isn't on the agenda. The first teahouse could be thirty or more miles away and, crucially, I haven't got enough food or water to last me anything like that distance at the current rate of progress. Thumbing a lift has become justifiable since it is no longer physically possible to ride, but a lift might be a long time in coming as there is little traffic and the infrequently passing lorries are almost always fully laden, with no room for a bicycle. Nevertheless I have little doubt that sooner or later I'll be able to flag down a vehicle because in Xinjiang, as everywhere else in Asia, I am an object of considerable curiosity. Curiosity nearly drove me insane in India, but here in the Gobi it might save my life.

Heroism must be so much easier in the absence of alternatives. I elect to continue walking but to keep an eye (and an ear) open for lorries travelling east and to wave one down if there appears to be space on board for a man and a bicycle.

A number of fully laden leviathans drone past before a lorry loaded with forty-five-gallon oil drums stops unbidden just ahead of me. The co-driver, a tall, lean Chinaman, is offering me a ride. He clambers onto the drums and indicates that I should toss the loaded bicycle up to him, for he has no concept of its weight. With a sensation of mingled relief and regret I detach the panniers and pass them up first, and then the bicycle itself before joining him in the cab.

Buffeted by the wind, the lorry battles its way up the hill in low gear for over half an hour, its engine defiantly propelling twenty tonnes into a gale that had me on my knees. Although I have always been aware that the internal combustion engine is a miraculous invention, never before have I appreciated that fact quite as much as I do now – but then it is greedily slurping on a full tank of diesel and it was lack of food and water that did for me in the end rather than the wind itself.

Communication, as always, is difficult but we do our best. The lorry is going all the way to Lanzhou, which is more than halfway from the border to Beijing, but my objective is still to cycle as much of the route as I possibly can, so Hami, roughly a hundred miles away, will do. The driver makes signs that they'll be stopping there to eat. He and his co-driver are aged thirty-four and thirty respectively and are both Han Chinese from Lanzhou. They drive regularly between Lanzhou and Xinjiang, each round trip taking a week. The driver has a small mobile phone attached to his belt that rings three times during the journey, the boss presumably checking where the load is (something I can't imagine happening in India or Pakistan).

Beyond the mountains the horizons recede once more and a flat, slate-coloured surface of dried mud and gravel stretches away as far as the eye can see. Not a single teahouse or café. I inform my new acquaintances that I too used to drive lorries in England and ask them if I'm riding in a *Dong Feng*, the most common local marque and Chinese for 'East Wind'.

I am.

'Yufredden!' says the co-driver.

Does he mean 'friend'? I shake his hand. 'Thank you!'

He wants my address.

Fine. He can have it when we get to Hami. I'll send them postcards from Beijing or Moscow. They have helped me out of what might have become a very sticky situation.

We eat noodle soup and share a meat and vegetable dish at a truck stop next to a tyre repairer on the far side of Hami. Although my technique has come on in leaps and bounds since that first meal in Tashkurgan when I had to ask for a spoon, I'm still a little self-conscious when using chopsticks in front of the Chinese. I can manipulate them neatly enough, but to them I must still be painfully slow. Sitting hunched over their steaming bowls, shovelling in the food and slurping loudly as they vacuum up their noodles, they are fast and pragmatic eaters, unconstrained by extraneous western interpretations of 'table etiquette' or decorum.

After the meal my bicycle is passed down to me and we exchange addresses, shake hands, and bid each other good-bye. The wind seems either to have forgotten about me or, having demonstrated its power, is content to let me be for a while, and for the next three blissful hours I manage to average a brisk 15 mph before finishing the day under the road in a nice quiet culvert.

The dawn air is cold when the alarm sounds at 6 a.m. I decide to wait for half an hour in the hope that it'll get appreciably warmer when the sun comes up, but it doesn't and I need to relieve myself so I leave the warmth of my sleeping bag with reluctance. Shivering in the chill blast of the wind, I don fleece and jacket and replace my draughty Indian-made trousers with warmer thermal tights from home. It is too cold even to eat; I'll have to get on the bike and generate some warmth first.

The wind is strong and steady, and once more I have to ride directly into it. 'Why don't you take a day off?' I shout at it in frustration.

My morale has taken a beating over the last couple of days. If Beijing still seems a very long way away indeed, Vladivostok might as well be on the moon and I badly need some benign conditions to restore confidence. Starving and weary of the wind's sadism, I manage to beg food and drink at a ramshackle tyre place right in the middle of nowhere. They give me a huge plate loaded with an entire chicken, several potatoes, and a lot of garlic and red chilli peppers. I wash it down with a couple of cans of *Jianlibao*, an orange and honey flavoured fizz for which I've developed a craving in this thirsty place. The price, eighty yuan, is a shock, but worth paying perhaps for the subsequent lifting of my spirits.

The headwind persists, and cruelly, the road begins another long climb across more featureless desert. It's like attempting to cycle through molasses. When I dismount after two more backbreaking hours of attrition for a much-needed rest, leaning the bike against the parapet of another culvert, my average speed for the day has crept up to just over 8 mph.

Why the hell am I doing this?

Hungry once more, I sit down on the parapet and inspect the meagre rations inside the food bag, still full of sand from that stormy first night after I left Turpan. It is wet sand because one of the auxiliary water bottles has obligingly sprung a leak. Discarding the bottle and throwing away the cucumber I bought in Turpan, I turn the bag inside out to empty it of grit, and after attempting to wipe off the grains still clinging to the jars of Marmite and jam, I spread the remains of the jam on two halves of bread-roll and wolf them down with water.

For the rest of the day I mechanically churn out the miles, counting off the kilometres on the stone markers and taking frequent rests to ease my aching back. The wind has eased a little, but before long the road begins to climb again. By now my crotch and feet have joined my back in the clamour for relief, but a mountain range will have to be crossed before I make it to Xingxingxia, where I hope to get a meal and a bed for the night.

Despite the imminent prospect of even more hard work, I can never bring myself to resent the mountains, not even now that I am drained of energy and aching. Unlike the maverick wind they are never capricious, or spiteful, or disingenuous; marked on maps and usually visible from some way off, they give you every opportunity to avoid them if you so wish and they don't unexpectedly change direction or ambush you or capsize you. What you see is what you get; they are simply there, indifferent rather than hostile, honest adversaries commanding respect rather than hatred. Indeed, finding their beauty and the challenge they represent irresistible, I have deliberately sought them out on several occasions during this journey.

I lie down next to the bicycle on the parapet of a culvert in a state of exhaustion, the blood still racing around veins and arteries and making me tingle from head to toe. Too debilitating to maintain for long, the anger has gone, to be replaced by a sense of wonder at where I am and what I'm doing. At such moments there is no longer any need to ask myself *why*. The sky is a lovely untainted blue and the late afternoon sun is making the rusty mountains glow. Apart from the drone and rattle of the occasional passing lorry, there is nothing to interrupt the desert's awesome hush.

Is this what they mean by Inner Peace? If so, I have found it not in the overcrowded cities or the teeming plains of India, but fleetingly on the lonely roads and in the remote desert and mountain landscapes of Iran, Northern Pakistan and China. Maybe God doesn't speak to us because we are always making too much noise (even in places of worship) to hear Him. If ever I come to acknowledge a divine presence the conversion will come at a moment and in a place like this, surrounded by silence and alone amidst a flawless natural beauty and grandeur that fill me with instinctive humility. My mind is uncluttered and receptive, alive to possibilities, a blank sheet of paper waiting to be filled.

Unlike the Uighurs I find the desert silence peaceful rather than overwhelming, and the knowledge that areas of such isolation still exist in the world is immensely reassuring. Nevertheless their number is steadily diminishing and a nightmare vision suddenly comes to me of the Gobi in a hundred years time, criss-crossed by six-lane highways connecting concrete playgrounds filled with casinos and neon, its silence rent by the hideous sound of wealthy Chinese disporting themselves on virgin sand with trial bikes and dune buggies. The idea is both obscene and sacrilegious, like urinating on an altar or breaking wind beneath the echoing dome of Esfahan's imposing Masjed-e Imam mosque.

I'd love to sleep out in this magical place, cradled by the mountains and watched over by the stars, but I need food and water and Xingxingxia, where East Turkestan at last ends and Gansu Province begins, is only a matter of six or seven miles away, on the other side of the mountain range. I have become preoccupied solely by the essentials of survival and the simple, all-consuming objective of whittling away, kilometre by kilometre, the distance separating me from my destination. Having shorn life of complications, this extraordinary adventure has engaged me utterly, body and soul, demonstrating the gulf between existing and living. It has given me time to think and the space in which I can be myself. It has restored my pride. It has liberated me from cynicism and purged me of envy, and during those moments when my soul is fleetingly bathed in this fierce, sweet serenity, it has perhaps even brought me closer to God.

Chapter Twenty-One
The End of the Civilised World

A settlement formed around the Great Wall's final, westernmost fortress (built by the Ming in 1372) to support the garrison. For the Chinese – who had the same dread of the vast empty spaces beyond as their Uighur neighbours – Jiayuguan not only marked the western boundary of their empire, but the end of the civilised world. The Silk Road pioneers would have set forth on the next leg of their journey westwards with much the same misgivings as European sailors setting out to discover the New World.

These days, however, Jiayuguan is a modern, concrete oasis city that appears to have been designed by architects armed with setsquares, protractors and slide-rules but lacking in both imagination and a sense of humour – neither of which characteristics, come to think of it, tend to be associated with communists. Having emerged, dishevelled and weather-beaten, from the darkness, chaos and ghastly geometrical anarchy of the desert and mountain landscapes beyond the Wall, I check into the Xiongguan Hotel.

*

Like those pioneers of the Silk Road, I had little idea what I was letting myself in for as, thousands of miles, several time zones and exactly a year ago, I let myself quietly out of my sleeping friend's house and cycled down Northwood Lane. The asphalt surface of the Vladivostok Road was glistening after the night's heavy rain, and large puddles reflected the pastel shades of blue, white and grey of a treacherous sky. Most people would have known it as the Kidderminster Road, but the road offers endless possibilities and will ultimately take you to wherever you most want to go – which is probably why I have had a lifelong love affair with it.

Stourport. *WHEN RED LIGHT SHOWS WAIT HERE*

Worcester. I paused in a lay-by to refuel by ruminatively munching my way through two flapjacks. The principle feeling was one of unreality. I couldn't quite bring myself to believe after all the planning and preparation that it had finally started; in a minute the alarm clock would go off and I'd wake up to the realisation that it had all been a dream, and that it was time to get up, drink my coffee and cycle to the office.

But Evesham wasn't on the way to work.

Nor was Broadway. I still hadn't woken up.

The challenge of Fish Hill had been the first of countless tests, each successful outcome a significant boost to my confidence. I can remember dreading it as probably the longest and steepest ascent between Bewdley and Budapest, but I made it up to the top without incident, relieved and pleasantly surprised that I hadn't been overwhelmed by the weight of the loaded bicycle.

SPEED CAMERAS

At least I wouldn't have to worry about *those* in the coming months.

Bourton-on-the Hill.

Moreton-in-the-Marsh.

I cycled through Chipping Norton, soaked but undeterred by a heavy downpour.

Woodstock.

Pubs. Bus stops. Newsagents.

PLEASE DRIVE CAREFULLY

Village greens. Pelican crossings. Dry-stone walls. Public footpaths. Bridleways. I tried hard to take an interest in the tidy countryside and the neat towns and villages but they had become too familiar. That was one of the reasons I had chosen to go away. I remember wondering if I'd come to miss them one day.

*

China is a tyrant: when the wind is blowing against you, you have to cycle extra hours to achieve a respectable daily distance; and when for once it has extended the hand of friendship to propel you on your way, you feel compelled to cycle until you drop in order to make as much progress as possible before another of its mood swings. Goaded beyond measure by the wind's whimsical and obstructive power, I have succumbed all too easily to the delusion that it is something more than a meteorological phenomenon caused by fluctuations in barometric pressure, and to the vanity that I have become the unique focus of its spite. It played cat and mouse with me all the way from Xingxingxia, stalking me across the gravel and scrub and the rocky escarpments looming out of the empty, biscuit-dry expanses of the Gobi. It chased me into isolated villages where it lashed the forlorn lines of beleaguered single-storey, white-tiled buildings that lined the road, lifting surface dust into the air and bending poplars while I rested and refreshed myself on noodles and bowls of green tea. It would lie in wait outside culverts, agitating desert shrubs and piling up the sand while I slept. Spending several weeks cycling across deserts on one's own probably affects the mind, but it was uncanny how often it would suddenly blow a little stronger as soon as I changed up a gear (as if to say 'hey, not so fast, sonny!') and I became bitterly, furiously convinced that it begrudged me every mile of progress.

Strange that Rawicz never mentioned the storms in his book. He had crossed the Gobi from north to south and I am moving from west to east, so at some point in that vast wilderness his footsteps and my tyre marks would inevitably have intersected. Alois held that it was a waste of time to fight too hard against a gale and I've since had ample opportunity to discover that that remarkable man was as correct in this matter as he was in almost everything else (with the possible exception of crocodiles). The harder you struggle, the greater the resistance you meet – almost as if the bicycle has been anchored to a giant elastic band. Stand on the pedals for extra power and you merely present the wind with a greater target. All I could do was select a suitable gear, try to establish a rhythm (which isn't easy when the breeze is blowing in violent gusts) and plug away, drawing extra strength from a fund of anger. I was never again forced to dismount and push and I never had to thumb a lift. On occasions, usually towards the end of the day when I was already exhausted by long hours of struggle, the wind would ease or change direction and I'd be faced with the cruel dilemma of whether to stop for the night or to continue for an hour or two more, ignoring the ache in my back and the soreness in my crotch and feet in order to take advantage of the more benign conditions.

A further refinement in torture were the phantom villages marked on the map but which turned out not to exist, and I'd have to make meagre supplies of food and water last a little longer. Since I become very reliant on the information provided by maps and trip computer in desolate, uninhabited and lonely places, this was an alarming and potentially dangerous development, particularly as provisions were rarely obtained easily in the first place. Village shops stocked cigarettes, lighters, Pot-Noodles, chewing-gum and beer but few sold the items I considered essential for survival (such as bread, fresh fruit and vegetables, jam, spreads, mineral water and milk). So I filled my water bottles with boiled water from the thermos flasks provided in restaurants and dormitories and made do with bars of chocolate, biscuits and a sweet-tasting drink sold in small white plastic bottles. It tasted quite pleasant and I hoped it was nutritious, but I never found out what it was. Much of the food, concealed in cellophane packaging, was equally unidentifiable.

During one unforgettable day, when in addition to the wind I had to contend with two punctures and an attack of diarrhoea, I thought briefly of giving up. Although most of the trains that rumbled past were locomotives trailing long lines of tankers full of crude oil on its way from the wells sunk beneath the sands of East Turkestan to refineries in central and eastern China, the proximity of the railway line was a constant reminder that there is an easier way to travel.

Clack-clack, clack-clack. Those tiny wooden clogs on the key ring dangling from the bar-bag. *Klompjes* is the diminutive of *Klompen*, the delightfully onomatopoeic Dutch word for clogs. Blissfully unaware of the gales, Little Clogs would have passed this very spot nearly a week ago, speeding towards Lanzhou in a comfortable soft-sleeper and either asleep or gazing out of the window, musing no doubt how marvellous it would have been to cycle through this desolate landscape.

I toyed with the idea of getting a lift to Jiayuguan, a bus to Lanzhou, the train to Beijing and then flying home. No more headwinds, punctures or backache. But even as my strength was ebbing and my morale was at its lowest, I eschewed temptation. Harder to bear than all the aches and pains and the frustration was the prospect of damaged pride and returning home with the sense of an opportunity lost, a dream unfulfilled, a job only half done.

So I didn't give up. All I needed to make it across China was an impartial wind, a trouble-free bicycle, reasonable health, and a minimum of two visa extensions. Not too much to ask, you'd have thought.

*

Like Xinjiang, Gansu province is a rugged, remote area of desert and mountains and Chinese control of the area in the past has been similarly intermittent. The landscape in the Hexi Corridor, a narrow six-hundred-mile strip of desert that runs between soaring mountain ranges, was often spectacular. Oases, so luminously green that they hurt the eyes, would surge miraculously out of the sand and the air would suddenly be full of the sound of cuckoos and running water from irrigation channels provided by snowmelt from the colossal Qilian Shan, whose scintillating peaks were sometimes visible looming out of the hazy beyond. There were greenhouses and vine trellises and shepherds tending their flocks behind screens of poplars. Then, just as abruptly, the green would be replaced by sepia as the desert took over once more. Whoever controlled this narrow funnel of land squeezed between the Longshou Shan, Inner Mongolia and the Gobi Desert to the north and the mighty Qilian Shan and the Tibetan Plateau to the south would have had effective control of the Silk Road, for there was no alternative route for the caravans to take.

As I moved east the majority of the oasis dwellers changed imperceptibly from Uighur to Han Chinese, and as always, encounters with people occurred most often when I needed to eat. At Lake Karakul a Czech law student who had spent six months working as an I.T. expert in Beijing had warned that the Han Chinese were considerably less welcoming towards foreigners than the Turkic peoples of East Turkestan and would seize any opportunity to steal from us, considering it clever rather than morally wrong to put one over on the foreign devils. Although it was indistinguishable from any of the other dismal roadside pit stops, Anxi is reputedly the geographical heart of Asia, the midway point between the Urals and the South China Sea, and equidistant from the Arctic Ocean and Kanniyakumari, where the Indian peninsular dwindles to its southernmost point. I spent an agreeable night there, food, accommodation and excellent company provided by two charming teenage Han Chinese girls full of shy smiles and innocent giggles. If they were swindlers it was an extraordinarily effective disguise. Elsewhere the Chinese seized my maps and pored over them and clustered round the bicycle and leaned over my shoulder as I wrote my diary with every bit as much enthusiasm as the Uighurs. Some would persist in asking me questions, even though it must have been plain that I didn't understand a word they were saying. Occasionally they were a little too insistent, one twerp in sunglasses babbling at me determinedly as if at any moment I'd suddenly erupt with a stream of fluent Mandarin. His only English words were *Hello* and *Thankyouverymuch*.

Unable to express myself, unable to understand anything said and unable to read a Chinese menu, I have effectively become deaf, dumb and illiterate. At Yumenzhen two women welcomed me into their café, and realising immediately that there was a communication problem, ushered me into the kitchen to show me what they had. More normally I was met by blank incomprehension and laughter and presented with an indecipherable menu. Nevertheless, encounters were generally vigorous and good-humoured (if occasionally frustrating) and came as a relief from the brooding indifference of the desert and the solitary hours of exertion on the road. The food was invariably cheap and filling, and if I was ripped off I was never aware of it.

The Chinese are capable of great kindness too. The Internet café at Chinese Telecom in Jiayuguan being closed, a girl from the office next door forsook her post and walked with me for ten minutes along the baking boulevards to show me to an alternative establishment. Perhaps the most pleasant surprise of all has been the attitude of those fearsome instruments of repression, the police. I had been expecting them to be obstructive, antagonistic and a major source of trouble, but hitherto they have left me alone and the two policemen manning the tollbooths outside Xingxingxia had waved me through with broad grins.

*

Eating meatballs and noodles at a pavement café at the end of the civilised world a year to the day after leaving home, I mull over exactly what it is (apart from the food) that makes China feel so different from the Indian subcontinent. Dwarfed by the asymmetrical, snow-laden skyscrapers of the Qilian Shan, everything in Jiayuguan is neat and tidy, and *planned*, a victory of order over chaos. Buildings and streets are all ninety-degree angles, straight edges and parallel lines, and broad, smooth avenues with broad, smooth cycle paths and pavements to either side impart a sense of order and space. In India, where pavements are characterised by missing flagstones and gaping holes and the very idea of a cycle path is risible, chaos defiantly prevails. Although there are pedal rickshaws and tricycle carts here too, the cars and buses are modern in appearance and, unlike their uncouth Indian equivalents, don't trail clouds of black smoke.

Whereas religion permeates every aspect of Indian life, this is a secular society. The roads are safer because the Chinese place their trust in themselves rather than in God, and consequently drivers are more disciplined (and more restrained in their use of the horn) than their Indian and Pakistani counterparts. Chinese women, moreover, are on equal terms with men and aren't afraid to expose their legs and arms or display affection to the opposite sex in public.

There are no cows or stray dogs wandering the streets and the donkey carts were left behind at the city limits, hence no cowpats, dog mess or donkey dung. Litter is placed in bins regularly posted along the pavements. It is difficult to equate this rectangular, pristine, frightfully civilised city's white-tiled concrete and glass apartment blocks and department stores with its romantic past as a garrison town and a staging post of the Silk Route.

It's a year since I last ate a flapjack – and that alarm clock still hasn't gone off.

This is one hell of a dream.

*

I leave Jiayuguan on an excellent road surface and with a strong wind at my back. Cycling through a large oasis at an effortless 25 mph, a sensation all the sweeter for the bitter duels over the preceding weeks, I understand something of the joy a yachtsman must experience when a fair wind fills the sails. At the visa office the police were courteous and efficient and gave me my first extension and a receipt for 320 yuan, so for all of a blissful two hours I have everything I could wish for: excellent health, a benign wind, that vital visa extension, and a trouble-free bicycle.

Then, while resting with a Cola in the sunlit square of a village, I discover that the back tyre is soft. Feeling as deflated as the tyre, I drag the bicycle into an area of shade, hating it. A group of men gathers to watch me get my hands dirty.

I ignore them.

The puncture is yet another of those neat, distressing perforations on the rim side of the tube that bedevilled me between Puri and Delhi. I only have Indian patches left and I have little faith in anything manufactured in India. After I've stowed away the tools, pumped up the tyre and reloaded the bicycle, I discover that the bystanders have brought me a bowl of water and some soap powder so that I can wash the oil and road grime from my hands and arms.

What lovely people! Their kindness and thoughtfulness almost made it worth having the puncture. *'Xiexie!'* (Thank you!) and *'Zaijian!'* (Goodbye!) I say to the group as I pedal off.

Barely ten minutes after leaving them behind I become grimly aware that the tyre is still losing air, and in high dudgeon I march the wretched contraption into a culvert and rip out the inner tube.

Little more than an hour later I hear the dreaded hiss of escaping air again. Staving off despair, I turn the bicycle upside-down in a piece of desert and repair another slit in the rim side of the tube with an Indian patch, aware of the futility of continuing to cure the symptom while the cause remains as baffling as ever. I am reminded of those dreadful days in Greece when I finally realised that I wasn't going to reach Istanbul without new tyres and tubes, and the doubt is likewise beginning to grow that I'll make it as far as Lanzhou to order new tubes and rim tapes.

After the fourth puncture of the day I inform my bicycle through clenched teeth that it is a useless, overpriced heap of junk. If there had been a sledgehammer conveniently to hand at that moment I don't think I'd have been responsible for my actions.

Is this just another test of my resolve? I had been confident that the new tyres, tubes and rim-tapes I fitted in Delhi would signal an end to this misery. Fortunately I am not yet short of glue or patches, but for how much longer can I resist the bus if this continues? How many more blasted punctures will I have to repair before I decide that I can't go on? Four in a day must be a record; Klompjes, with less heavy-duty tyres, had only six during her entire trip.

I cycle on to the next village. Two puncture-free miles having become cause for celebration, I order food at a café. With the wind engaged elsewhere I'd normally press on for at least another hour, but although I am undaunted by the thought of the extra miles, I just don't think I could cope with yet another puncture repair. A dormitory bed is available for ten yuan so I decide to take it.

Leaving five other people snoring in the three remaining beds, I set off again at dawn. With the wind remaining encouragingly non-committal, I make a lightning start for the second day running as the road descends steeply between lager-coloured cliffs. All too soon it levels out, leaving the barren hills behind and running from oasis to oasis alongside the railway line and sad, crumbling fragments of the ruined Great Wall. People are pedalling sedately off to work on their black single-speed Flying Pigeon clunkers (why don't *they* get punctures?) or already busy with hoes and shovels in the adjacent fields. I cover just over fifty miles before the first puncture of the day. It says something for my state of mind that I'd happily settle for only a single puncture every fifty miles until I get to Lanzhou.

The next morning, 2,683 kilometres from Beijing, the wind is waiting for me. It seems to me that hardly a day in China has been problem-free since Kashgar; the ill health that dogged me across the Taklamakan was followed by hurricanes in the Gobi and the current dispiriting outbreak of punctures in the Hexi Corridor. I can only be grateful that thus far I haven't very often had to fight my battles on more than one front.

I manage nearly an hour of debilitating low-speed slog before coming across a group of buildings on the left. No closer to understanding the 56,000-character Chinese alphabet, I have to rely on a finely honed instinct to tell me that one of them is a café. The pleasant couple running it seem to understand perfectly the need for a large breakfast: the plate of spicy vegetables with rice would have been sufficient on its own but the lady brings me a huge, steaming bowl of egg and tomato soup to accompany it. By the time I've finished I can eat no more, the wind has dropped and the air outside is gloriously still.

No headwind, so I'll get a puncture next! I tell myself. Ten minutes later a bridge crosses the railway line and the air hisses out of the back tyre.

'You *bastard*!' snarls Bertie.

Jeeves glowers back stonily. He's heard this all before of course, many times over (and boy, is it boring).

'I've just about had it with you!' rasps Bertie (just in case there should be any doubt about the strength of his feelings).

Wooster and Jeeves? The relationship between man and machine has soured to the point that we have become more akin to Blackadder and Baldrick, or Basil and the hapless Manuel.

*

Although desert and bone-dry mountains still lurk in the background, the land is becoming more fertile and consequently more populous as I head east, and it is getting increasingly difficult to find places sufficiently secluded to camp out. Villages run into each other and people are cycling or walking along the road and at work in the fields. A significant freedom, and one that I had forgotten to appreciate, is gradually being taken away by the thickening traffic: I no longer have the road to myself. A conduit to civilisation and the most likely source of help should I have needed it, that narrow black ribbon had represented safety in the empty landscapes of the High Karakoram, the Tarim Basin and the Gobi Desert, but the deserts have at last been left behind and every square inch of this wide valley is either built upon or used for agriculture. The growth in traffic has turned the road from a lifeline into the most likely source of danger. Cars and lorries hurry past with blaring horns. The surface, rutted and broken by the pounding it has received, prohibits rapid progress and I resent the loss of peace and quiet.

Gluing another patch onto the recently perforated spare tube in the dusty evening sunshine with my back propped against a concealing wall and the Karrimat and sleeping bag laid out nearby, it strikes me that, despite all the punctures, I've still managed to average over eighty miles a day since leaving Jiayuguan. Following the latest repair I was ready to throw in the towel and asked the proprietor of a café near Yongshan about buses to Lanzhou, but of course he failed to understand the question. Suddenly grateful for the language barrier, I vow that as long as I can sustain a respectable daily mileage, and as long as I retain enough adhesive and patches (I retract what I said about products manufactured in India) I'll resist the temptation to jump onto a bus, no matter how filthy and dispirited I get.

I *won't* be beaten.

Chapter Twenty-Two
A Close Shave

'Is Lanzhou famous for anything?' I ask the students.

'Yes, it is famous for its pollution,' replies Muyong, without discernable irony.

I burst out laughing. 'Isn't it famous for anything a little nicer – like wine, or food?'

Lanzhou announced itself with a giant petrochemical complex and a chimney spouting flame. I cycled on past miles of factories and warehouses towards the centre, the city seeming far bigger than it actually is because its three million inhabitants are squeezed into a narrow valley that extends along the Yellow River from west to east for fully thirteen miles.

We are sitting on the grass of the football field on the university campus, a large tree-lined park intersected by paths connecting shabby concrete tower blocks. Something of the city's setting reminds me of the French city of Grenoble: multi-storey office and apartment blocks rise well beyond the spider's web of power lines that feed the trolleybuses but are dwarfed by a backdrop of mountains. Apart from its pollution, Lanzhou, the gateway to China's Wild West, is apparently best known for a certain beef and noodles dish.

I met Muyong Xiang and Guo Qiang at the Internet café. They hail from opposite ends of China – Jilin in Manchuria and Urumqi in Xinjiang. Both are postgraduates, Muyong studying Chinese history and Guo engineering. We make our way past basketball and volleyball courts to the canteen where we devour noodles in a watery tomato and egg soup accompanied by a meat and pepper dish. Muyong produces a book written for Chinese students of English. It is a reasonably faithful portrait of Britain in the sixties, a dimly remembered land of Harold Wilson, black and white television, beehive hairdos, Twiggy, Morris Minors, Bobby Charlton and *Angel's Delight*. Chapters entitled 'The British Bobby' and 'Piccadilly Circus' are accompanied by black and white photographs. It may be adequate as a language guide but an accurate representation of the United Kingdom at the beginning of the new millennium it most certainly isn't.

Unlike the Soviet Union, China has thus far managed to implement and pursue a programme of economic reform without political disintegration. Barely three years after the Tiananmen Square massacre had demonstrated the ruthlessness of the Communist Party when faced by any threat to its hold on power, Deng unexpectedly announced in 1992 that 'to get rich is glorious'. I wonder if economic liberalisation is the price the government is willing to pay for political continuity, a sort of tacit compromise reached with the people along the lines of 'you can do pretty well whatever you damn-well like but only as long as you don't challenge our right to govern or mention nasty words like "human rights" or "democracy".'

Having made its pact with the devil, Chinese society at the turn of the millennium appears to be as competitive and as dedicated to making money as any in Western Europe. Vast and colourful advertisement hoardings on top of and on the sides of tower blocks exhort the population not to work harder for the motherland but to part with their earnings, and Lanzhou's wide pavements are seething with entrepreneurial activity. A plate of noodles can be bought for as little as two yuan from an abundance of cheap cafés and pavement kiosks. Vendors of soft drinks, ice cream and yoghurt recline on chairs next to their chest freezers. Spicy potatoes and cubes of tofu are barbecued on braziers and eaten off long cocktail sticks. I stroll past mouth-watering displays of melons, bananas, strawberries, apricots, lychees, nectarines, apples and oranges, all the fresh produce for which I longed but was unable to obtain during those weeks in the deserts. Purveyors of calculators, watches, wallets, nail-clippers, combs, electric shavers and other miscellaneous junk have spread their wares out upon the pavements on cloths. Shoeshine and shoe-repair guys and girls wait patiently for customers. Traffic, pedestrians and cyclists are swept up in a careless maelstrom reminiscent of Indian cities and the streets are lined with banks, restaurants, supermarkets, department stores along with smaller shops and cafés. Trolleybuses are driven back and forth along the broad, tree-lined avenues by incongruously tiny women. What a difference a border makes.

One afternoon my Chinese friends invite me to accompany them back to their hall of residence. Their room is scarcely larger than the one I had all to myself when I was at university and they have to share it with two others. There are two double bunk beds, a map of the USA on the wall, and several books and bits and pieces strewn about, the untidiness the result of too much gear and too little room rather than personal sloppiness or indiscipline. How the four of them manage to coexist in that tiny cell beats me. I suppose they must get used to it.

Muyong and Guo are rather serious young men. We drink tea and earnestly discuss British and Chinese politics, Marxism, socialism and capitalism, the differences that exist between the English spoken in America and the English spoken in the UK, and Britain's former colonies (did they benefit or suffer as a result of the British presence?). My opinions on all these matters, such as they are, are eagerly sought and digested. When disparaging references to past British imperialism and present American 'aggression' are repeatedly made, I can't resist asking them if they regard Tibet as part of China and tentatively suggest that a lot of people both inside and outside Tibet might take issue with their assertion that the country has belonged to China since the fourteenth century. Their reaction, however, is one of astonishment that anyone could possibly think otherwise. Never having been exposed to a carefully reasoned counter-argument (and I'm nowhere near well informed enough to provide it), the students are as implacable in their way as Milo – but living in a country in which people are sentenced to 're-education through labour' or long prison terms for the expression of views deemed 'harmful to the state', they can be forgiven their intransigence. Free and unfettered access to ideas and information are a threat to the regime and, as in Iran, the media is strictly controlled. Internet sites offering alternative perceptions of the present and recent past to those officially sanctioned by the Government are blocked or closed.

Was Tibet 'invaded' or 'liberated'? The little I know is only what I've been told; like Muyong, Guo and other educated Chinese, I have read the papers, listened to the radio and watched the occasional television documentary. Is history ever presented entirely objectively? Politics muddy the truth and I might be as much a dupe to propaganda as they are, but at least we in the West are able to examine several alternative perspectives before choosing what to believe, and we are unlikely to be arrested for expressing our opinions. Although I'd love to explore the delicate political arenas of Tibet, Xinxiang and Tainanmen Square with a student of Chinese history, I decide that it might be wiser not to do so; I could land both my hosts and myself in all sorts of trouble.

Muyong and Guo, who both enthusiastically endorse Marxism, tell me with one voice that Mao was 'a very great man'. Politics are highly subjective and again our beliefs are diametrically opposed. How can the Chinese people be so forgiving? Mao's hideous brand of Marxist Communism plunged China into the dark ages and the country is still in the process of recovering. In the West he is considered a monster, right up there alongside Hitler and Stalin in the twentieth century's rogues gallery of megalomaniacs and mass murderers, and yet the Great Helmsman continues to be revered by the very people who suffered most from policies that combined economic sabotage and cultural vandalism to appalling effect.

The Mao personality cult will probably endure until such time that the party he helped found loses its stranglehold on power and alternative views are tolerated. When, feeling like a heretic, I cautiously venture that the Cultural Revolution is regarded in the West as a disaster, my friends do nevertheless concede that he made 'a few mistakes'. Amongst them, presumably, was 'The

Great Leap Forward', a catastrophic attempt at economic reform that resulted in an estimated thirty million people dying of starvation. The Cultural Revolution itself was an orgy of government-sponsored persecution during which Chinese society was plunged into collective madness and, like a scorpion surrounded by a ring of fire, systematically set out to destroy itself. Millions more died.

Some mistakes.

*

Because I have paid only for a bed (as opposed to a room), the other two beds in what is effectively a three-bed dormitory can be occupied at any time. A German backpacker from Frankfurt has been replaced by Cyrille, a stocky and bespectacled twenty-nine-year-old French physiotherapist. He has just arrived by train from Turpan after travelling the overland route from Dunkirk and plans to make his way eventually to Japan or South Korea to teach English. Two years ago he spent a year on a Chinese Junk as a crewman, mapping coral reefs and researching marine life in the Southern Pacific Ocean.

One evening we make our way to a street filled with cafés and stalls offering cheap food. Ignoring the stalls displaying pig's trotters, hen's feet and other dubious local delicacies, we select a number of long cocktail sticks laden with cauliflower, tofu, broccoli, seaweed, potatoes, mushrooms and meatballs. The food is taken off the sticks, cooked, and served in a single large bowl from which we help ourselves with our chopsticks, companionably sharing our microbes as well as our dinner.

Our stomachs satiated, we mingle with the crowds in the city's main square – a huge open rectangle of concrete flagstones surrounding grassy borders. A giant screen is showing a Chinese movie but we settle down instead with ice creams at a pavement café to study the Chinese at play. People are milling around in the soft glow provided by street lamps, by the light emanating from shop fronts and by the vast illuminated billboards and flashing neon signs on surrounding tower blocks. At neighbouring tables men are engaged in a noisy drinking game that reminds me of the *hic haec hoc* paper-wraps-stone, scissors-cut-paper, stone-blunts-scissors game I used to play at school. The square is full of beautiful women wearing platform shoes and dressed in mini-skirts, and I wonder what Mao's Red Guards would have made of the ostentatious self-expression, conspicuous individuality and rampant consumerism on display. Plenty of them must still be alive. Do they yearn for the 'good old days', when they rampaged through China eliminating anything and anybody that symbolised China's 'exploitative', 'bourgeois' or 'capitalist' past, closing down universities and secondary schools, murdering or sending intellectuals to work in the fields, destroying the work of writers and artists and ransacking temples and monasteries? The Cultural Revolution was a surge of oppression sparked in 1966 by none other than the students of Beijing University – whose successors ironically formed the majority of those demonstrating for greater freedoms in Tiananmen Square in 1989.

'I'm not like this normally,' apologises Cyrille, staring goggle-eyed at yet another slim, scantily clad beauty gliding gracefully past our table. 'It's just that I've spent so much time in Iran, Pakistan and India, where women cover themselves up and hide themselves away.'

I feel dangerously susceptible myself. Mini-skirts and platform shoes are in vogue and the warm evening air is encouraging an exposure of flesh that would have been considered scandalous in any of the Islamic countries. Added to which I happen to find Chinese women extraordinarily attractive anyway.

While waiting for the lift to take us down to breakfast the next morning we play our own version of the Chinese drinking game (which involves a great deal of incoherent shouting accompanied by enigmatic hand signals) for the benefit of a bemused lady on the service desk.

A young woman dressed in a red and gold uniform ushers us to a table in the hotel's empty dining room.

'*Meilli!*' (You're beautiful!), beams Cyrille, eyeing her lecherously. His glasses are very strong and make his eyes appear twice their normal size, giving him something of the appearance of a startled owl. Clearly a proponent of The Direct Approach, he doesn't seem to lack confidence in his dealings with the opposite sex.

She merely smiles and shakes her head.

'I don't think she liked it very much when I said that,' remarks Cyrille dolefully.

'Of course she did! All women like to be told that they're beautiful. She was just a little embarrassed, that's all. You'd be the same if a woman you'd never met before told you that you were gorgeous.'

'I don't know – it has never happened to me.'

We are the only two people eating. There must be at least half a dozen waitresses standing around looking bored in the cavernous restaurant. To my astonishment the woman returns with a note and hands it to Cyrille.

'*We are good friends. You teach me English, I teach you Chinese,*' he reads, grinning triumphantly. He is smoother with the ladies than he is with his chopsticks, complaining initially that the noodles are the wrong size (which reminds me of British Rail's infamous *wrong type of snow* excuse) and then that the chopsticks aren't his preferred type. A bad workman.

'You're distracted by love,' I suggest. 'Or lust, more likely.'

'Lust?'

I can't think of the equivalent French word. His pocket English-French dictionary translates it as *désir*, but that doesn't seem quite specific enough somehow. 'It means more than that,' I insist, groping for a definition. 'You *love* a woman's soul, but you *lust* after her body. Do you understand?'

He nods his head vigorously, but he is equally incapable of finding a translation. 'Perhaps we don't have a word for it because in France we don't understand the difference!' he sniggers into his noodles.

*

Following Cyrille's departure from Lanzhou, depression settles upon me like a heavy grey cloud. Having suffered no less than ten punctures during the six-day ride from Jiayuguan, it was obvious that I wasn't going to get much further without new tubes, patches and rim tape, and that amusing, irreverent Frenchman was an excellent antidote to the frustration caused by the delay in their arrival. After a week of waiting I am beginning to feel trapped. I have calculated that it will take me roughly seventeen cycling days plus a bare minimum of two rest days (say three weeks) to get to Beijing, and approximately the same time to cycle from there to the Russian border post at Heihe. Although I have already obtained a second visa extension from the local PSB, there will be little time to spare for delays caused by headwinds and any health or mechanical problems.

The other two beds in the room are taken for a night by two American students. Nice chaps, but there isn't time to establish any real rapport with them and they depart early in the morning to take a bus to the *Bingling Si*, a warren of Buddhist grottoes fifty miles away. People come and go but always I stay; Lanzhou has become a prison. I am woken every morning not by the sound of cuckoos exchanging greetings but the muffled concert of horns on the busy street five floors below the window. If that doesn't do the trick Chinese pop music blares out from about 9 a.m. onwards, presumably from a nearby discotheque or dance hall. By sometime tomorrow I'll have finished reading the Beeb's *From Our Own Correspondent Volume 4* and another defence against boredom will have been breached.

Deciding that I can bear the confines of the hotel room no longer, I sally forth in search of a bite to eat. Round the corner from the hotel on Pingliang Lu are two or three hairdressing salons where the girls appear to be more than usually friendly, shouting greetings in English and Chinese as I walk past. Cyrille informed me that many such establishments in China double as brothels, and although they were unable to confirm it, the two Americans had heard the same rumour. I'll have to get my head shaved before leaving Lanzhou and I have time on my hands, so on an impulse I decide to put the matter to the test myself.

The only girl in the salon is wearing a tight-fitting knitted black pullover and faded denim jeans. Of course she speaks no English, but I manage to convey to her that I'd like my head shaved and ask her how much she charges. Unable to understand her reply, I indicate that she should trace the number with her forefinger on the counter. Instead, with much smiling and giggling, she seizes my wrist and traces '10' in the palm of my hand.

She is undoubtedly flirting. I'd never before realised that the palm of my hand was an erogenous zone, but this is clearly a most erogenous young lady. I decline her offer of a massage and she gets to work, laying her left hand caressingly and rather unnecessarily on my scalp while she carefully scrapes away the stubble with her right. Meanwhile, I study the absorbed expression of her lovely face in the mirror, all too aware of her physical proximity and her slender, coltish grace. When the tickling of my scalp causes me to sneeze violently (a dangerous thing to do when someone is holding a razor to your head), she bursts into another fit of giggles and I grin back at her reflection.

Shave satisfactorily completed, she repeats the offer of a massage.

Smiling, I shake my head.

With much sighing and giggling, she says something that sounds like 'Chicken Chicken?'

I feign puzzlement.

She takes my hand again and, looking into my eyes, draws '150' in my palm, makes a sign which leaves absolutely no room for further doubt, and brazenly points to a door leading to a flight of stairs.

I smile and shake my head again, but she chooses to misunderstand me and indicates that she's open to negotiation if I'd like to name a price more to my liking.

I'd hardly be human if I wasn't tempted. A beguiling blend of innocence and worldliness, she can't be any older than twenty. Alternating between tenderness and coquettishness, she is bewitchingly beautiful, with exquisite features and gleaming raven hair cascading down almost to her tiny waist. Why is she involved in this unwholesome business? What do her parents think? Are they even aware of what she does? Maybe in China there is no shame in practising this most ancient of professions.

Again I shake my head. I've never in my life paid for sex and, despite the considerable charms on offer, I have no intention of doing so now. It isn't a question of finances (I wouldn't dream of insulting her by suggesting that she isn't worth the paltry £12.50 for which she's asking) but a matter of principle. Does she ever enjoy what she does, or is each coupling a matter to be got over as quickly as possible so that she can take the money and move on to the next customer? I'd find sex humiliating in those circumstances, but having paid for it I'd have no right to expect anything else. If the attraction isn't mutual then there is surely very little pleasure to be experienced by either partner (which is partly why I find the motivation behind rape so incomprehensible). Nevertheless, the thousands of miles cycled over the past year have endowed me with the physique of an athlete, and it may not be entirely beyond the bounds of possibility that she *does* fancy me a little bit. Perhaps she is even a little curious to find out if intimacy with a western man is any different to what she is used to, and if I could only be persuaded that she wants me instead of my dollars I'd be more than happy to enlighten her.

What I really need, though, cannot be bought or sold on a street corner. Under no obligation to explain but liking her enough to want to all the same, I fumble in my bag for the photocopies I made of Cyrille's pocket Mandarin–English dictionary, searching for words that will somehow allow me to express myself in a way that she'll understand. I point to the Chinese word for *young*, but that's not really what I mean at all. Although the disparity in our ages is a factor that makes me a little uneasy, why should it? She isn't a child and it's not as if I'd be taking anything from her that she hasn't already lost, doubtless many times over. And after all, she is playing the role of seducer, not me; I've forgotten that she's a whore.

'You're really lovely and extremely tempting,' I say to her in English, finally giving up the struggle and handing her ten yuan for the haircut, 'but I just don't think I'd be very proud of myself afterwards.'

I drift towards the Internet café sensing that the decision had owed more to instinct and precedent than logic or reason. I've turned down numerous offers of sex from prostitutes at the truck stops and in the lay-bys of Eastern Europe and Russia, but never before have I been tempted as at that hairdressing salon in Lanzhou. Not only was I attracted by the girl's beauty, but also by her manner. I found myself *liking* her, and I'd sensed instinctively that she had liked me too; her invitation held the promise not just of intense erotic pleasure, but fun. Why then didn't I accept it?

I had hoped to leave something of my personality at home with the majority of my belongings, to discard some of the customs and codes of conduct imposed by the way of life I had left behind and travel light in every sense, but although I have shed a few homebred inhibitions along the way, certain attitudes (as I discovered most notably in India) are clearly very deeply ingrained. Self-esteem was in the end too high a price to pay for short-term gratification. I left home to rediscover my pride and self-respect, not to lose them, and it has been precisely the refusal to compromise on certain principles that has made this journey so memorable. Without it I'd have accepted the lifts offered in Turkey and Iran, jumped onto buses and trains in India, and given up in the Gobi.

Maybe there is a different type of trip to be made, one in which ethics and scruples can be left behind and reclaimed along with the furniture and hi-fi upon returning home. Perhaps I'll attempt it one day.

On the way back to the hotel I buy three of the delicious chilled yoghurts sold in glass jars from a stall and sit down in the warm darkness at a nearby table to consume them. There is something about Lanzhou at night that lifts the spirits – the temperature of the air, the soft radiance of the street lights and the illuminated signboards, the smell of barbecuing food, the lively, bustling atmosphere with street cafés and pavement vendors still doing a roaring trade, and the general friendliness of its inhabitants. The stallholder smiles indulgently at me as I suck the yoghurt out through a straw. People are sitting out on the pavements playing endless tournaments of Chinese Chess. Despite Lanzhou's reputation as the most polluted city in China I have found the air far less offensive than the atmosphere in either Lahore or Delhi. Watching the bustle around me, I reflect that there are considerably worse places to be stuck.

Such as Nea Karvali. Or Kerman. Or Kidderminster.

The light is on in Room 510. The newcomer is Japanese. Although I feel desolate when people like Cyrille and even the Americans move on (accentuating my feelings of being trapped) I can't avoid experiencing a touch of resentment at each intrusion of a perfect stranger into what I've unwillingly come to regard as home.

My new roommate finishes his pot noodle and asks if I'd mind if he smokes.

I tell him I'd rather he did so outside.

*

Delivery of the new tubes was promised within four to seven days. Eight days after the parts left St John's Street Cycles in Bridgwater I phone the courier company's office in Beijing, and after being swatted like a shuttlecock back and forth between various departments, I am informed that my package is in customs. They promise to phone me back as soon as they have any news.

Yeah, right. Of course you will. Feed him some bullshit and he'll go away. They make me sick. It seems to me that you can decide to do something marvellous and original with your life and you can plan it down to the finest detail, but in the end all your determination and dedication and effort may come to nothing because at some point you are no longer the master of your own destiny. You are left having to rely upon people who share nothing of your commitment – wage slaves to whom the success or failure of your enterprise is of no account, mere numbers in a vast multinational machine that casually breaks its promises about delivery times.

While I continue to count the days a steady stream of travellers occupies beds two and three, none staying for long enough to get to know properly. I make further phone calls and regularly check at the hotel's reception desk to see if a parcel has been left for me, but the news is always the same: *'Meiyou!'* (No chance!).

A third visa extension has become essential if I am to get to Heihe. On the tenth day of my stay in Lanzhou I send an email to the courier company's head office setting out in some detail what I think of their lousy service and vowing that I'll never use it again and that I'll tell my friends not to use it either (and of course I've got loads of friends and they're all rich and powerful and make regular use of courier companies). An exercise in futility, but it does at least have the effect of making me feel better for a while.

'Massage! Massage!' coo the sirens as I walk back to the hotel past one of the hairdressing salons.

'Buyao!' (No thanks!) I shout back.

Chapter Twenty-Three
Smiling at China

'Good-bye! Good luck!' smiles one of the women on the fifth-floor service desk as their longest-serving prisoner leaves Room 510 for the last time and piles his gear into the lift.

The package containing the inner tubes and rim tapes finally arrived fully a week after it was promised, but after begging and pleading with the PSB I managed to obtain my third and final visa extension. Thus, for the first time since entering China, I can relax in the knowledge that I have ample time (in theory) to cross the rest of this relentlessly demanding country. It's a fantastic feeling.

A group of local worthies assembles outside the hotel to watch me oil the chain prior to departure and there is much 'OK, OK!' followed by the thumbs-up sign when they gather that my destination is Beijing. In England I'd have interpreted the reaction as one of sarcastic disbelief, but this is China and there is no doubting their sincerity. Although I spent a fortnight of frustration in Lanzhou, the greatest factor to influence my opinion of a place is the memories I retain of interactions with its people (which is why my love for France has endured despite the best efforts of French politicians to extinguish it), and for that reason I will always remember my time in China's most polluted city with affection. I'll miss the daily soak in the bath too.

East of the city the road climbs steeply onto the Loess Plateau amongst mountains made of baked, crumbling mud, beige in colour except for slender horizontal strips of vivid green where terraces have been carved into their sides. I had originally intended to take a more northerly route following the Yellow River and taking in Yinchuan, Baotou and Hohot, but rumours of fierce winds sweeping the grasslands of Inner Mongolia persuaded me to select a mountainous alternative.

After a long, kilometre-devouring freewheel between the beige and green striped staircases the road levels out to bisect a broad, fertile valley criss-crossed by deep canyons and ravines cut into the soft, crumbling soil by the river and its tributaries. The three hundred thousand square miles of the Loess Plateau used to be forested, but generations of farmers have cut down the trees and there is little left to bind the soil.

Because of the number of people at work on the land there appears to be little chance of camping out, but just as I'm resigning myself to the task of searching for a hotel or dormitory in the next town, I discover a cave cut into the baked mud of a cliff face and I gratefully scuttle into it like a hermit crab retreating into its shell. At first sight it appeared to be an ideal shelter, but a cursory examination of my sleeping quarters reveals what even I, despite limited anatomical knowledge, cannot fail to recognise as three human skulls. There are other bones strewn about upon the thick carpet of loess dust – tibias and fibulas, I think, and part of a pelvis – and for all I know there may be more buried beneath the mound of rubble at the back of the cave.

Has this homely grotto been the scene of a massacre? I think it more likely that these people (intellectuals murdered by the Red Guards during the Cultural Revolution perhaps, or victims of starvation during China's Great Leap Backwards) died elsewhere and their bodies were dumped here. Somehow I can't bring myself to believe that they died peacefully of old age. Death clearly visited them a long time ago, for the bones are dry and bleached, and if souls do indeed survive the destruction of the body and move on, these have long since checked out. Reasoning that I have more to fear from a nocturnal visit by the living than an awakening of the dead, I clear a space for my sleeping bag. The dark holes in the skulls where the eyes used to be are a little disconcerting, but they all have such lovely welcoming smiles. Using one as a convenient prop for the bicycle, I sleep soundly amongst human remains.

*

Beyond Guyuan the G309, narrower and more rustic than its more frequented cousin the G312, climbs steeply into the mountains, affording me a dramatic view of the concrete metropolis sprawled out in the valley below beneath a stormy sky. The asphalt becomes intermittent before disappearing entirely, and the tyres bump and skid over washboard corrugations and loose rubble. Violent gusts of wind laden with dust and grit sandblast exposed areas of skin and force me to shut my eyes, and for a while I have to dismount and walk. The valley below has been enveloped in a fog of what I can only suppose is airborne grit. Then the rain arrives, falling from the inky sky in stair rods. What will China visit upon me next? Swarms of killer bees? Snakebite? I'm rarely permitted the luxury of being bored by this country.

I eat at a restaurant in a village lashed by the wind and rain. Crowds of people are milling aimlessly in the road amongst tethered cows and donkeys, presumably brought in from the surrounding fields to shelter from the dust storm. About forty yokels immediately surround the bicycle and people peer through the door to watch the alien eat his noodles – I may well be the only foreigner they have ever seen. By the time I remount the bicycle the wind has dropped, the rain has disappeared, and the sun is shining innocently once more from a cloudless sky.

Long, steep climbs continue to be followed by brief, exhilarating periods of freewheeling. After three days without a puncture I am halfway to forgiving the bicycle its previous misdemeanours, but at the summit of another long climb there is a report like a gunshot, loss of control is instantaneous and it falls from underneath me. I pick myself up from the road unhurt, but with a premonition of disaster. The inner tube in the front tyre has burst and the split in the rubber is so wide that it will be impossible to repair. With the sun hot on my back I replace the tube and re-inflate the tyre, but just as I'm putting away my tools there is a second deafening bang and the tyre capsizes again.

For a few moments I allow rage and despair to overwhelm me. The bicycle is the most obvious outlet for my fury, but sense prevails and I manage to resist the temptation to hurl it to the ground and give it a good kicking. I walk around in tight circles swearing at it instead. Two brand-new tubes have been ruptured beyond repair in the space of minutes and I am close to tears. I have no idea why they are bursting and I have only two spares left.

Calm down! Think!

The fate of my venture is hanging in the balance; if I fail to discover the reason behind the destruction of the tubes the journey will finish on this very spot as soon as I run out of spares. On previous occasions people have materialised as if by magic to offer help when I've been most in need of it, but this time it's up to me. It is already late afternoon. I have enough bananas and bread left to provide a meagre supper and breakfast, so I drag the bicycle into a secluded hollow next to a steeply sloping cornfield where I judge that I'll be able to spend the night undisturbed.

Reflecting that I can at least count myself fortunate that the tyre burst while I was ascending the hill at 5 mph instead of freewheeling down the other side at speeds in excess of 30 mph (in which case I'd be in hospital or a morgue by now), I lever the tyre off the rim once more. Unlike the previous rashes of random rim-side pinpricks (for which I still have no explanation), the two larger lacerations have occurred in exactly the same position on each tube, almost directly opposite the valve. The tyre has been levered on and off the rim so often that the metal tyre levers I borrowed from Klompjes have cut into the tough rubber, exposing sections of the wire that runs round each inner circumference; it has to be beyond coincidence that both tubes have split directly opposite the worst-affected area. Blessing the impulse that made me retain one of the worn tyres I replaced in Delhi as a spare, I pump four bars of pressure into the replacement tube, all the while holding my breath and waiting for another bang.

No bang and the tyre remains firm.

After sleeping peacefully I wake up to the early morning concert of rural China: the crowing of a rooster, the call of any number of unseen cuckoos, and the braying of a donkey. Confident now that my diagnosis of last night was correct, I set off after a nauseating breakfast consisting of a banana so bruised that it was all but pureed.

The road continues to rear and plunge incessantly, but beyond Caomiao the going at last becomes easier with a long descent to a broad valley dividing wide staircases of crops cut into mustard-coloured massifs. Convoys of combine harvesters are being driven in the opposite direction but I have yet to see one at work in the fields, which are being harvested with scythes. Sheaves of wheat have been piled up and, as in parts of India, peasants have spread the harvest out on the road so that passing vehicles can carry out the task of separating the wheat from the chaff. I cycle warily past a number of beehives reflecting that life in this part of China can have changed little for centuries.

When darkening skies are followed by rumblings of thunder and showers of heavy rain, people scurry for shelter in the villages. Within seconds my singlet is usually sopping wet and I have to proceed with circumspection owing to the strong gusts of wind, but each downpour never lasts for long and it takes little time for the wind and the sunshine to dry me out. Stimulated by the bucolic landscape and persistent bursts of meteorological intemperance, the orchestra that has taken up residence inside my head is performing Beethoven's Pastoral Symphony.

*

Although the language barrier has been at its most impenetrable in China, the Chinese are amongst the most welcoming people I've met anywhere and gatherings of curious spectators in towns and villages are generally rendered less oppressive by a strong female presence. At the crossroads village of Banqiao a knot of onlookers forms as I treat myself to a can of Jianlibao and an ice cream, and when I signal by pointing to my mouth and patting my stomach that I'm still hungry and looking for something a little more substantial to eat, a young woman beckons to me and the entire entourage follows in a state of barely repressed excitement. I find myself in a quadrangle surrounded on each side by the familiar white-tiled buildings, one of which proves to be a canteen. Everyone takes their place around the table to watch me eating my noodles with green beans, but I have become nimble and precise with my chopsticks and my self-consciousness has diminished. To distract them I show them the photocopied Chinese-English dictionary, and between mouthfuls I watch them struggle to pronounce the English words. Although one girl appears to speak a smattering of English, I don't think that she can quite pluck up the courage to address me. When a uniformed man arrives with less inhibitions and barks 'Hellohowareyou!' like an incantation and I reply 'I'm fine thank you, how are you?' there are triumphant cheers and uproarious laughter. Like so many others I've eaten in China, the meal is free.

*

A narrow, rocky canyon divides the pine-clad hills beyond Heshuilaocheng. People and livestock have been left behind in the wide, cultivated valleys of the Loess Plateau and for the last hour I have had the road more or less to myself, so when it winds its way steeply up a mountainside to enter a long, unlit tunnel, I decide that I won't bother to switch on the rear light because it involves the hassle of stopping and dismounting. Halfway through I hear the purposeful roar of a lorry entering the tunnel behind me.

Isn't that just bloody typical? Intimidated by the steady crescendo into unnecessary panic, I attempt to move over to the edge of the road before dismounting and switching on the light – a bad mistake because I can't see in the blackness. The front wheel hits a hidden kerb and the bicycle crashes to the ground.

You stupid idiot!! I am spread-eagled on the road in pitch-darkness right in the path of the oncoming lorry. The sound of its engine has become a deafening, terrifying clamour.

Get up! There is nothing unnecessary about my panic now. *QUICKLY!!* Adrenaline pumping, I untangle myself from the bicycle and scramble awkwardly to my feet, unaware that I've cut my knee.

Switch on the light! Frantically, I haul the bicycle upright and fumble blindly for the switch. *HURRY!!!* I breathe a sigh of relief as I locate it, cowering into the tunnel wall as the lorry thunders past only seconds later.

A car that passed me earlier has stopped just beyond the circle of daylight at the other end of the tunnel. The driver, unaware of the drama that has just taken place in the filthy black hole behind us, makes signs for me to stop and produces a notebook. As I write down my name and address for him, I wonder if he has noticed that my hands are trembling. Although the third visa extension removed any requirement to make haste, hurrying has become a habit. The sixth fall of the journey was due entirely to my own stupidity. If I'm not careful this obsession with momentum will be the death of me; I vow that never again will I place my life at risk to save a few meaningless seconds.

The *insh'allah* fatalism of Islam and the Hindu's abdication of responsibility in the name of religion can appear irrational and deeply perplexing to the sceptical, existentialist European but the Chinese are a secular people too, and for all that their language remains unfathomable and very few speak any English, I have discerned a greater meeting of minds. Although they appear able to appreciate something of the enormity of the distance I have covered there is never any hint that they doubt the sanity of embarking upon such an enterprise – even though (unlike in the other Asian countries) there is little tradition of pilgrimage to explain it away. My achievement in coming so far is miraculous and needs no justification, and not only do I receive delighted grins and thumbs-up signs at roadside halts but very often a free meal too. With actions expressing their admiration more forcefully than any words, language has become largely superfluous. When notebooks and pens are eagerly produced I write down my name, postal address, phone number and email address. To the Indians, Pakistanis and Iranians I remained a fascinating and bewildering phenomenon, but the Han Chinese have welcomed me as a conquering hero. Maybe all they want is my autograph.

They are every bit as enchanting in Shaanxi Province as they were in Gansu. A youth shouts a greeting to me from a tawdry gaggle of roadside tyre stores, workshops and cafés a few miles south of Tan'an, and on an impulse I cycle over to ask him if there is anywhere a cyclist can rest his weary body overnight. He leads me to a building where a young woman smiles radiantly and shows me to a room in which there are two beds. As soon as I've wheeled in the bicycle and propped it against a wall they usher me to a table in the restaurant with great fuss and ceremony and the woman, who really does have the most breathtaking smile, pours water into a basin so that I can shave and wash the sweat and dust from my face and arms.

People inevitably converge to watch me eat. Owing perhaps to an all but imperceptible difference in their attitude or body language (so much more important when verbal communication is virtually impossible), I have found Chinese inquisitiveness less intrusive and alienating than the Indian variety. We manage to converse after a fashion, but only by pointing to words in the dictionary. I produce my maps and a teenage boy hurries off to find his English textbook. The young woman who showed me to my sleeping quarters remains in the background, waiting upon my every need, offering me more food and attentively topping up my bowl of tea. Every time I glance up her eyes are upon me, and her smile is beginning to interfere with my pulse rate.

After I've finished eating she follows me into my room and watches intently as I retrieve my diary from a pannier. Then she sits down opposite me at a table in the restaurant, gazing at me as I write and smiling sweetly and brilliantly every time our eyes meet. I establish that her name is Gao. Her behaviour is electrifying but disturbing too, raising far more questions than it answers because she runs the café with her husband who is blithely drinking beer with some friends at another table. They have two children.

After finishing the day's entry in my diary, mildly frustrated by my inability to communicate more effectively, I decide to retire early. Gao enters the darkened room several times while I'm in bed, ostensibly to hang up some clothes, but she never fails to glance in my direction before she leaves. I lie there in the semi-darkness, the U2 song *I Still Haven't Found What I'm Looking For* replaying itself inside my head and preventing sleep:

I have climbed the highest mountains
I have run through the fields
Only to be with you.
I have run, I have crawled
I have scaled these city walls
Only to be with you.

At length I doze off to a puerile fantasy involving being woken by her soft lips being applied to mine.

It is the gentle pressure of her hand on my shoulder that wakes me up, however. She is perched daintily on my bed in the semi-darkness brandishing a 100-yuan note. My initial reaction is one of slight unease – I've already paid for my meal and accommodation, so why is she demanding more money from me? The next thought that surfaces from the mental confusion is that she's offering me her body for a hundred yuan, but she has never remotely struck me as 'that kind of gal'. For a start, her clothes don't fit the bill. If she had swapped her unflattering outfit of plain jacket and loose-fitting trousers for a skimpy skirt or dress I might have thought otherwise, but she has dressed to cook and clean rather than to seduce potential clients, and she isn't wearing any make-up. With the darkness adding intimacy and a sense of conspiracy to an already charged atmosphere it takes several minutes of *sotto voce* exchanges and sign language (during which I wonder distractedly how she'd react if I pulled her down on top of me and kissed her) before I realise that she is asking me if I have change for the note.

I fish out my money belt and give her two fifties.

There follows more sign language and a good deal of incomprehension. She appears to be asking if I'd like her to leave and let me get some sleep.

It is the oddest of questions. Of course I don't want her to go. She is intriguing and exotic and her smile makes me dizzy, but I can think of only one reason why she should stay. She is sitting dangerously close and I am naked under my blanket. She appears to be in no hurry to depart with her change and she quite literally hasn't been able to take her eyes off me all evening. Was the 100-yuan note just a pretext for another chance of making contact? I'd have interpreted her behaviour in a western woman as the clearest of all green lights, but I am painfully aware that in the Far East the game of seduction might be played out according to very different rules.

Life is full of little ironies. In a Lanzhou salon I was fully aware that I was being propositioned, but unable to determine that the girl was attracted to me for the right reasons, I held back. Now, as certain as I can possibly be that Gao finds me every bit as exciting as I find her, I can't quite decide if she is attempting to seduce me or not. A beautiful damsel marooned in an ugly roadside pit stop in the middle of nowhere, bored by a routine of dull and repetitive chores (and maybe – who knows? – by her husband too) is naturally excited and curious when a mysterious, travel-stained stranger from a distant land appears unexpectedly on a black charger, choosing this most forlorn and unlikely of places to interrupt a great quest. Although he is clearly tired, he carries himself with pride, for he has crossed towering mountain ranges, traversed burning deserts and immense plains, and ridden through cyclones, blizzards, hurricanes, sandstorms, thunder and lightning. He has survived Pakistani food and Indian drivers and defied the demons in the deserts beyond the Great Wall. He has cheated death by dead fish and stoning in Indus Kohistan, and braved the roaring metal dragons in the black mountain lairs of Turkey and China. He has been pursued by the progeny of Beelzebub and by dogs with eyes the size of dinner plates. He has slept with the dead. He has worn out two sets of tyres, two chains and a pair of boots.

Only to be with you.

Of all this she knows nothing of course, but maybe she guesses a little of it. Feminine fascination is the most potent of drugs and I could so easily become intoxicated by it. Ever since leaving Europe I have been the object of considerable interest and curiosity, but until China its source was invariably male. Because in China women have been free for the first time since Istanbul to express that interest, I should be particularly wary of misinterpreting it for something else. Gao's husband (a pleasant chap who welcomed me with great warmth and offered me food, shelter and a beer) is in the next room, for heaven's sake. Isn't he a little troubled by the fact that his gorgeous wife is alone in the stranger's bedroom? Either he has every reason to trust her completely, or he takes her entirely for granted and simply doesn't care what we get up to together. They might be estranged. Or perhaps she is on the game after all, using prostitution with his blessing as a way to gain extra income to support her family.

Not the least of her charms, however, is the captivating transparency of her fascination and I can't bring myself to believe that she regards me as a client. If that were the case I'm sure she'd have found a way of spelling it out to me just as the Lanzhou hairdresser did. That bewitching smile and her glimmering eyes make her husband seem distant and irrelevant and I long to reach out for her, just to kiss her hand or her cheek and see what develops, but it would surely be considered reprehensible behaviour in any culture to accept a man's hospitality and then make a pass at his wife, and even if she was to make a move herself, I don't think I'd be able to take advantage without ultimately feeling ashamed of myself.

I still haven't found what I'm looking for.

Many years ago I was lucky enough to find it, but I let it slip through my fingers. Maybe it only happens once in a lifetime; I imagine that some people spend their entire lives in a futile search for it.

Not knowing what else to do, I signal to Gao that I'm going to go to sleep. It seems that I'm not cut out to play the role of Sir Lancelot to her Guinevere.

She gets to her feet and drifts silently out of the room, a vanishing dream.

I always preferred Gawain to Lancelot anyway. I spend the rest of a sleepless night wishing that she'd come back.

*

Yan'an is choked with traffic and, like Lanzhou, hemmed into a narrow valley by mountains. I find my way through by trusting to instinct and the guidebook's street plan, but later I get lost in a much smaller town called Yaodian, where I find myself cycling along a road that I know from the direction of the sun and the lie of the land doesn't correspond to the one marked on my maps. And yet the signpost had clearly indicated 'straight on' for Yulin.

Or had it? Had I been half-asleep, still dreaming about Gao, when I passed it? Geocenter and the larger scale Nelles roadmaps are unanimous in their belief that I should instead have turned left and taken the road to Qinghuabian, but a shopkeeper and an elderly lady both confirm that this is indeed the right way to Yulin. Unconvinced, I cycle back to check the signpost only to find that I had been right first time: Yulin is straight on. Maps inevitably become outdated, particularly in a country in which major improvements are being made to the road network. The evidence of China's booming economy can be seen not only in the construction sites and new buildings sprouting up in the cities, but also in the extensive road-building projects. All over the country brand-new highways are being built alongside and on top of the old roads and there are frequent diversions onto hurriedly improvised dirt tracks or the stony beds of the new roads.

Whereas Indians undeniably brought out the worst in my nature at times, the Chinese continue to bring out the best in me. I am rapidly forming the opinion that not knowing a language has its advantages and that words can be a distraction. In their absence I have become hypersensitive to body language and facial expressions. So much can be conveyed by a single smile: welcome, admiration, friendship, delight, recognition, greetings, and even unease or embarrassment.

Hullo! I come in peace! Let's be friends! says my smile as I stop beside a roadside stall for a drink.

Gosh! Welcome to our country, stranger! What can I do for you? replies the smile of the vendeuse.

Chinese women are so delightfully uninhibited. Gao's smile had said plainer than any words *I think you're amazing!* and mine had replied *Wow! You're gorgeous!* We might have put less energy into smiling at each other if we'd been able to talk. Her husband had been the only person about when I got up and I had been fearful that I wouldn't get a chance to say goodbye to her before I left, but she emerged shortly afterwards clad in a short, patterned dress, looking sleepy and tousled and wholly kissable. As soon as she understood that I wanted to photograph her she went back into the building and reappeared with her hair immaculate and wearing a long red dress, clearly anxious to look her best. She needn't have worried: some women look glamorous whatever they wear and I had appreciated her every bit as much in her dowdy, shapeless work clothes.

I came to the reluctant conclusion last night that she was inviolable, but a day later, still drunk with the power of that smile, I have no idea whether I was right or not. My boyhood fantasies, fuelled by the exploits of heroes like Ivanhoe, King Arthur and Robin Hood and by legends such as the Siege of Troy, had been conveniently free of moral dilemmas; beautiful damsels were always plainly in distress and had always been in obvious need of rescuing. There had never been the slightest ambiguity about the matter; if they were married it was invariably against their will to sadistic brutes who starved and cruelly beat them until they were dispatched to eternal damnation by a clean sweep of my shining sword. But sadistic brutes don't offer you a beer, and the worst crime of which Gao's inoffensive husband had appeared capable was indifference (although I suppose that in some circumstances that can be crueller than any beating). I was never able to work out quite at which point reality ended and my imagination took over, and principles intervened in the end just as they had done in Lanzhou (albeit for very different reasons). They are becoming the most boring and tiresome baggage to carry around; I really ought to have left home without them.

Chris! You should've f***ed her! an email from the brother in New York lamented, referring without preamble to the episode in the Lanzhou hairdressing salon. *I don't think you understand. Your readership is crying out for some romantic (or better, sexual) interest in the unfolding narrative. First the*

Dutch girl and now, not screwing a pro. I dunno. If you write a book about this, you'll find it easier to get published with some kind of parallel romantic subplot (preferably with some syrupy-sweet ending) that unfolds with the ups and downs of the road.

During one of his more contemplative moments in the Baluchistan desert Ralf expressed the opinion that *some people* (including both himself and me) *just aren't meant to do the 'Honey, I'm home!' thing*, but despite the latest manifestation of an unfortunate propensity to fall for utterly unsuitable women, I have never seen myself as one of them. Whereas Ralf is a dyed-in-the-wool cynic, I'm a hopeless romantic, persisting in the belief that love conquers all and that it can ambush you when you least expect it and in the most extraordinary places.

Klompjes would have been the ideal partner in so many ways. She liked me for all the right reasons and there was no husband or partner to complicate matters. She was adventurous, spirited, charming, sweet and funny, and came as close to understanding me as any woman probably ever will. One evening in Delhi she had expressed concern in her uninhibited Dutch way that it was too early to go to sleep.

'Don't worry! After reading *City of Joy* in a foreign language for half an hour you'll be ready to sleep.'

'I can think of much nicer ways.'

'I don't know what you mean,' I lied.

'I think it is quite strange for two single people to share a room for all this time and not... well, share the bed too.'

'Do you? Why? You didn't share beds with Martin.'

'No, but I didn't like him that way.'

For two months we fulfilled in each other the physical requirement to love and be loved, but although the relationship was satisfying and fun and affectionate, it never crossed the border into mutual passion. Klompjes offered me something that is beyond price, but I was unable to accept it. It is a bitter irony that a married woman with whom I was barely able to communicate was nevertheless capable of the one vital thing that Klompjes wasn't: she had the ability to make my pulse race with a single glance or smile.

I'm doing my damnedest, but syrupy-sweet endings, my brother, are far easier to contrive in works of fiction.

Chapter Twenty-Four
Man With No Name

Directed by pointing fingers, I eventually find myself standing in the reception area of a large hotel arranged around a drab, concrete courtyard. The streets of Qingjian are packed and about forty people with nothing better to do have followed me in. Perspiring heavily after a long, hot ride and irritated by the press of bodies, I turn to address the multitude. 'Do you all need a room too?' I ask it peevishly.

Both the sarcasm and the meaning of the words themselves are predictably lost on them, and I am astonished (and dismayed) that the receptionists are prepared to tolerate the invasion. When I pick up a pen to write down my details in the registration book forty people lean over my shoulder with bated breath, but the resentment soon disappears because they are so helpful. Willing hands heave the loaded bicycle up a steep flight of steps and I find myself sharing a pleasant, spacious four-bed dormitory with my bicycle and about twenty onlookers.

I am desperate for a chance to wash, shave, write my diary and put my feet up, but I keep on getting visitors, many of them delegations of teenage girls from the local middle school eager to practise their English. How on earth they got to know that I was staying at the hotel, never mind which room I was in, I have no idea. They are sweet, well meaning and ever so slightly dizzy. Their English, it has to be said, is poor.

Three of them cheerfully announce that I'll be coming to school with them tomorrow.

No, I won't. I hate to disappoint them, but I have no intention of postponing my plan to cycle on to Liulin. Really. I'm polite, but firm. Sandstorms, thunderstorms, blizzards, hurricanes, mountain ranges and intense heat I can cope with, but being paraded before hordes of overexcited and inquisitive schoolgirls like a trophy *(Hey, everybody! Look what we've found!)* just isn't for me. I am far from certain moreover that the teachers would welcome my unexpected and undoubtedly disruptive presence in their classes. I employ the

251

old 'limited time on my visa' excuse, which I'm not sure they understand and no longer applies anyway, but I lie without a qualm.

Writing is a slow business with all the distractions and it is getting dark. The strip light in my room isn't working and a replacement is sent for. Some schoolgirls want to pose with me for photographs (using *my* camera if you please) but fortunately there's nobody around to take the photo. Others entreat me to 'tell them about England', but I can think of absolutely nothing to say. The television is showing grainy cartoons in high volume Chinese because some misguided soul has thoughtfully switched it on for me. At length two men arrive with the replacement light, but that doesn't work either and I'm transferred to another room. One lad who speaks no English at all is waiting patiently for me to finish writing because he wants to take me somewhere to eat, but the heat – suffocating even after nightfall – has robbed me of my appetite. Eventually he too departs and at last I have the room to myself.

The hotel's lavatories are situated in a separate block. Since crossing the Bosphorus I've encountered some fairly grisly examples of the squat toilet (in which you place your feet upon parallel porcelain steps and squat over a hole) but the full horror of the Asian latrine finds its apotheosis in China. A narrow strip of concrete spans a trench filled with a stinking pile of excrement alive with fat, squirming maggots. You carefully position your posterior over one of the half-dozen rectangular slots cut into the concrete and release your bomb in the company of up to five other people grunting and straining. Owing to the inaccuracy of some squatters, the lip of each slot is daubed with shit and plump, long-tailed maggots wriggle exultantly around your feet. It was in India that I first came across the phenomenon of social defecation, but never until I arrived in China did I expect to be participating in the ritual myself.

*

At a drinks stop in a village east of Suide a chair is brought out for me and I sit there on the pavement eating an ice cream and rehydrating with icy bottles of orange fizz and mineral water. I can hear children chanting inside the school opposite and I wonder if they are rehearsing their revolutionary slogans. Do they still bother with all that stuff these days? Communism is yesterday's failed experiment and present-day China embodies almost nothing of its ideals (apart from the Communist Party's inalienable right to govern). An audience has materialised as usual from nowhere, so my piece of pavement has become quite crowded. I'd love to have a photograph taken of me sprawled in a chair calmly eating and drinking while twenty or thirty people of all ages and both sexes discuss me and gape at me, but of course the spontaneity of the scene would be lost as soon as they realised that they were being photographed. An attractive young woman is standing at the gates of the school and the woman who sold me my drinks is trying to persuade her to come over, but she appears to be too timid.

'English teacher!' explains a voice in the crowd.

The shopkeeper signals that I should walk over and introduce myself, but sat on my throne amongst my entourage, I indicate with an imperious wave of my arm that the young woman should come over to me instead. She is eventually persuaded (with much general mirth) to approach, but she is very self-conscious and all she can ask is if I'm from England. Either she isn't as accustomed as I am to holding conversations in front of thirty onlookers or she is fearful that I might expose any inadequacies in her English. A pity.

*

At Songjiachuan the road crosses the Yellow River and enters Shanxi Province. Shanxi accounts for a third of China's known iron and coal deposits, and the yellow loess dust of Shaanxi and Eastern Gansu has been replaced by coal dust. The road to Liulin is lined with squalid villages of grimy brick or tiled buildings that run into each other. Coal is heaped upon the pavements, in yards next to the railway and upon lorries.

The first four and a half hours of cycling east from Liulin are uphill as the road wends its way up a valley before climbing steeply into the Luliang Shan. Mines have pushed up forests of chimneys, and slag heaps abound. Coal dust lies thickly on the verges and hangs in the air, covering everything in a patina of grime. The road surface is cracked and lumpy, disintegrating under the pounding of the pale-blue lorries that shudder past in low gear, themselves breaking up under the weight of their loads of coal. Two of them have collided with each other and appear to have been abandoned, and several have stopped at the side of the road with their engines bellowing impotently. Others, more seriously afflicted, stand mute with bonnets gaping or cabs tilted while bits of engine or transmission are surgically removed by prone figures working beneath. By the time I stop just outside Lishi for a meal after overtaking a lorry labouring up a gradient, I have taken on the appearance of a particularly disreputable Victorian chimney-sweep, covered in coal dust and the soot vomited out by geriatric diesel engines.

I book into a hotel in Fenyang that boasts rooms with colour television, air conditioning, hot water, an en suite bathroom and complementary sachets of green tea for just fifty yuan. Following a luxurious soak in a hot bath I bask in an equally warm reception at a café across the road. An English-speaking teacher volunteers the information that today has been the hottest of the year so far, the temperature having peaked at thirty-eight degrees Celsius.

'We think you're great!' he says solemnly.

The feeling is fully reciprocated; never have I encountered such generous and frank admiration. The Chinese don't deserve their reprehensible government.

*

I've had Beijing in my sights for so long now that each remaining day separating me from my objective is in danger of simply becoming an obstacle to be overcome rather than an adventure to be relished. Between Fenyang and Taiyuan the road at last leaves the mountains and crosses a wide plain. The sky is overcast and a haze of smog reduces visibility. Smoke rises from burning stubble and the blue coal lorries clatter past at regular intervals, the drivers aggressively sounding their overused horns. Some of the worst culprits for chucking out undigested diesel are the noisy little three-wheeler, two-stroke, belt-driven pick-up trucks that ply the roads all over China. Exposed areas of skin have become black with soot and coal-dust, and my eyes are red-rimmed and smarting but I can regularly wash my face and arms in the basins of water that are always provided at cafés. It is so hot that I sweat more eating noodles and drinking green tea than when cycling.

I am still having problems with the language. The waitresses in a roadside restaurant giggle vacuously when I ask in my best Mandarin for noodles and egg so I march into the kitchen and point to some raw noodle mixture and some eggshells, and the resulting noodles served with omelette and tomato is exactly what I wanted. A bemused café owner learns that I have ridden all the way from the UK on a tomato, and it takes me an hour to find my way out of Taiyuan because there are no signs that mean anything at all to me. Asking for directions is the usual frustrating business; there is a limit to the number of ways that you can pronounce a simple, two-syllable name like Datong and I must have tried them all. With each blank, uncomprehending stare I have to go through the laborious ritual of getting the guidebook out of my bar-bag, finding the Datong section, and pointing to the Chinese characters. Apart from the unfathomable alphabet the biggest obstacle to communication, I think, is that several words are spelt in exactly the same way and distinguished only by the intonation used. You literally have to sing them. This has the effect of greatly increasing the number of variables in the way a word can be uttered and therefore multiplies the number of ways in which you can make yourself misunderstood. Each syllable can be howled in four different ways: high, rising, falling-rising and falling. Given that the apparently innocuous monosyllable *ma* can mean 'mother', 'horse', 'scold' or 'swear', or 'hemp' or 'numb' (depending upon the way you warble it), 'Datong' suddenly looks very complicated indeed.

THE KEY TO GOOD INVESTMENT IS A DEVELOPING MARKET
trumpets a huge roadside billboard. Mao must be turning in his mausoleum.
The Communist Party risks appearing more and more of an anachronism as
the economy, fuelled by the cheap labour provided by migrant workers,
continues to forge ahead. Manufacturing costs are about 10 per cent of those
of the USA, Japan and Western Europe and the economy has quadrupled in
size over the last twenty years.

*

The China of my imagination, a flat, intensely populated land of endless rice
paddies, resolutely refuses to materialise. Beyond Daying the road leaves the
Hutuo River and climbs into the foothills of the Wutai Shan, a chain of
mountains that reach heights in excess of three thousand metres. At Shentangbao
several hairpin bends lead to a high pass overlooked by fortified watchtowers
and another precipitous, cork-screwing descent.

After spending a cosy night concealed amongst massive blocks of stone in
an abandoned quarry, I discover that the rear carrier has fractured, a victim no
doubt of the consistently poor road surface of the G108. Having experimented
unsuccessfully with cable-ties, I dismount opposite a man welding a
wheelbarrow on a building site in Laiyuan. He summons a couple of colleagues
and together they have a go at the carrier, but the two ends won't merge and
if anything their efforts have made the situation worse. Undaunted, they
improvise a repair by cutting a length of concrete-reinforcement steel and
tying it parallel to the broken support with copper wire, their work cheerfully
abandoned. They refuse to accept the fifty yuan I offer them for their trouble,
and I cycle off with the carrier as good as new (but with recently-added
character) and with ample cause once again to marvel at the magnanimity of
the Chinese.

An hour later the road forks and a sign in Chinese and Latin characters
indicates Beijing to the left and Tianjin to the right. I take the left hand fork and
the road immediately begins to climb steeply. For the first time for over a
hundred miles the surface is good, so I'm astonished to find great chunks
inexplicably dug out of it by 'repairers'. It is infuriating because I have to slow
to a crawl to cross each stretch of rubble and I spend a good deal of time
wrestling – between curses – with the question as to why people have been
paid to vandalise a perfectly good road. It is an enigma as insoluble as the
Naked Lady I saw walking along the verge yesterday. She was middle-aged,
unattractive, stark-naked and beyond doubt utterly bonkers. Some of the
excavated sections are so rough that I have to dismount, and I conclude
eventually that the only reason to dig up an excellent road surface must be to

encourage through traffic to use an alternative route to Beijing – but why then the signpost?

If the aim was indeed to discourage through traffic then they appear to have succeeded, for the road, climbing via countless hairpin bends into jagged green peaks, is almost deserted. During a pause to rest my aching back I sit on a concrete parapet, listening to the patter of drizzle, the buzz of insects and the warbling of the birds. The vegetation looks almost sub-tropical and the massive green-clad mountainsides take me back to those gruelling days on the Black Sea Coast. Sheep grazing on a distant hillside look like maggots.

On a steep, twisting downhill stretch beyond a lofty pass I spot an isolated café. The place appears to be run by two girls, aged eighteen and twenty. There is a father with his young tot and a couple of young men are wandering around to no great purpose. The father, a scrawny little runt of a character who appears to be mentally as well as physically compromised, is one of the very few truly annoying people I've met in China, persistently calling out to me in English. Since his only two words are *Hello* and *Bye-bye* conversation quickly becomes rather monotonous. With the help of graphic sign language he indicates that I'll be able to get a good f**k in Beijing and I wonder how on earth he knows – I can't imagine that any woman would sleep with him for fun.

One of the younger guys tells me that he is twenty-eight and unemployed. He used to drive one of those smoke-belching little three-wheeled pick-up trucks until he overturned it one evening after downing eight beers. His elbow is in a brace as a result of the accident and he finds using his left arm awkward. After confiding with a smirk that the elder of the two girls is 'his property', he points suggestively to the younger girl who brought me my food and writes *I love you* in biro in the palm of his hand. I'm faintly embarrassed by this juvenile behaviour but the girl, who is very sweet and lovely but far too young, is acutely discomfited by it and furious with him.

After dinner we stroll up the hill in the darkness and sit for a while on a section of road overlooking the twinkling lights of a village deep in one of the valleys. Spectacular flashes of sheet lightning are illuminating the sky over the mountains to the east.

*

I get up at dawn. Mist has veiled the mountaintops. Beijing is only about 130 miles away and I'm anxious to make a start.

The others surface one by one.

'Hello!' screams the runt.

'I think you mean "good-bye!" don't you?' I retort, mounting my steed.

'Hello!'

'Bye-bye!'

I have become the Man With No Name, the mysterious stranger riding into people's lives but always moving on – just like Charles Bronson in *Once Upon A Time In The West* (all I need is a soundtrack by Ennio Morricone). 'Harmonica' (the character played by Bronson) had been obsessed by revenge and was probably more than a little deranged – but then there had been no shortage of people back home who thought exactly the same of an individual prepared to cycle alone across Asia.

Chapter Twenty-Five
Homeward Bound

Dear Mr. Smith,
I am pleased to tell you that the telex number of your invitation has arrived at the Russian embassy in Beijing. You can collect it there, it has been deposited on your name.

In Marco Polo's time travelling merchants risked ambush by bandits and warlords, but the greatest obstacle to the modern traveller is bureaucracy.

Dear Sabine,
I spent all this morning queuing in sweltering heat outside the Russian embassy here in Beijing, only to be told that they had NOT received the telex! The woman there checked on her computer twice, using both my passport number and my date of birth as references, but she had no record of it. Please, please send it again IMMEDIATELY so that I can get things going tomorrow (before the weekend). Please also send me an email to confirm that you have sent it and that I will be able to collect it tomorrow.

Instead of getting a well-merited opportunity to relax and do some sightseeing I am shuttling between my hotel, the Russian embassy and an Internet café on the other side of Beijing because the German travel agency I've authorised to provide the documents necessary for my visa application has evidently failed to telex them through. The conditions outside the Russian embassy are unspeakable.

Dear Mr. Smith,
Attached to this mail I send you a copy of your invitation as prove to the Russian Embassy. Our Russian colleagues again have assured to us that there is a telex at the Embassy but you can also get your visa with this copy of the invitation. Hope there will be no more difficulties tomorrow.

After hours of pushing and shoving in a sweaty scrum of identically stress-laden and desperate people in the blazing sunshine outside the embassy gates for the second time, faxed copies and pleas are rejected alike. The spirit of Andrei Gromyko, the stonewalling Soviet foreign minister, lives on in the staff of Russia's Beijing embassy and once again I reel dazedly back to the tube station with a resounding *nyet* ringing in my ears.

Dear Sabine,
I printed out the invitation and took it along to the Russian Embassy this morning. However there is still no record on their computer that they ever received the original telex and they will not accept copies. It also appears that the invitation is unsatisfactory because for a business visa they require a letter of invitation addressed to me from a Russian company giving full details of the company's particulars, including the company registration number. I would suggest that you send the original telex again, plus the necessary supporting documents. Perhaps one of your Russian colleagues can contact the embassy to find out EXACTLY what they require. If this matter is not satisfactorily sorted out by the middle of next week, I will have to swallow my disappointment and make alternative plans, avoiding Russia. Naturally in this case I will expect my money to be refunded in full.

Amongst the arcane requirements for a Russian visa are a letter of invitation from a Russian resident or company, an itinerary specifying the arrival and departure dates at each hotel (out of the question if you're travelling by bicycle) and, in some instances, even a plane ticket out of the country – as if any western tourist would seriously entertain the idea of emigrating illegally to a crime-ridden, poverty-stricken, moribund mess like Russia.

Dear Mr. Smith,
I talked again to our Russian Colleagues today, they have checked with the Russian Foreign Ministry and they confirmed again that the telex was sent to Bejing. They were also surprised that the printout was not accepted because this is an official invitation which so far has been accepted at every other embassy. Nevertheless, they will try to phone Bejing themselves to find out what is wrong - although they don't expect too much from it. In the meantime they will get a knew invitation for you which should be at Bejing on Thursday. I hope that their efforts will successful and will contact you again as soon as there are news.

Others before me have successfully circumvented the tangle of red tape to cycle independently in Russia but the Beijing embassy is notorious as one of the most uncompromising of them all.

Hi Sabine,
Will the new invitation be at the Beijing Embassy on Tuesday or Thursday?
I will await confirmation from you that it has arrived before trying again.
If your Russian colleagues could get the name of a contact there with whom
they have spoken and who knows about my application it might be helpful.
I have to say that I am not very optimistic. I have cycled more than 26500kms
through eleven countries in 13 months to get this far and Russia is the first
which has given me any problems at all. Their visa regulations are absurd.
As soon as you get news that the new invitation has arrived at the embassy,
please let me know. I don't want to be waiting for much longer.

As soon as the dinosaurs in the Kremlin wake up to the fact that their bankrupt country needs every tourist dollar it can get the application procedure will be simplified, but their slumber has continued into the new millennium.

Hi Mr. Smith,
It will arrive on Tuesday - sorry for the mistake in typing. Of course I will
give you the confirmation as soon as I know it is there.

I kill time by travelling on the underground and drifting around Beijing on foot. Pizza Huts, McDonalds, Kentucky Fried Chicken, Baskin Robbins, Starbucks (and other western chains that I've never heard of before) have spread like chickenpox across the face of China's capital city and I indulge myself endlessly on coffee and fast food, endorsing globalisation and welcoming the change from noodles and green tea. Tiananmen Square is a vast and rather bleak concrete apron and the Forbidden City, full of tour groups, is interesting and an impressive size but unable to match the serene beauty of either the Taj Mahal or the Golden Temple – and it pales into insignificance next to the recollection of the morning sunshine glinting off the snows of Nanga Parbat.

Dear Sabine,
Can I assume that the telex has arrived at the embassy today and go to
collect it tomorrow morning (Wednesday?)

Harmonica would have shot the bastards at the embassy and galloped off to the border, but then he wouldn't have required a visa; he wouldn't have had a passport and he hadn't even needed a name. Some aspects of life at least were simpler in nineteenth-century America.

Dear Mr. Smith,
Our Russian colleagues sent a new invitation to the embassy and assured us
that you can collect it there by now. I hope you won't have any more trouble now.

Amen to that. I don't have the energy to deal with any more trouble. A toilet attendant and a yoghurt vendor attempt to overcharge me on the way back to the hotel, and a couple of delightful and thoroughly unchaste young women shave my head.

Dear Sabine,
I have just returned from yet another unsuccessful visit to the Russian embassy. Still no record of a telex in my name on their computer. I have now wasted three mornings waiting outside their visa department and I cannot see any solution to the problems. I have therefore reluctantly decided to cancel my plans to cycle on to Vladivostok and to make alternative arrangements. Please therefore reimburse my credit card account in full, and send me an email to confirm that you have done this.

Implacably tightening its grip and denying me the oxygen of hope, the cold, dead hand of bureaucracy has finally asphyxiated the fragile dream.

Dear Mr. Smith,
Sorry for the delayed answer. Of course we regret the trouble you had at the embassy in Bejing - but nevertheless the telex was definitely forwarded there and our Russian colleagues have cross-checked again that the telex was there. Since we had sent the telex correctly there might have been some other reasons why the embassy in Bejing did not grant the visa. Maybe because of the means of transport you had chosen - maybe there were some other reasons. Anyway we have fulfilled our part of the contract and have sent the telex and thus cannot reimburse the amount to your credit card account.

*

Thirty-five thousand feet below the Air China 747 I can make out a flat, unpopulated landscape of forests and lakes and winding rivers glimmering silver in the sunshine.

Siberia.

Mesmerised by the sight, I can feel only the most painful regret that I'm flying over instead of cycling (or at least travelling by train) across one of the remotest places on earth, a mysterious land that has intrigued me since childhood.

Why don't you fly, Christopher?

Because I yearn to feel sunshine, wind and rain on my face, to hear a foreign country's birdsong and traffic, to taste its food and drink its water, to smell its farms and factories, to bump over its dreadful roads and to feel its hard, lumpy ground beneath me as I sleep out in its birch and pine forests with its dust mingling with the salt on my skin. Most of all I want to meet its people and to witness – and perhaps even sample – a way of life different to my own.

I had imagined the final months of the journey so clearly. A final three-week push through Manchuria to the border was to have been followed by a two-week ride on rough roads from Blagovescensk to Vladivostok, where I'd have leaned the bicycle up in the city's central square to allow myself to savour a priceless Perfect Moment. The six-day trans-Siberian train ride across Russia to Moscow would have been the ultimate reward for the previous months of toil, a glorious week of watching the Siberian landscape slide by without effort, aching or anxiety. Heaven must be an endless succession of Perfect Moments and on that train I fancy that I'd have caught more than just a glimpse of Paradise.

The power of that vision had sustained me across two continents and thirteen countries but things rarely turn out exactly as you expect when travelling – which is precisely why I've always found it so worthwhile. Sweeping away all my preconceptions, China had been a case in point; positively the last thing I'd anticipated was that I'd fall head over heels in love with the country and its people.

For a fee, a local travel agency offered to arrange a visa, tickets for either the Trans-Mongolian or Trans-Manchurian trains that run direct from Beijing to Moscow, hotel bookings and onward transport out of Russia. In order to comply with the stringent regulations limiting baggage, however, I'd have had to dismantle the bicycle and shoehorn it into a box no larger than 30.5 x 159 x 67cm. I doubted that this would have been possible but the sad truth is that I wasn't even prepared to try. The denial of the Russian visa had knocked all the fight out of me and I'd had enough of travel agents and their promises.

I considered using up the weeks remaining on my Chinese visa by cycling on to Vietnam or Laos, but Beijing was already like an oven and the heat would only have intensified on the route south. I toyed with the idea of taking a leaf out of Alois' book by flying to San Francisco and cycling across the States but decided that, like southeast Asia, the USA wasn't quite worth the trouble. Considerably closer than either, Ulan Baator and Outer Mongolia offered something of the remoteness and end-of-the-earth appeal of Vladivostok, but I found that I could no longer face the prospect of fighting hurricane-force winds. The journey had lost its focus and I was no longer able to find sufficient motivation to put my body through extra weeks of sweat and soreness. Vladivostok had been an obsession; denied it, I felt rudderless.

Haven't you done enough? demanded an insidious little voice that had been getting harder and harder to ignore.

For most people I think the answer would have been an unequivocal *yes*, but then I'm not 'most people'. Nevertheless, I capitulated; I allowed it to persuade me to buy a one-way ticket to Frankfurt for five hundred US dollars. Undoubtedly I should have fought harder, but having arrived in Beijing physically battered and emotionally drained by the crossing of China, I'd had little fight left. The passion that had burned so brightly for so many months had died, consumed perhaps by the sheer intensity of the Chinese experience. A Russian visa alone would have been sufficient to rekindle it and keep the embers smouldering for the extra five or six weeks it would have taken to reach Vladivostok.

The little that remained of my previous energy deserted me entirely after I booked the flight back to Europe. Those final days in China were swelteringly hot and punctuated by thunderstorms and deluges of rain. I spent time in Internet cafés acknowledging sympathetic emails, and in the warm evenings I sat on the hotel's terrace and drank cold Chinese beer with a friendly bunch of European and Antipodean backpackers. Seven of us shared the cost of a minibus for the daytrip to a crumbling, overgrown, but nonetheless impressive section of the Great Wall as it wound its way steeply across the mountains at Huanghuacheng.

*

Whereas in Asia I was subjected to a degree of scrutiny that in the West is the preserve only of celebrities, no one in Germany (apart from Ralf) has any idea that I have just cycled 16,500 miles across two continents. During the ten hours it took for the Air China Jumbo Jet to fly from Beijing to Frankfurt I reverted from being extraordinary to ordinary, and although it was difficult to deal with at times, I even find myself missing the attention. I've become just another touring cyclist and it's odd no longer being surrounded by crowds of people whenever I stop at a filling station or supermarket to buy provisions; the metamorphosis back from Superman to Clark Kent was achieved in only a few hours and it takes a little time to readjust.

Vorsprung durch technik. Doesn't that mean 'Advance through technology'? Those who choose to advance through Germany by alternative means find themselves marginalised. Full of bossy directives to use cycle paths that are poorly signposted, poorly surfaced and have a nasty habit of depositing you in the middle of nowhere and with no idea where to go next, this is anything but my idea of a cycling paradise. With many of the main roads classified as expressways (and consequently out of bounds to cyclists along with the dual carriageways and autobahns) I have been obliged time after time to backtrack and search for an alternative route. After several false starts I found myself heading away from Frankfurt Airport along a bumpy, un-surfaced cycle track that led me through a wood.

Roads in the developing world may have been chaotic and dangerous, but there was a glorious sense of freedom out there. No Big Brother telling you what you must or mustn't do, or where you could or couldn't go. You could do anything and go anywhere you liked and people usually did, cycling or driving exuberantly against the traffic flow and joyfully ignoring traffic lights. Weaving in and out of the congestion in the cities and racing for the small gaps of empty road, high on adrenalin, I came to enjoy taking on the locals and beating them at their own game, but in Germany any such improvisation by road-users is strictly *verboten* and only the weather is allowed to be unpredictable. Intervals of bright sunshine alternate with overcast skies and occasional thundery showers of rain. I camp out in damp woods with enormous orange slugs for company, dozing off in my sleeping bag to the whispering of the trees and the distant pealing of church bells.

A free spirit amongst people who celebrate regulation and conformity, Ralf fails to answer his bell when I call and a neighbour informs me that he is holidaying in Austria with his mother. I have no idea when he'll be back, so there is nothing for it but to turn westwards, towards Holland. So desperate am I to leave Germany that I cover the 111 miles from Vlotho to Enschede in a single day.

*

'Do you like Holland then?' Klompjes challenges me after a day spent sunbathing amongst hordes of Dutch and German sun-seekers on the beach at Zandvoort.

It took me only a day and a half to cross the Netherlands from east to west; European countries are positively Lilliputian after Asia. Unencumbered by panniers, the bicycle feels abnormally light as we accelerate along cycle paths criss-crossing an area of woods, canals and pasture. I know she is dying for me to say yes, but I have a perverse reluctance to yield. 'I think cycling in Holland is a bit like cycling the Karakoram Highway, but without the mountains. Show me a mountain and *then* ask me,' I tease her. Holland is pleasant enough and altogether less irritating than Germany, but I can find little splendid or dramatic or inspirational in the tidy landscape. Maybe it feels too much like home.

*

After a day and a half's cycle ride from Haarlem I arrive – true to form about three hours ahead of schedule – in a nondescript German town called Wesel. I while away the time in a café next to the railway station by eating sandwiches, drinking coffee and studying *Bild*, which appears to be a Teutonic version of *The Sun*. Along with the German football league tables, the paper contains several pictures of scantily dressed women and a feature that appears to be about some lunatic's attempt to create a Hitler clone.

'Hey, Dude!' A victim of queuing traffic on the autobahns, Ralf is just as typically an hour late. He tells me contritely that if he hadn't driven illegally and unethically down the hard shoulder for the final twenty kilometres he'd have been even later and I feel more strongly than ever that he was born in the wrong country. He was probably born on the wrong planet.

After placing the bicycle in the back of his little van we head along the network of autobahns to Germany's industrial heartland, where VFL Bochum are to play Karlsruhe. A coltish beauty wearing a Kicker T-shirt and very little else intercepts us outside the ground and Ralf explains that she is offering a year's subscription to the magazine at a discount price.

'Have you informed her that you've been using pages torn from the magazine as toilet paper?' I ask him.

'Don't worry about my English friend!' he reassures her. 'He's mentally retarded.'

After savouring a few moments over a couple of beers and a *Ruhrstadion Wurst* outside the compact, modern stadium, we squeeze into the end occupied by the most vocal Bochum supporters. German football fans are very much like their English counterparts; there is a lot of triumphal singing and waving and when the chant turns to *Sieg! Sieg! Sieg!* I feel as if I'm at a Nuremburg rally.

'I take it that you understood that bit!' Ralf's sardonic voice rises above the general German hubbub. I have gathered that the object of his devotion is the Birmingham City of German football: a big-city club that has achieved little during its long history. At the end of last season the team was relegated to the Second Division.

The essential ghastliness of being a football supporter is the same the world over; notwithstanding the occasional explosions of unrestrained joy, anger and apprehension are the dominant emotions experienced during the average ninety minutes. Pre-match optimism following a victory in the opening game of the season reaches a peak when Bochum score an early goal, but Karlsruhe equalise almost immediately and the game degenerates into scrappiness and tedium. The Bochum players are idolised during brief periods of domination, but as soon as a misplaced pass or poor control causes a move to break down they are vilified. Exasperated cries of *Mon, mon, mon!* signal disapproval and frustration, and when the cunning Wosz (arguably Bochum's only creative player) is sent off in the second half after a second booking for the odious offence of 'diving', the roars and whistles of fury reach a crescendo. Things are beginning to look bleak for the home crowd, but Bochum's ten men manage to hold out for an unsatisfactory draw. When a disappointed Ralf comments as we make our way back to the van that it was 'a shitty game', I assure him that as a Spurs fan I've witnessed infinitely worse.

Surrounded by a level of squalor evocative of some of the more sordid Asian hotels, we spend the evening in Ralf's flat watching the day's football highlights on television and reminiscing in a desultory fashion about the weeks we spent cycling together through Iran and Baluchistan.

'We made a good team,' Ralf maintains. 'If it wasn't for you I'd still be savouring moments somewhere in Baluchistan, and if it wasn't for me you'd have been twice round the world by now.'

If it hadn't been for Ralf I might never have cycled across Baluchistan at all.

*

Laconic and unsociable to the end, Harmonica spurned the affections of the rich and beautiful young widow whose husband he had avenged along with his own murdered brother, and the film ends with him riding inscrutably into the sunset to bury the corpse of a recently departed colleague. How does one fill the vacuum when a lifetime's obsession is suddenly ended – replace it with another? The film leaves this intriguing question unanswered, so I will have to find my own solution. Riding west through Belgium and France, into the sunset and an uncertain future in which I am to be reunited with an address and a national security number, I still have to bury the corpse of a recently departed dream.

As far as I know I've never seen the barman before and his face betrays not a flicker of recognition as he pours out my Perrier water. His voice is clear and firm but fifteen months is more than enough time to make a complete recovery from a sore throat or a touch of laryngitis, and ample time too to forget the details of someone's face. As he neither comments on the presence of the bicycle outside nor attempts to engage me in conversation, however, I conclude that this can't be the man who tossed me a lifeline when I'd been floundering in a quicksand of despair on that distant June day.

What a pity. I cycled back this way expressly to shake his hand and thank him for changing my life.

Unsure whether to count the previous fifteen months as a success or a failure, I sip my Perrier. A *Perfect Moment*, I think, can be defined as a glimpse of Paradise. Although such occasions are by definition scarce and ephemeral, their recollection will endure for a lifetime. The Ovit Dagi Gecidi, 'Pakistan Railways', Kanniyakumari, Amritsar, Nanga Parbat, the Gobi Desert, Gao's smile… these are memories that will illuminate my life like beacons. They will act as co-ordinates whenever I become lost or uncertain of the way, providing a cerebral slide-show to remind me who I am when I am in danger of forgetting. The journey produced more Perfect Moments than I'd have any right to expect in any 'normal' fifteen-month period, but their supply was interrupted and the passion extinguished a relatively paltry 1,200 miles from Vladivostok.

Satisfactory but migt have done better.

Not unlike most of my school reports then. The people who wrote those testimonials puzzle me now: how can anyone's performance be described as satisfactory if they could have done better?

But perhaps I shouldn't be too hard on myself. Rowan Hague, a young New Zealand woman I met in Beijing, told me that I was 'an amazing man', and although she was unable to express herself in words that I could understand, Gao's eyes and her smile said as much.

An Amazing Man. Maybe I could indeed have done better, but that's not bad for a mid-term report. Sat at this very table fifteen months ago, unwillingly contemplating the ignominy of an immediate return home, I'd have been only too glad to settle for a 16,500-mile cycle ride to Beijing; I'd have been delighted then just to make it as far as Istanbul.

The end is near. Over the past fifteen months I've lived a life that's full and I've travelled a few highways. And more, much more than this, I did it My Way.

Instead of flying, I cycled.

Epilogue: Riding Home in the Rain (II)

When the alarm clock cheeps its unwelcome message at 5.20 a.m. he rolls over and stretches out an arm to switch on the radio. Propped up on the pillows, he drains a pint glass of water while listening to the 5.30 news and sports headlines on Radio Five. It has been the wettest July for ten years and the nation's rat population has swollen to sixty million, a phenomenon blamed on a growing tendency to drop litter (particularly fast food) on the ground instead of using bins. That's one rat for every man, woman and child in the British Isles, and they are emerging from their natural habitat of the sewers and taking to the streets.

Musing that litterbugs should be deported en masse to India (where there are no litterbins and the rat is venerated) and wondering how on earth one conducts a census of the rat population, he heaves himself reluctantly to his feet, gets dressed, and pads downstairs to the kitchen. When the kettle comes to the boil he pours himself a cup of coffee and, after a precautionary sniff, adds the milk. The carton is two days past its 'use-by' date, but having survived the stuff he had to eat in Pakistan he feels splendidly invulnerable to food poisoning.

He takes his coffee to the desk in the alcove on the first floor landing that serves as a study and switches on the computer. For the next hour he is utterly absorbed, his practised fingers tapping periodically at the keys and his whole attention riveted to the screen in front of him. He is reliving his adventures on India's Grand Trunk Road, referring to the diary he kept and trawling his memory for significant events, encounters and emotions. Sometimes he thinks that writing a book is a little like starting out with a great, shapeless lump of clay and attempting to fashion something useful or decorative from it.

Just before seven he wheels his bicycle out onto the empty street and cycles rapidly out of Bewdley. It is a fine morning and, fuelled by a heady mixture of caffeine, dodgy milk and fresh air, he ruminates about God and Destiny and wonders why so many people fail to use indicators on roundabouts. Do winners of the National Lottery feel that God or the hand of Fate has decided to

269

single them out? If God had anything to do with the Lottery the winners would surely be selected from the ranks of the meek and the humble and the repentant – in which case 99.9 per cent of the population would be disqualified and the entire system would collapse. And since the participants are motivated entirely by greed, God probably heaves a sigh, shakes his head, and washes his hands of the whole unsavoury business.

He turns right off the Worcester Road and cycles down Lincomb Lane, enjoying the greater peace of the tiny one-track lanes as they wend their way between tall hedgerows, past farm buildings and isolated homesteads, and through an undulating landscape of woods, cornfields, and meadows in which horses, cattle and sheep are grazing. Delivered from the sulphurous burps of catalytic converters, he can smell the burgeoning greenery all around him.

Was it an act of Fate, Destiny or God that, having just cycled approximately 18,000 miles and halfway across the world in fifteen months amongst some of the most dangerous drivers on the planet with hardly a scratch to show for it, he should have had two accidents within weeks of returning home? Or had it merely been bad luck? On the first occasion an elderly woman overtaking him in heavy rain less than a mile from home failed to leave him enough room, hitting his right calf a glancing blow and knocking her wing-mirror off on his arm. Fortunately all he suffered as a result was bruising, but the second accident brought more serious consequences. A forty-tonne articulated lorry drove into the back of the bicycle one December evening on a perfectly straight road, the driver having evidently failed to see him despite his back light and reflective waistcoat. He was thrown clear by the collision, and although he didn't appreciate his good fortune at the time, the gorse bush that broke his fall at least provided a cushioned (albeit prickly) landing. If he'd been hurled into a bus shelter, a lamppost, through a shop window, or even onto a pavement, he would have been left with more serious injuries than a triple fracture to the left shoulder, a broken left wrist and a fracture to the base of the right thumb. Although the mudguard and rear carrier were badly buckled and had to be written-off, the bicycle also survived.

Either accident would have been a thousand times more likely on any of India's roads than on the B4194 or the A4025. Had someone been trying to tell him something? For example that danger ambushes you at times and in places you least expect it? That our lives hang only by the slenderest of threads and since tomorrow may never arrive it is best to make the most of all our todays? It is the sound of the collision that he remembers above everything else, a hideous grinding of metal upon metal a couple of seconds before he was flung through the air. Several months later the metallic clang of automotive wheels on a loose manhole cover or the scrunching of missed gears immediately behind the bicycle still bring him out in a cold sweat.

He exchanges 'Good mornings' with the friendly middle-aged woman who is usually out walking her dog in Doverdale Lane, two lives intersecting for an instant before going in their separate directions again. Does she ever wonder where he has come from and where he is going in such a hurry? Should he be obliged to stop (to repair a puncture, for example) would she ask *Where from? What is your good name? What is your salary?*

He smiles at the memory.

Energised by the exercise, radiating heat and tingling with well-being, he arrives at work, fifty-two minutes and 12.6 miles after leaving home. It is only after he has coupled the tractor unit to the trailer that he realises that he forgot to have any breakfast.

*

The Returning Hero had been subjected to a mixed reception.

His friends and family, most of whom had travelled extensively themselves and had read his emails, understood something of the nature of his achievement and were excited by his return. His GP had urged him to present a slideshow at a village church and his solicitor had interrupted his soliloquy about compensation for the accident on several occasions to question him about the journey, his eyes drawn as if by a magnet to the map of China on the dining-room wall.

The *Kidderminster Times* devoted half of Page 18 to a brief interview, the campaign to prevent the downgrading of the local hospital naturally being considered more relevant to local people than some half-wit's quixotic decision to cycle all the way to China.

The nice, friendly woman at the local bakery asked him where he'd been all this time.

He told her.

'Oh, really?' she replied absently, as if he'd just cycled to Blackpool or Brighton instead of Beijing.

He supposes that to most people Blackpool and Brighton are a very long way to go on a bicycle too. He is proud of what he achieved but it has to be said that many have little desire to make such a journey, even in their dreams. For those who have found fulfilment closer to home the idea of cycling halfway across the world must appear at the very least baffling, and quite possibly even stupid. Many have no conception either of the distance covered during such a journey or of the planning, dedication and sheer effort involved, and since they evidently share little of his curiosity about the wide world beyond the West Midlands, he feels that there is little point in attempting to enlighten them. Some probably aren't even sure where China is.

In those more geographically aware, respect for a feat that they acknowledge is way beyond their capacity is often tinged with puzzlement. 'I can understand the sense of adventure and the attraction of seeing these places, but wouldn't it have been much nicer to do it by motorbike?' queried a bemused work colleague.

No. Sometimes it is preferable to do things the hard way. Quite apart from the physical rewards, he derives considerable satisfaction from the knowledge that his own lungs and legs have powered him half way across the world; the achievement would have been far less had he been slumped like a sack of potatoes behind or over an internal combustion engine. *He* had been the engine. His legs had been the pistons that transmitted power to the wheels, his lungs the air filters, his stomach and guts the carburettors and combustion chambers, and his passion had distributed the vital spark to the plugs. Apart from that early scare in France and the occasional loss of power or breakdown caused by contaminated Asian fuel, the engine had performed excellently throughout – and since foreign motor vehicles are prohibited from entering China it would have been impossible to travel that particular route by motorbike anyway.

The impression persists that the Chinese, notwithstanding the language barrier, understood the motives behind making such a journey far better than his fellow countrymen, some of whom dismiss him as a crank. Maybe these pages are a plea for understanding.

'China? *By bicycle?* Sad tw*t!' exclaimed the yardman at the Express Distribution depot with a grin and a dismissive shake of the head.

He thinks that the saddest people of all are those who have either lost touch with or given up on their dreams.

*

As he drives down the M5 he makes inroads into his sandwiches to quieten the messages from a stomach still wondering what happened to breakfast. His present job is a far cry from the more challenging excursions he used to make ten years ago to Russia and Kazakhstan. That had been pioneering, edge-of-the-seat stuff, the task of keeping six axles pointing in the same direction on sheet-ice a foot thick in sub-zero, diesel-waxing temperatures the ultimate driving challenge. Although he had loved it at the time, he has no wish to return to that way of life. He has chosen to do an undemanding job the better to concentrate on his writing, but the whole project is a huge gamble, a test of faith. He believes that he writes well and that he has something interesting to say, but what if nobody else shares that belief? The pressure to succeed is immense: if he fails, all that time and energy will have been wasted and he might be stuck with lorry driving for the rest of his life. He vacillates between optimism and an almost vertiginous feeling of panic. Whenever his faith wavers he feels that he is standing on the edge of a precipice.

The motorways are full of swaying caravans. Surrounded by the vast, windswept emptiness of the Gobi, he had cause to marvel at the miraculous nature of the internal combustion engine, but now it is merely the tool by which he earns his living. It occurs to him that he can't remember if he attached the safety-clip when coupling to the trailer, so he stops at Strensham Services to check. Some tasks are so automatic that you have no recollection of having completed them.

Existing as opposed to Living.

The store at Neath is reached in the normal time of exactly two hours thirty-five minutes from leaving the depot in Droitwich, and Haverfordwest is a further hour and a half from Neath. During delays at stores and the statutory forty-five-minute daily break he modifies sections of his manuscript with a pencil. After yawning his way back to the depot, ten hours having elapsed since he left it, he reverses the trailer onto one of the loading bays, fuels up and parks the Scania, and drops the keys and completed paperwork back in the transport office, every action unthinking and automatic. *Cogito ergo sum* – I think, therefore I am; I *don't* think, therefore I am *not*.

'You haven't planned your day very well!' says Vikki, grinning maliciously. The sky is heavy with unshed rain.

'I expect the day to plan itself around *me*!' he replies.

'I don't think it's going to this time!' Schadenfreude is writ large upon her mocking face.

Although the bicycle offers a ready solution to the twenty-first-century problems of pollution, traffic congestion and declining public health (a survey recently estimated roughly half of the UK's population to be overweight), most people aren't ready for it yet. They still think he's nuts to cycle into work and back every day.

'You cycle all the way from *Bewdley*? But that's *miles*!'

Yes. (But in the context of a 16,500-mile ride to Beijing, twenty-five miles a day is a breeze.)

'Aren't you out of breath?'

No.

'You must be very fit!'

Yes.

They have forgotten what their legs are for. When he thinks of the pleasure and the physical benefits he derives from cycling and the money it saves him – after all, there is no need to tax, insure, MoT or put petrol into the bicycle – he can only conclude that they are insane *not* to cycle to and from work every day.

It is too warm to bother with the waterproofs; a good soaking never hurt anyone and he'd rather be drenched with rain than sweat. At Dunhampton the heavens open and he recalls the ride in the rain in Southern India. *He who is wet does not fear the rain.*

No longer Gandalf, Bertie Wooster, Basil Fawlty or Charles Bronson, Christopher James Aston Smith (National Insurance Number KZ707284J) squelches rather than walks into his house, he peels of his saturated clothes and takes a shower. The cascading hot water – for over a year such a rare and sensory delight – has become just another routine, and routine anaesthetises sensation.

In a recent email Ralf posed the following question: *You wrote 'I'm clinging to the hope that it* (the journey) *will change me in some way, enabling me to return home with new ideas, different priorities, more maturity...' How about it – did u become more 'aloissy'? And what are Y-fronts?*

Of course I haven't! he wrote back. *I'm just a little older, a little wiser and a little more cynical than before...*

Actually those fifteen months taught him a little about the planet and the people that inhabit it, and a good deal about himself. They reinforced his belief that, despite the media revolution, the world remains an awesome and beautiful place that has lost nothing of its power to astonish, and that, given adequate maintenance and the appropriate fuel, the human body is the most sophisticated, durable and versatile of engines. The experience instilled in him a vivid awareness of the friendship and love that he had left behind, but he was amply compensated by the simple human kindness and solidarity he found flourishing in the most remote and unlikely of places. In a world riven by political and religious dissent, he discovered that basic human decency is an instinct that invariably prevails despite the hatred disseminated by bigots and fanatics, and he returned home with his faith in human nature and the existence of a brotherhood of man restored. The source of a thousand memories and insights, the journey had been a fantastic, illuminating voyage of discovery that had reaffirmed the extent to which it is possible to follow and live out one's wildest dreams. He has no regrets that he made it, and that in the end is all the justification it needs. No regrets.

Sometimes he is asked if he'll go on another big trip.

'Maybe,' he replies.

Now visit www.cycleuktochina.com for a photographic record of the journey.

'WHY DON'T YOU FLY?'

LIST OF EQUIPMENT

How much baggage one ultimately takes and which items one reluctantly leaves behind is in the end a very personal decision. Everything has to be pared down to the absolute minimum and with hindsight I could perhaps have packed fewer articles of clothing, for clothes are easily and cheaply obtained (and repaired) in most Asian countries, but in general I feel that I got it more or less right first time. The only omissions that I really came to regret were an altimeter, a gel saddle-cover and a Chinese–English dictionary or phrasebook. On future expeditions I'd take a compact digital camera now that they have become more affordable.

BICYCLE (for more anatomical information visit www.sjscycles.com)

I opted for S.J.S. Cycles' Thorn EXP, a custom-made long-haul expedition bicycle with Reynolds 725 steel tubing. 26-inch wheels made for a low centre of gravity and stability under heavy loads, and in keeping with a philosophy that favoured toughness and longevity over high average speeds, I selected Vredestein Spider 26 x 1.9 tyres. I judged 24 gears to be sufficient and a 26-42-52 crank-set was duly married to an eight-speed 11-34 cassette. The massive 52-tooth outer chain-ring enabled the maintenance of high cruising speeds on well-maintained asphalt, whilst on Turkey's precipitous Black Sea Coast road I was twice obliged to use bottom gear. After some initial misgivings (I'd never used cleats before) I opted for Shimano M535 SPD pedals, both for extra push-pull torque on hills and to ensure that my feet were always firmly anchored to the optimum position on the pedals. Disengaging my boots never proved to be a problem when coming to a halt, and even during falls my feet automatically separated themselves from the pedals. Luggage was placed in Carradice panniers (mounted front and rear), an Agu bar-bag, and a standard kit bag that was slung on top of the rear panniers and secured to the rack with a bungee strap. A Cateye Enduro 2 trip computer logged daily times and distances.

SLEEPING
Outdoor Research Advanced Bivvy Sack (lighter and more compact than a tent and offers greater concealment when camping rough)
Mountain Equipment Lightline lightweight three-season down sleeping bag
    Cotton liner
    Karrimat sleeping mat
    Mosquito net

EATING AND DRINKING
MSR Dragonfly multi-fuel stove and fuel bottle
Matches and / or cigarette lighters
Titanium saucepan and frying-pan set (expensive but very light)
Aluminium knife, fork and spoon set (including sharp, serrated knife)
Plastic mug
Three frame-mounted water bottles
Collapsible plastic water bottles to augment capacity in dry areas
Katadyn water filter (heavy and expensive but the best)
Pot scourer and tea towel
Small container of cooking oil
Bags of pasta and / or rice – indestructible emergency food rations

CLOTHING
Helmet
Spare glasses and sunglasses
Waterproof, breathable cycling jacket
Waterproof trousers (never used)
3 pairs of cycling trousers / leggings
1 pair of shorts
3 pairs of padded cycling shorts (doubling as underpants and swimwear)
3 polo shirts
2 singlets
1 long-sleeved thermal vest
1 fleece
2 pairs of gloves (of differing thickness)
Balaclava
Cleated cycling boots

Sandals
5 pairs of socks
2 money-belts

HEALTH AND HYGIENE

Razor, spare blades and pocket mirror
Shower-gel
Universal sink / bath plug
Toothbrush and toothpaste
Toilet roll (but I came to dispense with this luxury)
Nail-clippers
Tweezers
Small towel
Suncream
Multivitamin tablets (for areas in which local fare is either scarce or inedible)
Rehydration tablets (for areas in which local fare is too deadly to keep down – or up)
Nurofen
Immodium
Spray-on mosquito repellent and coils
Anti-malarial prophylactics (very expensive and never used)
Iodine water-purification tablets
Savlon antiseptic cream
Lifesystems Travel Medical Pack (containing a disconcerting assortment of antiseptic wipes, dressings, sutures, plasters, bandages, safety pins, scissors, syringes and sterile needles, sterile scalpel, Paracetemol, disposable gloves and basic instructions)

TOOLS AND SPARES

Topeak 'Alien' bicycle multi-tool (incorporating spare tyre levers, ring spanners, Allen keys, Philips and flat-head screwdrivers, a small knife, a spoke key, a bottle-opener and a chain tool)
Pliers and cable cutters
Adjustable spanner
Insulating tape
12 cable-ties and four bungee straps – invaluable for impromptu repairs and bodges
Cable lock
2 spare tyres
4 spare inner tubes and plenty of patches and glue for repairs
Tyre levers (I prefer metal ones as the plastic equivalents tend to break, but care is needed to prevent damage to tyres and wheel rims)

Pump (attached to bicycle frame)

Spare mini-pump in case of theft or malfunction of the above vital piece of equipment

Spare chain and cassette

Bolt and ring spanner for removal of cassette

Spare set of brake and gear cables

Spare set of brake pads

Spare spokes

Spare batteries for lights, trip computer, watch and camera

Refillable can of lubricating oil

MISCELLANEOUS

Passport, travellers cheques, credit card, cash in US dollars contained in 2 money-belts

Wallet containing separate, emergency stash of cash and travellers cheques

Insurance documents and inoculation certificates

Passport photos for visa applications

Driving licence and International Driving Permit (well, you never know!)

Photocopies of vital documents stored in a separate location

Dog Dazer

Maps

A5 'day to a page' diary

Biros

Small address book

Airmail pad and envelopes (rendered virtually obsolete these days by email)

Guidebooks (left with a reliable friend in stamped, self-addressed envelopes to be sent poste restante when required)

Wristwatch with alarm

Compact Canon Ixus Z70 camera and plenty of film (APS film not easily found and very expensive in Asia)

1 or 2 books (undeniably a luxury but in my opinion worth the extra weight)

1 15m length of cord

LIST OF ILLUSTRATIONS

(visit www.cycleuktochina.com)

Section One

19. Rising sun and perforated asphalt near Loralai, Baluchistan.
20. Teahouse, Mekhtar, Baluchistan.
21. Serenity, Amritsar.
22. Chaos, Amritsar.
23. Transport café, Rajasthan.
24. Scavenging cows breakfasting in Jaisalmer.
25. Palolem, Goa.
26. Elliott and Sandra: we discovered in Goa that our journeys had much in common.
27. India's 'Land's End' at Kanniyakumari.
28. Towering over Madurai's streets: part of the massive Shri Meenakshi temple.
29. This unusual load was viewed during the descent from Kodaikanal.
30. 'Oh no you don't!' The camera-shy Raners.
31. Most people would have flown – or at least taken the bus or train.
32. Destitution meets indifference on the Howrah Bridge, Calcutta.
33. Washing buffaloes in the Ganges, Varanasi.
34. A losing battle.
35. A wall in Agra. All over India colourful murals are used to advertise products and services.
36. Krishna the chef, surrounded by his pots and pans.
37. Traffic on the Grand Trunk Road near Ludhiana (photograph courtesy of Carla Smit).
38. Roadside encounter.
39. Re-entry into Pakistan at Wagah.
40. 'Piccadilly Circus', Lahore (photograph courtesy of Carla Smit).
41. Wild-eyed, bearded men wearing turbans congregate at a teahouse near Gujrat, Pakistan.
42. A mobile work of art.
43. Friendly natives of Indus Kohistan (complete with AK 47).
44, 45 & 46. Klompjes, Rosie and the Karakoram Highway.
47. The weather closed in during the final ascent to the Khunjerab Pass (photograph courtesy of Carla Smit).
48. Beyond the pass the shining domes of the Pamirs replaced the saw-toothed ridges and tapering steeples of the Karakorams.
49. Downtown Kashgar, where order and symmetry prevailed.
50. The livestock section of Kashgar's celebrated Sunday market, where they did not (photograph courtesy of Carla Smit).
51. Lorry drivers break their journey across the Taklamakan to examine an unusual phenomenon.
52. Puncture repairs were tackled with a combination of fury and resignation (photograph courtesy of Carla Smit).

Section Two

76. The mud walls encircling Bam's spectacular Old City date from the twelfth century.
77. A few months earlier two Swedish cyclists had their tent raked by automatic gunfire while camping out in this area. They survived but their bicycles were wrecked.
78. Fugitive from routine.
79. The walls of the fortress city of Jaisalmer tower over the desert in western Rajasthan. Formerly an important trading centre, the tourist trade now provides the bulk of its income.
80. Elliott prepares a barbecue on Agonda beach, Goa.
81. One of the fifty-metre-high gopurams of Madurai's Shri Meenakshi Temple.
82. The proprietor of a hotel in Kodaikanaal had a piranha smile that widened at the prospect of money. I agreed to his demand for a 'New Year's Gift' only if he'd let me photograph him.
83. Mysore's Summer Palace.
84. Calcutta or Kolkata? It will take more than a few strokes of a pen to erase the legacies of the Raj.
85. A street in Varanasi. The sheer density of the crowds began to trouble me in Northern India.
86. *Flawless and almost hypnotically beautiful, the visual equivalent of a piece of Bach or Mozart:* the Taj Mahal.
87. A man presides inscrutably over the Karakoram Highway from a chair made from slabs of stone. The reception wasn't always warm in Indus Kohistan.
88. The cycling became hard work in the thinner air and the landscape ever more barren as we gained height.
89. Beyond the Khunjerab Pass, high, drifting clouds in the Chinese sky speckled the glowing beige slopes of the Pamirs with darker areas of shadow, *like doubt invading a restless mind.*
90. Dilapidated villages occasionally provided a reprieve from the emptiness of the Taklamakan Desert.
100. Lanzhou, reputedly China's most polluted city, where I had to wait for over two weeks for a delivery of inner tubes.
101. A world away from the rapidly modernising urban landscapes (as epitomised by Lanzhou), roadside villages in rural China often consisted of little more than a ramshackle collection of cafés, automotive repair shops, a dormitory and sometimes a filling station, the inhabitants owing their livelihoods entirely to the custom of passing traffic.
102. Tiananmen Square, Beijing.